When Pirates Ruled the Waves

Paul Harris has worked variously, since his days in pirate radio in the late '60s and early '70s, as a writer (more than forty books), publisher, international printing consultant and journalist.

He covered the wars in Yugoslavia 1991-5 for press, radio and TV and, for ten years, worked as an analyst on global insurgency and terrorism for *Janes Intelligence Review*. His work took him to Sri Lanka, where he was also Colombo correspondent for *The Daily Telegraph*, and to such exotic hotspots as Nepal, Assam, Manipur, Meghalayah, Aceh, East Timor, Uganda, Eritrea, Sudan, Nagorno Karabakh, The Saharawi Arab Democratic Republic and to China, where he worked on *The Shanghai Daily* newspaper.

He is now endeavouring to live a quiet life in a small, remote country marked by hot weather and a lack of insurrection or drama. He works as a lecturer on cruise ships in Asia and Europe. His most recent book is *Delightfully Imperfect: A Year in Sri Lanka at the Galle Face Hotel,* also published by Kennedy & Boyd.

When Pirates Ruled the Waves

SIXTH EDITION

Paul Harris

Published by
Kennedy and Boyd
an imprint of
Zeticula
57 St Vincent Crescent
Glasgow
G3 8NQ
Scotland, U.K.

http://www.kennedyandboyd.co.uk
admin@kennedyandboyd.co.uk

First published July 1968 by Impulse Publications Ltd
Second edition September 1968
Third edition July 1969
Fourth edition August 1970

Republished 1977 as *Broadcasting from the High Seas* by Paul Harris Publishing, incorporating the text of *To Be a Pirate King* (Impulse, 1971)

ISBN 1-904999-37-9 Paperback
ISBN 978-1-904999-37-9 Paperback

Contents

Photographs

Preface

It is almost forty years since the British government banned a hardy crew of 20th century buccaneers: the enormously popular pirate radio ships like Radio Caroline, Radio London and Radio Scotland were summarily removed from the airwaves, and their anchorages, by the Marine Broadcasting Offences Act (1967).

I can recall quite clearly first tuning into what was then a truly innovative phenomenon in radio. It was a Sunday morning in the spring of 1964 and *The Observer* newspaper had a story on the front page about test transmissions from a radio ship called Radio Caroline anchored somewhere off the Thames estuary. Portable transistor radios were, in those days, still a relatively new arrival on the consumer goods shelves and they lacked the power and sensitivity to receive such weak signals. True enough, I could not receive Radio Caroline from my home in the north of Scotland on a transistor radio but, being something of a radio *afficionado* at the tender age of 15, a former Bomber Command radio receiver (type R1224A, if my memory does not deceive me) lurked in the attic and was connected to a 120 foot-long wire antenna in the garden below. I was not altogether sure why at the time, but I felt a very distinct thrill of excitement as I tuned the dial and heard, for the very first time, 'Good morning, this is Caroline on 199. Your all day music station'.

At the beginning of the 21st century it must be difficult to comprehend what a world virtually without popular music radio was like. At the beginning of the 1960s, most of the time there was no pop music to be heard on the airwaves. Indeed, some of the time there was no music at all. In the UK, the airwaves were the exclusive and unquestioned prerogative of the British Broadcasting Corporation which still strictly operated by the Reithian principles imposed by its *eminence grise* in the 1920s and '30s. The rights of musicians and composers were 'protected' by so-called needle time agreements which severely restricted the amount of recorded music played on the radio. The most popular records, or discs, were then covered by live bands playing vaguely ludicrous imitations of the real thing. There was no local radio at all, apart from Manx Radio which operated as a result of the peculiar constitutional status of the Isle of Man. There was no Radio One. There was, of course, the BBC Light Programme.

Of a Sunday afternoon, announcer Alan Freeman ('Hi there, pop pickers') presented *Pick of the Pops* which was regarded as the treat of the week with a couple of hours of authentic recorded popular music. A good ten minutes before the programme was broadcast, the family radiogram ('60s terminology for a combined radio and record player) was warmed up and tuned in. Usually, we recorded the programme for later delectation using a bizarre tape recording machine which fitted over the record deck and was driven by the motor of the record player. Apart from the odd disc played on lunchtime shows, that was your lot so far as pop music radio from the UK went.

There was, of course, Radio Luxembourg which broadcast from the Grand Duchy of the same name with its transmitters located far away in a distant foreign land. The signal you might receive reflected this. Luxembourg did not come on the air in English until seven in the evening and although the signal on 208 metres medium wave did improve as darkness fell, it was subject to many variables of weather, sun spot activity in the heavens, and the time of year. Inevitably, as your favourite new disc was played the signal would fade so as to become virtually indistinct. Incredibly, millions of listeners put up with these travails to hear some decent music.

The pirate radio ships arrived in a radio world bereft of any real choice in broadcasting; virtually bereft of pop music; and which made no concessions whatsoever to popular culture or mass tastes. I guess that was why I felt so excited as I tuned into that first broadcast from Radio Caroline, the forerunner of a miniature fleet of radio ships which would anchor off the British coast over the period 1964-67. Short-lived in terms of time, nevertheless the pirate radio phenomenon would completely revolutionise broadcasting in Britain directly leading to the creation of Radio One in 1967 and spawning the creation of BBC local radio and then commercial radio. Today, when a licence to broadcast on the airwaves is relatively easy to acquire, and the Internet is available to all, it is difficult to recall the assumed all encompassing rights of government to control all broadcasting.

And it was not just a matter of the pirate stations changing broadcasting for ever. Up until 1964, in the UK, culture and experience was dominated by middle class, middle of the road traditional values. These values were reflected nowhere so forcefully as at the BBC. The BBC endorsed, formalised and disseminated an ethos of subscription to such values in everything it broadcast from news to music. Subscription to alternative values was denied by the BBC's monopoly. The pirates would change that for ever, far beyond changing radio broadcasting. For millions of teenagers and other young people, all of a sudden *there was another way*. The definition of popular culture and access to freedom of expression was no longer the right of a privileged few. Pirate radio may have posed more questions than answers but it successfully challenged a whole series of assumed rights: rights to the airwaves, rights to hear the programmes of ones choice, rights to self-expression, and the right to question things which had never been up for discussion before.

And so, in the wake of offshore pirate radio, came a veritable revolution in music, dress, design, speech, human rights and attitudes. Of course, pirate radio cannot be scientifically linked to all this, and there were other influences at play. However, I do believe it was the catalyst in a much wider series of events.

Like tens of thousands of youngsters (the Free Radio Association, with which I was associated, had more than 100,000 members in 1967), I was passionate about the pirates, their product and about the issues they had raised. In the 1960s, for the first time, young people were emerging into a new world where they might express themselves, dress themselves and become players in their own right.

My first book, *When Pirates Ruled the Waves*, was written in longhand in my school holidays in the summers of 1966 and 1967. Accordingly, dear reader, much of this book, it has to be borne in mind, is the product of the thought processes and analysis of a 17 year-old schoolboy. The London book publishing industry, reflecting as it did those strong traditional values and attitudes, was incredibly snooty about the book. I approached no less than 32 publishers over a period of some six months. All turned the book down. The most common observation was there was 'no market' for such a book. Implicit in this was the feeling that young people would not buy books and that for older people this was a subject of absolutely no interest whatsoever.

With all the optimism and certainty of youth, I was convinced that these views were mistaken and that the publishers were all fools. But I was unsure about how to proceed until the last publisher I approached, Clive Bingley, wrote me a note inviting me to meet him at his office in London's Notting Hill Gate. Clive, now retired, was probably one of the shrewdest and most down to earth publishers in the UK during the '60s and '70s. In the early '70s, together with fellow publisher Lionel Leventhal, he would start a book fair in London for small and specialist publishers (SPEX) which would, in time, grow into the massive and successful London Book Fair (which he would sell for a vast sum of money to Reed Exhibitions).

Clive, direct as ever, sat behind his desk in his book-lined office and told me, "I'm not going to publish your book . . . that's because I publish books on librarianship." I had not done my research properly. "However, this is a good book and I believe it will sell. If you can't find a publisher to do it, then I shall help you to publish it yourself." Clive went on to give me a series of informal seminars on how to publish a book. Within three hours I had it all. Clive was dismissive of the mystique surrounding book publishing and he willingly shared all his knowledge of production, distributors, wholesalers, discounts and booksellers. It took no more than three hours.

In the heady atmosphere of the 1960s, where so much suddenly seemed to be so possible, I never doubted my ability to publish the book and make it the success the traditional publishers sought to deny me. I went to the university printers at the university where I was studying politics and international relations, handed over the typescript and politely asked for 2,000 copies, please. In July 1968, 2,000 copies were duly delivered to the offices of the Free Radio Association (FRA) in Rayleigh, Essex, together with a bill for £1,340, net 30 days. At that time, my sole source of income was a university grant of £360 a year so the bill pretty much equated to my total money for living for the next four years.

By now, however, my research skills had been honed a little. The FRA, headed up by the immensely committed Geoffrey 'Cup Cake' Pearl and his wife, June, offered the book to its members and soon sold several hundred copies. But it was a quarter-page advertisement on page three of the pop music weekly *Disc & Music Echo* which would really lift the project off the ground. Vast numbers of pirate radio 'nuts' read the paper as it covered developments on the scene in some detail. The journalist who wrote these pieces, David Hughes, told me in The Avenue pub on Shaftesbury Avenue, there were "thousands of nutters out there" and "they'll all want your book". I wanted to believe it but wasn't really sure. How come those genteel folks in book-lined offices in Bloomsbury don't know about this, I wondered?

I stuck the ad into the following Thursday's issue, with an accommodation address in central London. I didn't dare go into the office on Friday and delayed my visit until Monday lunchtime, not daring to hope I had any orders in response to the £35 advertisement . . . At the top floor offices of the agency in Southampton Row they were very put out. "Where have you been? Please take all this stuff away." The mail was stacked all over their office in bags, bundles and untidy heaps. The Post Office had made special deliveries to get rid of the mail from the sorting office. I opened some up and there, sure enough, were hundreds of orders at 37s 6d a time (just under two pounds in modern parlance). Most people, bewilderingly to me, had just popped cash in the envelopes. I emptied a few envelopes and went out and had a slap-up lunch.

Within a few more days all 2,000 copies had gone to the readers of *Disc & Music Echo*. News of this teenager's *success fou* had reached Fleet Street and my success story was all the rage in the Sunday papers, with the lead in Mandrake in *The Sunday Telegraph*. This brought urgent demands from the largest wholesalers in the country, W H Smith (known to *Private Eye* readers as W H Smug) for me to fill their warehouses with books (they had ignored it before publication and declined to stock). I sat for mornings on end in shop windows in London's Charing Cross Road signing copies and escorted by beautiful, nubile girls from some long-forgotten pop group whose publicist, Jonathan Northam, wanted to ride on the back of my glittering success story. At nineteen years old, I was rich, dining in the best eateries, escorted by tasty young women and living on the adrenalin of adulatory publicity. The '60s were indeed a good time for some of us.

Of course, it could not last for ever . . . But it would last a good few years. *When Pirates Ruled the Waves* would go through four editions, selling 10,000 copies, between 1968 and 1970. I would soon be driving a Mercedes and owning a couple of discotheques and a publishing business whilst roaming in the groves of academe when the inclination came to me. This was all very much a '60s success story. Youth was pre-eminent and cash was available in a way never experienced before.

The Beatles were, of course, the ultimate success story of the '60s. In the way one successful man seeks to meet others of like kind, I dropped in on the Apple Company's offices in Baker Street one morning and asked to speak to John Lennon. A secretary bird was about to shoo me away when John's Liverpool tones droned from behind a half-shut door. "Let the guy in." I marched into John's office. I was impressed. He had two stunningly beautiful mini-skirted girls, one on each knee. One was white skinned and blonde; the other as black as the ace of spades (as we used to say in the '60s before political correctness came in) with long straightened black hair.

"What you got man?" was John's question. I suppose everybody who visited him wanted to sell him something. I knew, however, what a great supporter he was of pirate radio and I whisked a copy of the first edition out of my bag. Balancing the girls delicately on his knees, he fanned the pages of my book. "Great, man. Great, man." Thus came John's considered verdict. Now to business. "How many you got, man?"

At this stage I made my first and possibly one of my greatest mistakes in business. I assumed John was asking how many I had with me to sell him that day (in fact, he wanted to know how much I had in my entire stock so he could buy the lot). "Twenty, John," I responded. "We'll take them all, man," said John levering the black bird off his knee. "Go and get the petty cash," John instructed her.

This was a bit of a surprise. Everybody else in London was asking for 30 days credit, and actually taking 90 to pay in those days. But Apple did business rather differently (in fact, it went bust shortly afterwards and one Saturday morning they gave everything away from their Baker Street shop). Anyway, my business dealings with John Lennon were highly satisfactory.

I wasn't so successful handling things with David Bowie. A friend and late 1960s 'mover and shaker' Dick Fox Davies, active in the radio and music scene, introduced me to Bowie in a pub in Beckenham. Bowie was looking for a five hundred pound investment to build him a recording studio in the basement of his flat nearby. In return I would get 10%, maybe 20%, of the Bowie action. "Look, David," I counselled him earnestly. "Just accept it. You've had your hit, *Space Odyssey*. But that's it. That sort of stuff has had its day." No cash for you mate.

Maybe my second great mistake in business. By now the mistakes are racking up at much the same rate as the successes. Shortly after the publication of *When Pirates Ruled the Waves* I took my new red Mercedes for a European peregrination. I visited Radio Luxembourg to look at a book project with them (non-starter) and then visited a Canadian living in The Netherlands called Timothy Thomason who ran an outfit called the International Broadcasters Society (IBS). The reality was rather less grand then the name. The IBS was the creation of Thomason and his wife, Berthe Beydals, run from a small upper-floor flat in the pleasant provincial town of Bussum. Our encounter in Bussum would lead, however, my own *entrée* to the world of pirate radio as a participant.

Out of our meeting, short-lived pirate radio ship Capital Radio would be born. Alas, business-wise this was not destined to be a success. Within months of launch, the Liechtenstein-registered M V *King David* would be aground on the beach at Noordwijk, and our hopes, and cash, washed up on shore. The full story of this period is recounted in some detail in these pages. The saga of Capital Radio, Radio Veronica and Radio North Sea International followed *When Pirates Ruled the Waves* in a separate book entitled *To Be a Pirate King*, which was published in book form in 1971. It was also serialised in the Dutch daily newspaper *De Telegraaf* in 1971.

The text of both books – *When Pirates Ruled the Waves* and *To Be a Pirate King* – were combined and re-published as *Broadcasting from the High Seas* in 1977. It was reprinted twice. Neither *When Pirates* nor its successors have been republished since 1978. The European pirate radio phenomenon died out, apart from various rebirths of Radio Caroline (reborn aboard the converted trawler *Ross Revenge* in 1983), and other stations like Radio Paradise (arrested by the Dutch authorities in 1981) and Laser 558 which took to the air in 1984 but which came and went amidst financial acrimony and chaos.

This new edition with the old title *When Pirates Ruled the Waves* incorporates virtually all of the 1977 content of *Broadcasting from the High Seas*. It was greatly facilitated by finding 95% of the original photographs used in the '60s and '70s books when moving house in 2005. More than half of these were taken by myself but others were given to me more than thirty years ago and their origin is somewhat hazy. But I do have on my original list of credits The Free Radio Association, the BBC, T D R Thomason, Eddy de Jongh, Theo Dencker, Radio Veronica, Radio Scotland, Radio London, Radio Essex, Radio 390, Radio 270, Radio Hauraki, The Press Association, ANP Foto, The Johnnie Walker Fan Club and Squire of Romford. Thank you all again and I hope you do not mind seeing these images in print again three or four decades on.

During the early 1970s the world of pirate radio ships crossed over dramatically with the world of espionage and this remains another, rather more curious, legacy of the pirate era. When I published *To Be a Pirate King*, *The Sunday Express* newspaper carried an article referring to my allegations about the activities of Radio North Sea International (RNI) and its owners, the two Swiss businessmen Erwin Meister and Edwin Bollier. A couple of days after the article, in the summer of 1971, a Special Branch officer appeared on my doorstep to make an appointment for me to meet 'someone'. "Who?" I asked, not unreasonably, I thought. "I'm not at liberty to disclose that information," advised Mr Plod.

A few days later, he returned with MI6's 'man in Scotland', retired Detective Superintendent Warren of the Perth police force. Warren made it clear that he knew I had been running and investing in Capital Radio. Ergo, I was liable to prosecution under the Marine Broadcasting Offences Act (1967). However, these things could be overlooked . . . I was invited to reveal what I knew about RNI and worked with MI6 on bringing their game to an end. The security services were specifically concerned with RNI's relations with the East German intelligence services; SIGINT (signals intelligence) equipment aboard the radio ship; and the station's participation in the previous British general election campaign. A patriot to the core, I rallied to the cause. Over the ensuing months, I would hand significant documents to MI6 detailing the activities, particularly, of the main man, Edwin Bollier.

Bollier was allowed to continue with his espionage activities but would re-emerge dramatically on the international scene in the wake of the Lockerbie bombing of December 21 1988. That night, jumbo jet Pan Am 103 was blown up over the Scottish border town of Lockerbie killing all 259 passengers plus eleven people on the ground.

In 2001, two Libyan intelligence officers went on trial in a specially convened Scottish court at Camp Zeist in The Netherlands, charged with downing the jet. What was most interesting to me, however, was the testimony at the trial of my old 'friend' . . . Edwin Bollier. I read the reports of the Camp Zeist testimony of the man who admitted to manufacturing the timer of the Lockerbie bomb with a mounting sense of incredulity. The security services knew from my own evidence supplied to them back in 1971 that Bollier was, at that time, working with the East German intelligence services. We all knew too well – thirty years ago and seventeen years before he provided the prime constituent part of the Lockerbie bomb – that he was, in Bond parlance, a thoroughly bad egg. But this was not in the world of James Bond: it was in the harsh reality of the Cold War that unscrupulous businessmen men like Bollier, operating out of neutral Switzerland and with Swiss passports, could operate internationally with virtual impunity.

Edwin Bollier and his partner Erwin Meister were then in their early thirties and termed themselves 'radio engineers'. Their partnership gave birth to the Zurich company Mebo Telecommunications AG, registered on March 24 1971, which operates to this day and which was named in a Lockerbie warrant issued by the Lord Advocate of Scotland in November 1991.

They first came to public attention at the beginning of 1970 when they launched their pirate radio ship onto international waters off the Dutch coast. How the Zurich radio repairmen who did a line in 'spy bug' transmitters came by the cash was a mystery. Radio North Sea International was bigger, better and flashier than any other pirate. Aboard a Norwegian coaster converted into the radio ship *Mebo II* in a Hamburg shipyard, it came on the air on January 23 1970. Painted in brilliant psychedelic colours and topped by a 50 metre high radio mast, it was, for me, a fascinating enigma from the start. Its conventional medium wave transmitter was more powerful than any other pirate radio ship, and most European national radio stations, and it also, surprisingly, broadcast on two short wave bands and on VHF. It was difficult to discern any commercial rationale behind the operation.

Controversy dogged the station. Its role in the June 1970 British General Election was extraordinary. It mounted a campaign against the then Labour Government, which lost the election, and was, in turn, jammed by the Post Office, a British naval radio station and the military.

As a journalist and worker with another pirate radio ship, Capital Radio, anchored just a few miles away, I was able to infiltrate the Mebo office operation which was located in a suite in the Grand Hotel in Scheveningen on the Dutch coast. From the window of the office we could see the pirate ships at anchor in a row offshore in international waters outside the jurisdiction of the Dutch authorities. Rather curiously, there was sometimes an out of area US Coastguard vessel to be seen anchored out there as well, and occasionally it actually anchored off our own Capital Radio vessel . . .

Meister and Bollier did not discuss their business with outsiders and were men of mystery with a well-polished public relations line. Bollier, with his psychedelic kipper ties and expensive Italian suits, was clearly the dominant partner although he left Meister to do most of the talking with people like me. When they talked between themselves they used *Schweizerdeutsch* which I found totally incomprehensible despite a reasonable grasp of normal German. I became aware of shipments of radio transmitter parts to East Germany and discovered in the outgoing mail copies of airfreight waybills addressed to the 'Institut fur Technische Untersuchungen' in East Berlin'. This equipment, of US origin, was being shipped by Mebo Telecommunications (then unregistered) of Zurich to East Berlin, via Amsterdam's Schiphol Airport. Such technology exports were banned under Federal US law. The Institut was a wing of East German intelligence, the *Stasi*.

I spirited away the mail that looked interesting, steamed it open using a technique learned from *The Eagle Annual* as a schoolboy, photocopied it, popped it back in the post and laid the copies securely aside for my next trip back to the UK (no email in those days and fax was a relatively new introduction). Back there, usually in Aberdeen, I would be contacted by a Special Branch officer who would set up my meetings with the man from MI6. Hardly surprisingly, I was dealt with on a 'need to know' basis but from the extensive questioning and discussions it became quite clear that 'W' was particularly interested in the East German connection and the interference by the radio ship in the general election.

This was distinctly low grade intelligence work far removed from the glamorous world of Bond. But in those days it was this sort of dull footwork which formed the bedrock of most intelligence operations. I was never paid a penny for my miniscule part in winning the Cold War. Anthony Wedgewood Benn – then Her Majesty's Postmaster General with responsibility for broadcasting matters – had secretly sworn a warrant for my arrest under the Marine Broadcasting Offences Act 1967 for my part in setting up Capital Radio. I was simply granted immunity from prosecution as was one of my colleagues, Scottish radio engineer aboard Capital, Ewan Macpherson.

However, evidence soon emerged that the activities of European and American intelligence agencies had borne fruit. On July 8 1971 the Dutch newspaper *De Telegraaf* published a leaked report from the CIA. It revealed that ten pirate radio ships, based on the Radio North Sea operation, were under construction in the Polish port of Gdansk. The programme was under the direction of the Institut fur Technische Untersuchungen. This was believed to be a Cold War riposte to the US-backed operations Radio Free Europe and Radio Liberty. It was also likely that such vessels would incorporate a SIGINT (signals intelligence) capability, which was also a feature of the North Sea operation. Publication of the report effectively compromised the whole operation and work on the ships ceased.

In May 1971, Radio North Sea was bombed by frogmen who attached plastic explosives to the hull. Rival Radio Veronica was blamed but in reality it was a botched job by the BVD (Dutch secret service). Meantime my own pirate ship had been cut adrift by night and had ended up on the beach at Noordwijk – right in front of the Grand Hotel. Radio North Sea was closed by Dutch government legislation in August 1974. In January 1977 it sailed from Rotterdam for Libya.

As the ship sailed, a photograph of Bollier's new patron, Colonel Ghadaffi, was pasted up in the studio. The ship was sold to Ghadaffi and used to broadcast the Koran. One day, Ghadaffi tired of his plaything, or maybe it had no use for him any longer. A Libyan air force jet fighter strafed the *Mebo II* and sent it to the bottom of the Mediterranean Sea.

The Swiss relationship with Ghadaffi was one which would flourish for ten years: right up to the fateful night of December 2 1987 when Flight Pan Am 103 would crash in flames onto the town of Lockerbie. That may not have been predictable. But might it have been preventable? The world's intelligence community knew all about Edwin Bollier. The enduring question must be why his activities were tolerated.

My own best guess is that following the evidence that he was so closely involved with the East German intelligence services, and the intensive CIA preventive activity around the projected series of radio ships, Bollier was 'turned' by the CIA and became *their* man. It was then a logical act to rein him in during the 1990s and require him to testify about supplying the timer for the Lockerbie bomb to those persons the US was determined to indict and find guilty of the crime (there can be little doubt the Libyans did *not* carry out the Lockerbie bombing). I suppose RNI remains as an indicator of what could have developed on the high seas if the development of pirate ships had remained untrammelled and unscrupulous operators had been allowed to move in.

Romance, adventurism and drama always seemed inextricably linked with the saga of the pirate radio ships. You might say these elements went with the territory – and the people who made it their own. Whether it derives from the romance of the rusty old ships themselves, the nascent power of broadcasting over its listeners, the emotive power of music, or simply the notion of boldly going where others fear to go, the story of the pirate radio ships around European coasts is a compelling and fascinating tale. Although made illegal by virtually every government in Europe, the pirates did relatively little harm whilst bringing enjoyment to vast numbers of people, and more than a little fulfilment to those intrepid modern buccaneers who were involved.

Paul Harris
July 2006

1

An idea is born

'The Irish breed rebels where the English breed gentlemen. The English like to watch the action; the Irish provide it.' These words, not surprisingly, are the words of an Irishman. They were spoken in December 1965, some twenty months after this particular Irishman had, in the true Irish fashion, brought about his own particular Easter Rebellion. His name was Ronan O'Rahilly, and the words which will always be associated with him are 'pirate radio". On Easter Saturday, 1964, a new sound was introduced to Britain – the sound of offshore commercial radio; the sound of 'Radio Caroline'.

The introduction of this, then new, medium of communication is usually attributed to this young, fiery Irishman. The story goes that the idea of pirate radio was born in a London Soho public-house a few months before Radio Caroline came on the air. Two men, one Irish, the other Australian, met there and discussed the business opportunities involved in it.

The Australian was Mr Allan Crawford. He was a man of considerable business acumen; he had been managing director of Southern Music, reputed to be the world's largest music publishing business, and he owned an Australian record company.

The Irishman was, of course, 23-year-old Ronan O'Rahilly. He had a background of rebellion against authority, which was to fit him in his future role. His grandfather was killed charging a British machine-gun post single-handed in the 1916 Easter Rising and Yeats wrote a poem about him. Ronan himself had been a rebel as a boy. He had earned the distinction of having been thrown out of seven different schools. He then left home and went over to London from Ireland in 1961.

'I looked upon my move as a challenge', he has said. He felt the time was right for some sort of revolution in British life, and resolved to be instrumental in bringing it about. First of all he founded an Actors' Studio based on American 'Method' type acting, but after that came a more important and successful project.

In his own words: 'Youth was busting out all over. There was a lot of money to be made. Things were really beginning to happen, and for the first time since the First World War Britain was swinging. Fortunately these ventures required hardly any money at all.'

The venture in question was the Scene Club in Great Windmill Street, Soho. Ronan knew exactly what British teenagers wanted, and understood that the growth of pop music and beat groups heralded a veritable pop culture of its own, which would forever be associated with the 1960s. Through the Scene Club he gave groups, like the subsequently highly successful Rolling Stones, their first break, and soon attracted 7,000 young members. It did not take long for the Irishman to realise that these young people would listen to pop music all day long, and an idea began to form in his mind.

The idea of Radio Caroline first began to take form in 1962. At this time O'Rahilly was the agent for Georgie Fame, a 'pop' singer who was soon to make the 'big time', but who then was virtually unknown. Every time the young agent tried to get a record company to cut a disc for him, however, the big concerns were not interested. When O'Rahilly went to Radio Luxembourg and offered to bring out his own record label if they would play it, he was told that they could not do so as most of the time on the station was booked by the big four record companies: the EMI, Decca, Pye and Philips groups.

In this way Ronan O'Rahilly became aware of the monopoly in the record business, and discovered that at that time independent companies were producing a mere one per cent of records sold. He became determined to change the situation. 'I wanted to break that monopoly so I started Caroline. I knew that if Caroline died the monopoly would grow.'

Ronan O'Rahilly was not, though, by any means the first 'pop' pirate. There had, in fact, been no less than eleven commercial radio stations on ships before Radio Caroline came on the air in March 1964. Most of these had broadcast pop music and commercials to Scandinavian and Northern European countries other than Britain, and most had been closed down.

In 1962 crew members of the Danish pirate radio ship Lucky Star were put under arrest by the Danish Navy and police following a court injunction gained against them by the Danish Government. Operating as Radio Mercur, the ship had been transmitting commercial programmes into Denmark since 1958 from an anchorage in international waters off the Danish coast.

In the same year, 1962, the Swedish pirate radio station Radio Nord, soon to reappear in a different form in the pirate radio world, had been silenced by order of the Swedish Government.

On the other side of the balance, when Radio Caroline came on the air, two pirates were successfully broadcasting from international waters. They were Radio Syd, off the Baltic coast of Sweden, and Radio Veronica, off Scheveningen on the Dutch coast.

The latter station had survived the animosity of the Dutch Government for over four years, and very successfully at that. A factor which probably influenced would-be British pirates was that Veronica was netting about £1 million per year from advertising revenue. Radio Veronica was, actually, the first pirate radio station to broadcast programmes in English. The station started transmissions in April 1960, and for some weeks in February and March 1961 had broadcast for a number of hours daily in English, in addition to normal Dutch language programmes.

*

At the beginning of 1964 Britain had not come under fire from the transmitters of the pirates. Ronan O'Rahilly set about remedying that situation.

His father, an Irish industrialist, had bought the entire port of Greenore in Eire from British Railways. After a search a suitable ship was found which would be strong enough to ride out any gale, for there would be no running to port in heavy seas for a pirate radio ship. The 188 foot-long motor vessel *Frederica* was found in a Dutch port and taken to Greenore, sixty miles north of Dublin. The ex-Danish passenger ferry was especially suitable for her new and exacting role. She had been used as a passenger ship in the Danish Islands and her hull had been specially strengthened to resist the pressure of ice. With the aid of £¼ million of Irish, British and Swiss money, O'Rahilly's Company, Planet Productions Ltd., rented the vessel from a Swiss company, Alraune.

Ronan O'Rahilly renamed the ship *Caroline*, after the daughter of the young Irish American who had become the first Roman Catholic President of the United States of America – John F. Kennedy. He chose the name when he was flying across to America and opened up his newspaper on a large picture of Caroline Kennedy. In O'Rahilly's words: 'She was smiling and she looked so young, so

The Radio Nord ship which broadcast to Swedish listeners from March 1961 for just over a year. In the foreground is Jack S. Kotschack, owner of the radio station.

fresh and happy. It was exactly the feeling I wanted to get across on the air. I chose the name on the spot.'

At Greenore the 763-ton, former passenger ferry assumed the role of a radio ship. The latest in broadcasting equipment, two 10 kW transmitters and a massive 168-foot high radio mast, was installed on board, and the ship was further strengthened to withstand the continuous assault of waves and winds. The broadcasting equipment was installed by Arthur Carrington, the pioneer of Britain's first aerial and undersea television transmissions, and who had formerly been employed by the BBC and the British Government on radar research and development. In this way it was ensured that the equipment was of the very highest standard so that no interference would be caused to other broadcasting services. The ship was also fitted out with two anchors designed to keep her steady in normal weather. The special anchoring equipment included one heavy-duty anchor for use in bad weather; in this situation the ship would sail into the weather, circling the anchor. All these preparations went on under conditions of great secrecy for two principal reasons.

Firstly, because of the danger of being forestalled by prohibitive legislation on the part of the British Government, O'Rahilly was convinced that once he got his station on the air it would prove tremendously popular; so popular that the Government would not dare to close it down. He, therefore, had to have the chance in the first place of putting Caroline on the air.

Secondly, a race against time was developing, for the 42-year-old Australian, Mr Allan Crawford, was pressing ahead with his own project, Radio Atlanta. Since 1962 Crawford had been thinking about broadcasting to Britain from a ship anchored outside territorial waters, long before he had discussed the idea with Ronan O'Rahilly. He had commenced preparations, working with London businessmen and an ex-Major, Oliver Smedley, and a theatrical impressario, Kitty Black. Both were to reappear later, dramatically, on the pirate scene.

Smedley had been given the task of making everything water-tight legally, which he did by setting up a number of interlocking companies in Britain and Liechtenstein. The company, however, lost its start on Radio Caroline when financial backing fell through after the Danish pirate ship *Lucky Star* was arrested by the Danish Government and towed into port. Although it transpired that this action took place only because a murder had been committed

*Radio Antwerpen broadcast to Flemish-speaking listeners from
off the coast of Belgium during 1962. On December 16, 1962,
the radio ship Uilenspiegel broke free from her anchor and went
aground on the Dutch coast at Cadzand. Only days previously the
Belgian Government had introduced legislation banning offshore
broadcasting stations.*

on board, it was sufficient to deter those interested in backing the British project. Millionaire property developer John Delaney originally agreed to put up £70,000, but the agreement fell through and the money had to be raised over nearly two years from small shareholders. After five months of formalities Smedley managed to obtain £55,000 from the Bank of England to take abroad in order to buy a vessel called the *Mi Amigo*, which was owned by a Swedish radio company and up for sale after the station had been prosecuted and closed down by the Swedish Government.

By the time the money was raised and formalities completed, however, the vessel had left Swedish waters and was crossing the Atlantic for the United States where it berthed in Galveston, Texas. Finally negotiations were completed and Crawford could press ahead. The Caroline project had a good start over him, and he did his best to get the 470-ton *Mi Amigo* fitted out as Radio Atlanta, at Galveston, as quickly as possible, and get in on the pirate radio business right at the beginning.

The *Mi Amigo* had an interesting history. The vessel had been built in 1920, and had served as a coaster until 1961. She then briefly joined the pirate radio business in 1962 as the Swedish pirate, Radio Nord.

It took the *Mi Amigo* twenty-seven days to cross the Atlantic, during which time she almost sank, but eventually arrived at Spain, where she was fitted with extra bilge keels to give her more stability. The ship, it turned out, though, needed a new radio mast and a pact was made with the rival Caroline organisation. In return for having Radio Atlanta's mast fitted at Greenore, it was agreed by Crawford that O'Rahilly could use his studios in London to tape-record programmes for Caroline.

As the two ships were being fitted out, in great secrecy, in Southern Ireland, both Crawford and O'Rahilly continued the search for backers and advertisers in Britain. Inevitably, rumours began to spread and leaks occurred.

On February 6th, 1964, the Postmaster-General, Mr Ernest Bevins, was questioned in the House of Commons about Radio Caroline. He asserted that broadcasting commercial radio programmes from a ship would break international rules and endanger international agreements about sharing radio frequencies. He said that it would almost certainly cause serious interference to radio communications in Britain and other countries, and hinted that legislation might be introduced to deal with it. This was to be the first of very many such threats by three Postmaster-Generals.

Mr O'Rahilly retorted, shortly before Radio Caroline went on the air: 'We have taken legal advice and we are certain that under international law they cannot touch us. Our company is registered in Switzerland, and does not come under the Minister.'

He certainly had had little difficulty in finding the necessary £250,000 for the project, and Mr Crawford had found backers ready to help finance Radio Atlanta with about £150,000.

By now the two companies were racing to get their rival ships to sea. Radio Atlanta experienced another setback. Its aerial mast failed to arrive on time; the *Mi Amigo* was ordered to leave the harbour at Greenore and anchor in the bay for seven stormy days, to make room for one of Mr O'Rahilly senior's coasters. During that week of gales the *Mi Amigo* very nearly ran aground and was saved only by the prompt and skilful action of her captain.

As the work on *Caroline* neared completion, O'Rahilly pretended to be unprepared and Crawford, in his turn, provided O'Rahilly with inexperienced technicians and misleading radio information.

But by the beginning of March work on the M.V. *Caroline* was complete and, with a Dutch crew on board, she left Greenore flying the Panamanian 'flag of convenience' and slowly made her way through the Channel. Her course and destination were followed closely by Mr Crawford, whose Radio Atlanta was nearing completion. It soon became clear that the *Caroline* would anchor off the south of England, and not the north as Crawford had believed she would do – leaving the south to Radio Atlanta. The course of the strange ship with its huge aerial mast was also closely followed elsewhere on shore. Shore radio stations were told that she was the *Caroline* 'heading south, destination Spain', but she made for the English Channel, not without inspection from a Royal Navy destroyer off Plymouth.

At 6 p.m. on Good Friday, March 27th, with strong winds whistling about her bows the *Caroline* dropped anchor five miles off Harwich in international waters. At 9 p.m. that night Radio Caroline put out her first test signal. The station was officially launched on Easter Sunday. Simon Dee, Britain's first pirate disc jockey, started the regular transmissions: 'Hello everybody. This is Radio Caroline broadcasting on 199, your all-day music station.' He had started more than he probably realised.

88,30 MHz

RADIO SYD

TRANSMISSION HOURS:
DAILY FROM 6.00 – 3.00 A.M.

MALMÖ 4 – SWEDEN

The M.V. Cheetah I, from which Radio Syd broadcast to Swedish listeners. The illustration is taken from the QSL card (Verification of Reception Report) issued in 1962, and it is to be noted that the station was broadcasting on FM (VHF) - a considerable technical achievement for the time and conditions.

The station announced that it would be broadcasting modern light music, a euphemism for 'pop', every day from 6 a.m. to 6 p.m. on 199 metres in the medium wave band. For the time being there would be no evening broadcast because of difficult reception, due to increased competition from continental stations after dark. As yet there was little advertising, though O'Rahilly claimed that advertisers were 'interested', but wanted to wait and see what kind of audience the station secured before committing themselves.

Meanwhile, on April 17th, the *Mi Amigo* had left Greenore and had given her destination as El Perroll. The authorities and the Radio Caroline organisation both followed her movements with great interest, but were left to guess at her destination. Nothing further was heard of the radio ship, which followed an erratic course, until she entered Falmouth, her 141-foot mast-shackle broken in a gale. The Captain had radioed a message to Lands End Radio requesting that workmen should travel to Falmouth from Greenore to carry out repairs, but the station refused to accept the message and it had had to be sent through a more co-operative Continental station.

After repairs she disappeared into the Channel and re-appeared on the 27th April off the Essex coast, where she anchored 3½ miles South-east of Frinton-on-Sea; within sight of her rival.

On the 9th of May, 1964, the second pirate radio station, Radio Atlanta, came on the air with test transmissions. She began transmitting on the same wavelength as her near-neighbour, Radio Caroline, when that station went off the air at 6 p.m. Between records disc jockey Bob Scott, of Radio Atlanta, emphasised that it was a test transmission: 'You are tuned to Radio Atlanta', he said, 'this is not a regular format, it is a test format. I repeat, this is a test transmission.'

Radio enthusiasts on the coast twelve miles away at Felixstowe reported that the signal strength was slightly higher than Caroline's. The station had six disc jockeys and, when it began regular broadcasting, was on the air twelve hours a day. Most of the disc jockeys, unlike those of Caroline, never set foot on board the ship, but instead recorded all their programmes in a studio in Soho. The tapes then had to be rushed out to the ship by the programme controller, Richard Harris, who drove down to Brightlingsea and put them on board the only tender the station could find – a gravel barge. Sometimes the tapes arrived with only minutes to spare, and Texan radio engineers Johnny Johnson and Bob Scott had to turn disc jockey. Ronan O'Rahilly, meanwhile, sent Allan Crawford a 'Good Luck' telegram.

The *Daily Mail* declared of the pirates: 'And whatever the official view of the Postmaster-General might be, the public seem to like it.'

This observation was borne out by a Gallup Poll which showed that in its first three weeks Radio Caroline gained nearly seven million listeners. This figure did not include listeners under the age of seventeen, and the total was from a potential audience of only twenty million people.

Mr Bevins and the authorities, though, were far from inactive.

On April 1st the General Post Office had officially requested the International Telecommunications Union (the body which controls all broadcasting throughout the world by regulating frequencies and powers of transmission) to help in stopping the pirate broadcasters. The ITU stated on April 3rd that it would remind Panama of a provision in international radio regulations that the use of broadcasting stations on board ships outside territorial waters was prohibited.

Mr Bevins informed the House of Commons on April 7th that Panama had accordingly withdrawn registration from the vessel *Caroline*, and that he was considering the possibility of legislation to deal with such broadcasting.

Official action against Radio Caroline came in her first week when the GPO cut off the ship-to-shore radio link, announcing that messages from the *Caroline* would be handled only in an emergency. Only the supply tender remained for communication with the land, as obviously arrangements about programmes, commercials and so on could not be made over the air. When the tender left Harwich for international waters H.M. Customs and Excise ruled that it was leaving the country and, therefore, those on board had to carry passports, stores were inspected, and the shipping agents had to additionally go through H.M. Waterguard, H.M. Immigrations and the Special Branch of the CID for each trip made. Other authorities involved were the Board of Trade, the Ministry of Transport, British Railways, the Port of Health Authority, Trinity House, and the Local Harbour Board!

The tenders, supplied by a Dutch salvage and ship delivery firm, travelled to *Caroline* about three or four times a week with food, fuel, water, relief crew, disc jockeys and, of course, records.

In May the first attempt by the British authorities to board a pirate station took place. Shortly after it took place Radio Caroline disc jockey Simon Dee broadcast a news flash:

The former Radio Nord ship photographed from the air as she prepares to drop anchor to take up her new role as Radio Atlanta.

At 12.20 p.m. today Her Majesty's vessel *Venturous*, flying the Blue Ensign, drew close to *Caroline* on the port side. Permission was asked to board to see our bonded stores. We replied that this was against the law appertaining to international waters and one man only would be allowed access in a lifeboat. This offer was not accepted and at 12.33 p.m. the *Venturous* drew off.

One wonders what would have happened if *Caroline* had been boarded. Would the sound of offshore radio have disappeared? It is not unreasonable to suspect that it might indeed have done.

Fears that the transmissions would affect air and sea navigation proved exaggerated, but Belgium complained of interference with its authorised programme service from Brussels. The Belgian authorities probably failed to appreciate the point of view of the enthusiastic journalist who telephoned Radio Atlanta from Antwerp to say that the programmes came over better than Radio Brussels!

Soon after Radio Caroline came on the air Phonographic Performances Ltd. announced its intention of securing a High Court injunction against the station. The Company, representing record companies, alleged infringement of the copyright laws.

In a statement, the Company said that counsel had advised that unauthorised broadcasting of its members' records on stations outside territorial waters and beamed to Britain, represented a breach of copyright. The statement added: 'Indiscriminate broadcasting of records is detrimental to the interests of the industry, musicians and artists.'

Rumours began of a link-up with Radio Atlanta to fight this threat. Mr O'Rahilly said in London: 'We are in the same business – possibly our relations will get closer. Approximately £250,000 has been spent on this venture and we mean to continue. We have had no communication from Phonographic Performances.'

At the same time, though, it was announced that the Performing Rights Society, an association of composers, authors and publishers of music, had invited Radio Caroline to become a member.

Phonographic Performances quickly found an ally in Mr Roy Mason, Labour MP for Barnsley, who established himself as an adversary of the pirates by putting down thirteen Commons questions seeking a ban on pirate radio ships. Certainly Mr Mason and the authorities seemed to be able to do little about the radio pirates' claimed audience of seven million listeners, although, technically, under the terms of the GPO Wireless Receiving Licence, it was an offence to listen to such unlicensed transmissions. Clearly, though, prosecution of seven million people was out of the question!

In a written Commons reply on May 12th, the day Radio Atlanta began regular transmissions, Mr Bevins said that transmissions from Radio Caroline had caused interference to British and Belgian maritime services during the first few days of broadcasting, though interference since had been 'negligible'. Serious interference, however, could recur at any time if the ship's powerful transmitters were not properly maintained. Mr Bevins stated that the phonographic industry had been in dose touch with the GPO on the subject, and he had also had representations from the Songwriters' Guild of Great Britain, which was anxious that the development of pirate broadcasting stations be stopped as soon as possible.

The same day Mr Bevins met the Conservative Party's Radio and TV Committee. At this meeting he spoke of his plans for pirate radio and local sound broadcasting in Britain. News that was leaked to the radio pirates about Mr Bevins' comments at the meeting made them jubilant; news to the effect that he had put off any action against them.

The headlines announced next day: 'Pirate radio ship No. 2 on the air – Bevins beaten.'

Although Mr Bevins' action was taken as a climb-down, his decision was based on the consideration that action by all the nations of Europe, rather than by Britain alone, was necessary.

That day Radio Atlanta had had an all-star send-off when it commenced transmissions at 6 p.m. Alma Cogan, Harry Secombe, Frank Ifield, Cliff Richard and The Shadows, Victor Sylvester, Edmundo Ros, Peter Finch and Rolf Harris were among show business personalities who wished Atlanta 'Good Luck'.

Mr Allan Crawford stated: 'We approached the stars and they all agreed to wish us well. This shows that they, as well as the public, want commercial radio.'

Mr Crawford exultantly claimed that the programmes had been picked up 'loud and clear' in South Wales and Belgium. He said: 'We waited until we went on the air before worrying about advertisers. Now we're looking for commercials.'

One of London's biggest advertising agencies was said to be planning to advertise with the pirate ships through its Dutch and French companies. On the advertising front it was Caroline which hit the jackpot the day following the Postmaster-General's rumoured decision. On May 13th £30,000 of advertising poured in.

A spokesman for the Caroline organisation explained: 'Many of the bookings were hanging fire to see what action the Postmaster-General would take. Now that he has decided to let us continue we have been flooded with inquiries. The bookings range from holiday camps to carpet firms.'

Meanwhile, Radio Atlanta was reported to be reaching more of the country than Caroline with her broadcasts from 6 a.m. to 6 p.m. on 200.6 metres, 'a cat's whisker' away from Radio Caroline on 199 metres. The competition for audiences and advertising had begun.

The trend in pirate radio gradually became, as the number of stations grew, to have more and more powerful transmitters covering a larger area, therefore a larger public, and therefore bringing in more money from advertisers. Two years later, as the situation began to get out of hand, it was to become a matter of 'bigger and better than you' in an undignified scramble for higher power transmitters and larger listening audiences.

This trend, and the associated dangers of pirate radio, were probably foreseen in an action taken on May i3th, the day Radio Caroline hit the jackpot in advertising revenue. A committee of government experts from the seventeen member countries of the Council of Europe adopted a draft European agreement for the suppression of pirate broadcasting. This draft agreement was aimed at making it illegal to transmit from radio stations at sea or from the air outside territorial limits to member countries, or to cause harmful interference to the radio services under those countries' authority. Under the agreement it would be an offence not only to operate such stations, but also to sponsor, service, supply or assist them. The experts' views were embodied in a recommendation to the Ministerial Committee of the Council of Europe, which was expected to consider the adoption of a convention along these lines towards the end of 1964. Once this was done the stations could be silenced through national legal action.

Mr Bevins stated in the House of Commons on June 2nd that such concerted action was needed. Whilst some Scandinavian countries and Belgium had already legislated on the matter, the Government considered that it would be wrong to introduce legislation at present which could be evaded because of the absence of corresponding legislation in other European countries. In reply to demands for the introduction of local sound broadcasting, because of favourable reaction to the pirates, Mr Bevins stressed that the

*Richard Harris, the moving force behind Radio Atlanta, in the
station's early primitive studios. He was later to claim that Ronan
O'Rahilly stole from him the notion of pirate pop radio.*

17

Government could not accept the establishment of pirates as a reason for making precipitate decisions on local BBC or commercial radio, although, in the next parliament, it would undertake the review foreshadowed in the 1962 White Paper.

Thus Mr Bevins temporarily shelved this increasingly knotty problem. He had examined the possibility of legislation by Britain acting on her own, and rejected it. Whether he did so for the reason he gave, that is, to wait for concerted action through the Council of Europe Convention expected at the end of the year, is doubtful. The fact remains that he encountered opposition from a group of back-benchers who argued that the pirate radio stations supplied a need. These back-benchers represented constituents who were enjoying the wares purveyed by the stations; and there was a General Election due at any time.

The second part of the Postmaster-General's statement high-lighted the fact that the success of the new stations had had the effect of reactivating arguments for and against commercial radio in Britain, rejected as undesirable in the Pilkington Report in 1962, and the National Broadcasting Development Committee renewed pressure for experimentation with local broadcasting stations to be financed and run by private companies.

On May 27th a third pirate set sail on the radio waves. The new station was Radio Sutch, organised and run by Mr David Sutch, otherwise known as 'Screaming Lord Sutch', a long-haired 'pop' singer of doubtful vocal attributes, and one-time plumber. He had succeeded in making news the year before, in August 1963, when he unsuccessfully contested Stratford Parliamentary by-election as an Independent Teenage candidate.

His departure, in the 60-foot fishing trawler *Cornucopia* smacked distinctly of comedy, bordering on the farcical. The vessel sailed flying the skull and crossbones, and a banner proclaiming 'Radio Sutch' was slung between the masts. Four men in leopard skins shinned the main mast or clung to the rigging as radio transmitting equipment was loaded aboard the trawler. Twenty-two year-old David Sutch wore a purple velvet cape, bright blue trousers and brandished a cutlass. River police and a harbour-master's launch cruised watchfully near the blue-painted trawler as Mr Sutch's manager, Mr Reg. Calvert, later to be the victim of one of the most dramatic incidents in connection with pirate radio, told reporters: 'This is definitely not a hoax or a stunt. I have seen record players

The Radio Caroline ship was a converted Danish ferry boat. This photograph was taken during the station's early days as she approached her mooring off the Isle of Man.

which will practically play upside down and we don't anticipate difficulty transmitting from a small boat.

' "Radio Sutch" will broadcast over a fifty mile radius on 200 metres. Daily programmes will be from 12 noon to 2 p.m., 5 to 8 p.m., and 12.15 to 2.15 a.m.

'The later night transmissions will include saucy bedtime stories. The sort of thing we may do is fade music of, say, *In an English Garden* to a five-minute reading of *Lady Chatterley's Lover*. There will be no smut but we may send up some BBC programmes.'

It was announced that Mr Calvert's daughter Elaine, 13, would compere one of the programmes, 'Candy's Pop Shop', during her school holidays.

Mr Sutch said that the station was to carry no advertisements, but included in the broadcasts would be tape recordings by little-known pop groups and singers. He hoped that any who subsequently became famous would contribute to the station's costs, which Mr Calvert estimated at £4,000 plus £300 a week to run. Mr Sutch had underwritten the costs of the first month's operation, and intended to broadcast himself over the station, although continuing to perform on shore.

As the *Cornucopia* sailed away down the Thames it was fully expected that the vessel would anchor at the stated destination, four miles off Shoeburyness, and start transmissions. Events, however, took a different, surprise turn.

Radio Sutch was due to begin broadcasts at noon on May 27th. Listeners on shore, however, tuned their sets to 200 metres in vain. Then came the news that on May 26th the Army Department had been notified that 'Lord' Sutch was moving into an abandoned, derelict gun tower, one of a group, at Shivering Sands, off the Essex coast. This distinctly odd-looking structure consisted of a complex of six separate forts perching zoo feet above the sea on stilts and joined together by narrow catwalks. During the war the fort had been used as an anti-aircraft gun emplacement, but since then had fallen into disuse and disrepair.

The only news of the pop pirates came from Mr Terry King, 'Lord' Sutch's agent in London, who announced that 'Lord' Sutch and his team had lost contact with his organisation on shore. Messages were to have been relayed to a shortwave receiver on the coast, but there was silence from Shivering Sands. Said Mr King: 'We are trying to establish communication. Installation of the equipment may have been delayed because of the 100 foot haul up the tower.'

In May 1964 pop singer 'Screaming' Lord Sutch sailed down the Thames amid a blaze of publicity and occupied one of the deserted anti-aircraft forts in the Estuary. He later sold out to his manager Reginald Calvert who started Radio City.

When the station eventually did open, it was found that it could only be heard over a small area and represented little threat to the more powerful and professional Caroline and Atlanta stations. The disc jockeys did not even introduce many of the records; frequently LPs were put on and the disc jockey waited until one side had played and then merely turned it over. At other times the station's lack of organisation was revealed by such pleas as: 'If any boat is coming this way we're running short of bread.'

Meanwhile, in Whitehall, the Army Department was investigating the ownership of the fort, or rather, one suspects, investigating to whom the buck could be passed. A spokesman admitted, 'They were our forts. I am finding out whether we still have responsibility.' If someone had claimed responsibility for the fort on Shivering Sands then subsequent tragedy could have been averted. No one, however, seemed interested in claiming any responsibility for evicting its newly acquired, non-paying tenants. Soon a scramble for the forts in the Thames was to take place as a direct result of this official inertia.

A notable development came in July when it was announced that Radio Caroline and Radio Atlanta had joined forces. This was the culmination of merger talks between Ronan O'Rahilly, of Caroline, and Allan Crawford, of Atlanta, which had been going on since before either ship came on the air; agreement was reached on July 2nd. Both now operated under the call 'Caroline' but the M.V. *Caroline* moved to a new position off Ramsey, Isle of Man, and the *Mi Amigo* stayed in its position off Frinton. The two stations were named Caroline North and Caroline South respectively. The reason for the move north was, in Mr O'Rahilly's words, because of 'the tremendous public response to commercial radio in the north'. The *Caroline* sailed to the Isle of Man at the beginning of July, broadcasting as she went.

At this time the Caroline company. Planet Productions Ltd, moved out of its offices in the building occupied by Queen Magazine and into Chesterfield Gardens in Mayfair. A studio was built, equipment and telephones installed, but the GPO refused to list the number in the Directory!

Already the first 'Save Radio Caroline' petition had been organised in Ipswich and in a few days nearly 5,000 signatures collected. It was to be the first of many such petitions, but in the end of the day they were all to prove of no avail.

2

The *Jolly Roger* flies high

During the summer of 1964 another station came on the air with test broadcasts. It was, though, different from any pirate station in most respects. It was land-based, low-powered and licensed by the GPO. After a long struggle, the people of the Isle of Man had won the right to their own local radio station.

The Isle of Man is a remarkable place for its size. It has its own Parliament, one of the oldest in the world, a TT race, a small flock of four-horned sheep and cats with no tails. Now it was unique in another respect. There had been agitation throughout Britain, especially at the time of the Pilkington Report, for local commercial radio, but it was the little Isle of Man which, cocking a snook at the rest of Britain, gained its own station first.

The man Manxmen had to thank for their new endowment was Mr T. H. Colbourn, Manx Radio's Chairman. Like O'Rahilly he had a reputation for being something of a rebel. Years before, when BBC TV failed to include the Isle of Man in their plans, he built his own TV mast, picked up the BBC transmissions, and broadcast them to the islanders. Dismayed and slightly taken aback at this display of initiative, the BBC later put up their own mast.

Mr Colbourn was a well-known, self-made Manx business man whose large radio and TV business serviced a great deal of the island's communications. He was described at the time by *The Observer* as 'a tall, lantern-jawed extrovert; he has a reputation of being difficult to work with, particularly if people try to make him observe formalities. He is the sort of man who says he likes a fight and really means it.'

Manx Radio was Colbourn's idea, and as a member of the Manx Government he was in a position to implement it. For two years the Manx Government had negotiated with the Home Office and the GPO for the right to have a local radio station. In March 1964 the GPO finally agreed to license a station, providing it could not be received outside the island.

At the beginning of June the GPO licence was sent to Pye, who were to build the station. It was only for VHF transmission, though, as the Medium Wave frequency offered by the GPO, 1,594 kc/s, on very low power, had been rejected earlier by Pye on technical grounds. Pye had requested the frequency of 539 kc/s, and had been backed by the Manx Government. The GPO rejected this as impossible on the grounds that the frequency would be heard on the mainland, and also that the British Government, under international agreement, was not allowed to allocate this frequency.

Mr Richard Meyer was appointed to run the station, and as a man with considerable experience in commercial broadcasting, he was not too taken with the idea of broadcasting on VHF only. VHF broadcasting is a comparative innovation, and it is only in the last ten years that receivers for VHF have really come on the market. They are expensive and sales of them are generally admitted to have been poor. Not surprisingly, therefore, there were few VHF receivers on the Isle of Man.

Another figure in this struggle was Sir Ronald Garvey, the island's Lieutenant-Governor. Previous to his post in the Isle of Man Sir Ronald had been Governor of Fiji where, under his auspices, a local radio station had been introduced. As he was keen to see a station on the air in the Isle of Man it was seen as no coincidence that two masts appeared on the twenty acre site next door to Sir Ronald's Government House.

Transmissions during the summer only took the form of test broadcasts, and it was not until November 2nd that regular broadcasting began on 1,594 kc/s, the frequency originally rejected as not feasible technically. The power available under the GPO licence, a mere 50 watts, one two-hundredth of Caroline's power, was somewhat grudgingly used by Meyer, who voiced the hope that it would soon be increased to a more powerful 2 kW. Colbourn declared that obviously the station was interested in broadcasting to the mainland. Meyer had much experience in such external broadcasting. He had been manager of the International Broadcasting Company which started Radio Luxembourg before the war, had been commercial manager of ATV and started television in the Rhodesian federation. Clearly, Meyer and Pye were not just interested in the small population of the Isle of Man. The idea of using the island as a base from which to transmit into more densely populated North-western England was obviously prominent in their minds.

It had been quite an achievement to gain this station for the little island and the chagrin of Meyer and Pye, when Radio Caroline arrived in Ramsey Bay and started pumping out 10 kW of power into the island and North-western England, can be easily understood.

Manx Radio began its operations from a caravan situated on a hillside outside Douglas. This site gave coverage of only half of the island and, since the original Post Office licence was for VHF only, a mere 10 per cent of Manxmen could hear the station at first. Things soon changed though. The station moved its headquarters to Douglas seafront; at Foxdale the station erected two twin 180-foot masts for the medium wave transmissions, and on the peak of Snaefell a VHF Transmitter was installed. The station gained an extension to its licence and began broadcasts on 1,295 kc/s, as well as 1,594 kc/s and VHF, on an increased power of 2 kW. On the new medium wave frequency Manx Radio could be well heard in much of the North of England.

Within the island, the station rapidly established itself as an integral part of local life, running regular features for Scouts, women's societies, classes in Manx Gaelic and a weekly twenty minute quiz for local schools. Services for housewives included shopping reports, 'Melting Pot', a feature in which practical domestic problems were answered, and 'Swap Shop' when the station acted, free of charge, as an exchange mart for listeners wishing to swap almost anything.

The value of local radio was displayed when three prisoners escaped from the island's gaol. As a result of the descriptions broadcast by Manx Radio, a farmer spotted them and they were caught within half an hour.

The smallest of businessmen and shopkeepers found themselves able to advertise over the station, with its low rates of £1 for thirty seconds, or 12s 6d for fifteen seconds. Eighty per cent of the station's advertising came from local sources and it was estimated that of the 50,000 islanders, about the same percentage were listeners to Manx Radio. The station's relations with Radio Caroline were to improve with time until the island developed a strong affection for the offshore broadcaster, but its relations with the BBC were distinctly unhappy. John Grierson, the station's general manager, has claimed that 'the BBC loathes us'. The BBC tried to monopolise the commentary on the TT races in 1965 by arranging with the Auto Cycle Union that only they should broadcast from the grandstand. When Manx Radio's protests failed, the small station set up its commentary box just outside the grandstand and broadcast a better and fuller commentary than its rival.

The station's ambition to have a more powerful transmitter broadcasting to both Britain and Europe grew stronger with time, and this eventually was to be the cause of a bitter feud between Tynwald and the British Government.

Thus by the summer of 1964, Britain had four commercial radio stations; three pirate radios, and one GPO licensed local radio station. By autumn 1964 there was also a General Election looming up, and the question of broadcasting looked like joining the list of subjects for political discussion.

Mr Bevins, in June, committed the Tories to reviewing the whole question of commercial broadcasting, should they be returned to power in the October election. The Labour Party ardently denounced, in the words of one of its M.P.s, the 'greedy, money-grabbing lobby agitating for commercial radio'. The Tories, inevitably, became associated with the commercial radio lobby, and the Labour Party with the kill-joys interested in preserving the sanctity of the BBC monopoly.

The fact remained that the pirates now had an estimated audience of nearly ten million, though perhaps a rather optimistic estimate. To many millions of people these stations were bringing pleasure and had clearly fulfilled a need for all-day light and popular music. It was with real feeling that one Tory M.P. estimated that if Mr Bevins were to come out against the pirate stations it would cost him thousands of votes. Thus at the Election the potentially explosive problem of the pirates, and the associated issue of commercial radio which they had raised, was pushed firmly under the counter lest it be detonated. The Tory Party could not lend itself to an irresponsible condonation of a practice the legality of which was in doubt, and the Labour Party, if it was to hope to win the Election, could not condemn the pirates.

As the smoke of the Election battle cleared and a new Post-master-General appeared, in the form of Mr Anthony Wedgwood Benn, two new offshore sounds had come on the air.

Following the lead of the Radio Sutch interlopers, in June another disused Ministry of Defence fort in the Thames had been seized. Radio Invicta, which billed itself as 'The Good-Music Station', came on the air from Red Sands Fort, abandoned since 1956 by the Ministry. This station broadcast from midnight to 6

Red Sands Fort in the Thames Estuary. Loading supplies for King Radio

p.m., and announced that it planned a twenty-four-hour service. Power at first was only 1 kW but later was raised.

The station lacked either the professional organisation or approach to broadcasting of Radio Caroline with pleas to listeners for 'any old records'. The station was run originally by a local fisherman of the name of Tom Pepper and two partners, Charlie Evans, the landlord of the Oddfellows Arms on Folkestone quay, and John Thompson, a Canadian who had been involved in a number of unsuccessful pirate projects.

During June, however, Pepper cut his partners out – something which they did not take too kindly to and a small-scale pirate war began. Someone smashed the fuel pumps of two of Pepper's supply boats, and the tyres of Charlie Evans's car were slashed as it stood outside his pub. Thugs employed by Pepper watched his former business colleagues, and tried to ruin any attempts to start another station or take over Radio Invicta.

In December, however, pirate radio claimed its first victim when Tom Pepper and two colleagues met a sticky end. On the night of December i6th, together with disc jockey Simon Ashley and engineer Martin Shaw, he was returning ashore from the fort when a sudden squall blew up and the supply boat, *The David*, began to fill with water and sank. Pepper tied himself to a board but froze to death in the cold winter waters. The unrecognisable body of one of the occupants of the boat was found as far away as Spain months later. There was, however, on it a three-inch spool of recording tape, which was dried out and played. It was a programme for Radio Invicta.

Rumour has, and will always, surround the death of Pepper. He was not a popular man, and immediately Thompson and Evans got together to replace Radio Invicta with another station on Red Sands Fort.

Broadcasting from a fort had its obvious advantages; the station was much cheaper to run than if it was on a ship, and for the DJs life was, of course, much more comfortable! Many people were asking, however, what right the 'pirates' on the forts in the Thames had to be there at all.

In the Second World War the forts had been constructed for the country's defence. The Army had constructed three in the Thames Estuary; Red Sands Towers, from which Radio Invicta broadcast, Shivering Sands Towers from which Radio Sutch operated and a third fort, the Great Nore, which was demolished immediately after the war as it stood in one of the main shipping lanes. These

M.V. Galaxy, *the Radio London ship, commenced broadcasting in December 1964.*

fort complexes all consisted of seven separate towers set on stilts about a hundred feet above the sea, and linked by narrow catwalks. In the war anti-aircraft guns had been mounted on the forts, but soon afterwards they were just abandoned.

The Navy also had four forts, of different design and construction, built off the East coast and in the Thames Estuary. These were Roughs Tower, seven miles south-east of Harwich, Sunk Head Tower, further south-east, Tongue Sands Tower, north of Margate, and Knock John Tower off Southend. These forts consisted of reinforced concrete, boat-shaped pontoons from which two cylindrical towers rose. On top of the towers was a platform on which there were the fort installations and living quarters. The forts were manned by 100 officers and men who had joined them while they were still under construction in the Thames. When work was completed they were floated out and sunk on the sea bed so that only the superstructure and a little of the twin towers supporting it were visible above the water. Apart from the protection against E-boat attack afforded by the large naval guns, the forts reported important intelligence information from their exposed positions.

After the 'pirates' took them over, there was much debate over whether or not the forts were still Crown property. No Government Department seemed keen to accept responsibility for the strange structures, and it appeared that those occupying them simply exercised a form of squatters' rights. In 1963 the War Office had tried to sell them – but no one had been interested and, since it would have meant more trouble and cost than was worthwhile to demolish them, they were completely forgotten about ... at least for a while.

In December the most powerful pirate yet took the air. The new pirate was called Radio London and operated from the converted ex-American minesweeper *Galaxy* registered in Liechtenstein. Originally the station anchored in the Thames Estuary within territorial waters, but immediately Ronan O'Rahilly of Radio Caroline contacted the owners, pointing out the fact and it was moved to a position off Harwich. O'Rahilly did not want offshore radio to get a bad name.

The ship itself had an interesting and colourful history to match its new romantic role. As a minesweeper it had disposed of nearly 500 mines and had taken part in a dramatic wartime rescue in which hundreds of men were saved from a sinking ship. The boat served as a cargo ship after the war, until she was bought by American

Disc jockeys on board Radio London. Extreme left is Tony Blackburn.

interests for conversion into a radio ship. To be fitted out she was taken to Miami where a 50 kW transmitter and a 212-foot high mast, 23 feet higher than Nelson's column, were installed.

The Bahamas-based Trust which owned the station, the Marine Investment Co. Inc. of Freeport, Grand Bahama Island, was backed by American businessmen to the tune of £½ million. Mr Philip Birch, a 35-year-old, shrewd businessman with a background as a J. Walter Thompson advertising executive in the United States, was appointed the station's managing director and brought with him to Radio London a slick, professional style of salesmanship and broadcasting. With its catchy American jingles and professional disc jockeys the station soon built up a large audience. Although the London transmitter was capable of transmitting a most effective 50 kW, which would cover most of southern England and the midlands, it at first only used 17 kW on 266 metres, conveniently near to the Light Programme medium-wave frequency. Developments now were coming thick and fast. In October Radio Sutch changed its name to the ill-fated name of Radio City. 'Lord' Sutch relinquished ownership of the station for the sum of £5,000 to Mr Reg. Calvert, who had been his manager. The station obtained a new 1 kW transmitter, and started broadcasting with its two transmitters on two different frequencies.

Pirate radio, with its romantic associations and lucrative temptations, began to capture the imagination of all sorts of people who went out in small boats with primitive transmitting equipment, a selection of 'pop' records and a record player. Stations identifying themselves as 'Radio Red Rose', from the Irish Sea, 'Radio Lambay', off the Irish coast and 'Radio Shannon' from the coaster D.S. *Viking* were all reported to have been heard. At the end of 1964 a 'Radio North Sea', which seemed to be of Dutch origin, was frequently heard. It then disappeared from the air as mysteriously as it had come. Amateurs quickly disappeared from the air, for to run a pirate station was expensive, and risky too.

Their precarious position was brought home to the pirate stations in December 1964, when Radio Noordzee, an offshore commercial radio station which had been directing commercial TV, as well as radio, to Holland since September 1st, was seized and silenced as a result of Dutch Government action.

Although radio advertising and commercial TV were not allowed in the Netherlands, Radio Noordzee had been transmitting to a reception area which included Amsterdam, Rotterdam, The Hague, Utrecht, and the coastal region. Many leading Dutch and foreign firms bought advertising time on the station at 6,000 to 9,000 guilders per minute (£600-900). At first the TV transmissions were run by a Dutch company called REM, Reclame Exploitatie Maatschapij, one of the promoters of which was a well-known Rotterdam shipbuilder, Mr Cornelius Verolme.

On September 16th legislation giving the Dutch Government power to apply Netherlands laws and administrative measures to fixed artificial structures built on the Netherlands part of the North Sea Continental Shelf, even if the installation concerned was outside Dutch territorial waters, was introduced to the Lower House of the States-General. Not only did the measure apply to Radio Noordzee, located on an artificial platform mounted on steel stilts in the sea-bed six miles north-west of the seaside resort of Noordwijk, but also to rigs used to drill for underseas deposits of gas and oil. The Minister of Justice, Dr Scholten, explained, however, that it would not apply to unlicensed radio stations operating from ships outside territorial waters, such as Radio Veronica.

The legislation was passed, by a large majority, on December 1st, 1964, coming into effect on December 5th, and three regulations implementing the Act were issued on December loth, and became operative on December 12th.

On the same day REM announced that it had ended its transmissions and that the radio and TV installations had been taken over by a foreign company. The Prime Minister of the Netherlands, Dr Marijnen, stated on December 16th that the floating platform had become the property of a Panamanian company, whilst the use of the transmitter/was in the hands of a British company named as High Seas Television Ltd of London.

At dawn the next day, in a dramatic air and sea operation, Radio Noordzee was seized by the Netherlands police and put out of action on the instructions of the Public Prosecutor of Amsterdam, Dr J. G. Hartsuijker. Early on the morning of the 17th, police officials sailed from Hook of Holland in the naval auxiliary vessel *Delfshaven* and took up a position 200 yards from the pirate radio. At the same time three naval helicopters flew low over the station and landed a boarding party of ten policemen who immediately tore down the station's aerials, found their way to the control room and put the transmitter out of action the announcer cut off in mid-sentence. Meanwhile, the police on the *Delfshaven* stood by with rope ladders and boarding gear, but no resistance was offered by the ten-man crew of the station.

In Amsterdam, Dr Hartsuijker explained that the action had been taken only after the radio station's Dutch lawyers had informed him that there would be no co-operation in any closedown attempt in conformity with the legislation passed by the States-General.

A London businessman, Mr Eric Bent, stated that he was the sole director of High Seas TV, which six weeks earlier had been given sole right by REM to operate Radio Noordzee. Mr Bent, who was also managing director of two London printing firms, said that 'an official protest' had been made to the Netherlands Government by the Dutch legal advisers of High Seas TV Ltd.

The Public Prosecutor of Amsterdam stated that there would be a preliminary judicial investigation with a view to summonses being served on the defendant, who could not at present be named. The Dutch authorities, however, one suspects, had got themselves into a legal tangle to try the finest of lawyers. They had succeeded in silencing Radio Noordzee, the legality of which action was seriously questioned, but legal proceedings presented severe difficulties in the manipulation of international law and its application to citizens outwith the Netherlands.

Nevertheless, Radio Noordzee remained as a reminder to the pirate radio operators of the basic insecurity of their tenure of the radio waves.

As the New Year came in the competition among the pirate radio stations was still comparatively mild, not reaching its peak until the beginning of 1966. Radio Caroline South headed the popularity stakes, and consequently the advertising stakes, but was being closely pursued by the new but rapidly established Radio London. Radio Caroline's ship in the North was next in number of listeners, having found a ready market for her wares in the North, the home of beat-groups and the currently popular 'Liverpool sound'. The much less powerful Radio City came bottom of the league.

Radio Invicta had left the air after the death of its owner and two members of its staff and in January it re-appeared under a new name – Radio King. It was rumoured for a while that the Irish pop group 'The Bachelors' had bought the station, but this proved to be untrue. The station was now run by Charlie Evans, who had been involved with Invicta before the now dead Tom Pepper had cut

Dutch marines and police invade the REM artificial island off the coast of the Netherlands. The Dutch navy vessel Delfshaven *is in the foreground with a marine helicopter overhead.*

him out, and also an ex-Radio Atlanta disc jockey, Mike Raven, was involved. Charlie Evans's original idea was to declare Red Sands Fort, from which the station broadcast, an independent Kingdom with himself as King, and the station called Radio King, for he reckoned that as the forts were on the high seas they did not belong to anyone, and therefore the first person to fly a flag there would be the owner. This idea was dropped though.

When Mike Raven arrived at the fort with broadcasting equipment on board a Whitstable fishing boat, a shock awaited him. As the boat approached the fort through the fog, with disc jockeys Frank Smith, who had been Eddie Gerrold of Radio Invicta, and Eddie Hinkins also on board, three men came running out shouting and waving. When they had climbed the 60-foot ladder to the platform set on stilts above the water they found the men there to be starving; they had been marooned on the fort for three weeks. Two disc jockeys, Roger Gomez and Bruce Holland, had gone out to the fort to make some test transmissions, but the transmitter had broken down. The water barrels had run dry and the tinned food ran out. They had lived for days on dehydrated peas eaten straight from the packet!

Eventually Mike Raven got Radio King on the air as a 'sweet music' rather than a 'pop' station, and in a few months it gained an audience in Kent of about 20,000. The station was run on a shoestring and encountered many difficulties; lack of financial backing, transmitter and generator trouble, and storms which caused the fort towers to move in the wind – they had been designed to give with the recoil of the anti-aircraft guns. During one storm lightning actually struck the transmitter aerial and sent the transmitter flashing and crackling.

The new Postmaster-General, Mr Anthony Wedgwood Benn, had been able to turn a blind eye to the pirate stations since he took over the running of the GPO in October 1964. Few incidents had occurred which could be the basis of awkward questions in the House, and the pressure of other events had diverted official and parliamentary attention from the pirates.

At the time of Radio City's increase in power, however, a complaint was made against the station for making radio communication difficult for trawlers. Mr Benn was called upon in March to give details of interference with radio communications by pirate radio stations. In a written answer he listed nineteen specific instances when transmissions from pirate stations had caused interference to ship-to-shore communications; in seven of these instances Radio Caroline was singled out as the offender.

It also emerged that during February an urgent radio report from a lightship to a shore base was held up for thirty minutes because both frequencies normally available were blocked, one by a pirate broadcasting station.

In April, though, came the most serious threat of interference with authorised communications. A new pirate station, using the name Radex, announced it would be on the air within the next couple of months. Not only would it broadcast 'pop' radio programmes round the clock, but also for twelve hours a day would broadcast TV programmes on Channel 6 on 405 lines, which was already allocated by the Government to the Radio Astronomy Services at Cambridge. The BBC and ITV had already been ordered by the Government not to use Channel 6 until space and astronomical investigations had been completed. The investigations of Radio Astronomy Services were reported to be of great importance to space research and astronomy.

Professor Martin Ryle, Director of the Radio Astronomy Observatory at Cambridge said: 'If this station comes on the air at the same time as we are working we just cannot operate. We are using two large radio telescopes and one would be put out of action. I am absolutely appalled by the incredibly feeble action being taken by Western Europe against these pirate radio stations. People just do not seem to be worrying. I am very worried by all this.'

A BBC engineer also asserted that the station would 'play havoc' with the valuable research of Radio Astronomy Services.

In the light of this it was expected that Mr Benn would be urged to speed legislation to take pirate broadcasters off the air when Parliament re-assembled after the Whitsun recess. The Postmaster-General had the weapon required, for in January the European Convention, to outlaw stations operating from outside territorial limits, had been signed.

But meanwhile the GPO admitted that it was powerless to deal with the proposed station. Radex planned to broadcast from a ship anchored off Whitstable to a potential audience of five million in South-east England and London. The station was reported to be backed by American business men to the tune of £1 million to cover running costs for a year. The company was registered in the

The Shivering Sands fort complex from which Radio City broadcast.

Bahamas. Fortunately for Mr Benn the proposed station, after two months had come and gone, showed no signs of materialising. In fact it emerged later that the American backers had withdrawn support from the Radex project, and it was called off. Thus Mr Benn managed to escape having to introduce legislation. Radex would almost certainly have brought matters to a head, but now the issue could be shelved. But every day the pirates remained on the air, the more popular they became, and the more difficult it would be to unseat them in the end.

The existing pirate stations continued to develop their facilities, and plans for new stations went ahead.

In March Reginald Calvert, the owner of Radio City, announced that he planned to start another pirate station from an ex-Royal Navy supply boat in the Bristol Channel, near Lundy Island, to cover South Wales and the West country.

Radio Caroline North started testing for two hours after midnight, requesting reception reports in English, German, Dutch, French and Spanish. Radio King similarly announced that it would shortly extend its programming into the night.

Announcements were made at the end of 1965 that a Radio Scotland would go on the air in December from either the Firth of Forth or the Firth of Clyde.

In June Radio City increased its power from 3½ kW to 10 kW and extended its broadcasting hours. As the station now had a much larger reception area and, consequently, a larger audience, it started to attract more advertising. An American religious organisation booked six hours a week for religious programmes of the evangelical 'hell-fire and damnation' type. At the rate of £125 an hour, these programmes alone covered the station's estimated weekly running costs of £600; a comparatively cheap operation when compared with the £5,000 to £10,000 a week running costs for a ship-borne station such as Radio London or Radio Caroline.

During September a clash between rival radio pirates occurred involving those on Radio City; not the first time they were to be involved in such a clash. Early in the month Mr Reg. Calvert landed about £3,000 worth of equipment on another deserted wartime fort, Knock John Tower, four miles from the Shivering Sands Fort. Radio City, rumoured at the time to be part of the Radio Caroline organisation, although Radio Caroline later denied any association with Radio City, had decided to use Knock John as a base to test equipment, not as another station. Trouble started a week later when Mr Roy Bates, a Southend businessman, decided to set up a pirate station, Radio Essex, on the tower.

Events then resembled pirate tales of old with both sides making landings on the fort. Radio City removed two Radio Essex men and took them by boat to Whitstable. Radio Essex hit back as soon as the Radio City garrison was diminished to three. Mr Bates landed with a boarding party and marooned the Radio City men on Shivering Sands. Radio City then planned to embark in force for Knock John where Mr Bates was working in the control room on his own transmitting gear. But after a month-long battle Mr Calvert announced: 'Probably Radio Essex hnd my men could share Knock John in future', and the battle was called off. Mr Calvert and Mr Bates eventually came to an agreement, and in November Radio Essex came on the air on 222 metres from Knock John Tower.

Radio Essex became the only localised offshore station and concentrated on the county of Essex. The station's DJs played easy listening music during the day and 'pop' during the night, using the identification 'The Voice of Essex'. The station also was the first pirate to broadcast regularly round the clock twenty-four hours a day.

Meanwhile, in September, King Radio became Radio 390 with new owners, programming, new frequency and increased power. The programming was totally different from the all-day 'pop' format of Caroline, London and City. Daytime programming consisted of 'Eve, the woman's magazine of the air'. In this the emphasis was on 'sweet', light music with announcements and talk kept down to the barest minimum. This light music programme was in sharp contrast to the mixture of endless pop and loquacious disc jockeys of the other pirates. Radio 390 soon gained a very large number of listeners who found the station far preferable, and proved that there was not only a need for a single pop music channel, so far unprovided by the BBC, but also for a single light music station. In December the BBC receiving station at Tatsfield estimated Radio 390 to be the most powerful of the pirate radio stations, and to have the widest effective coverage, with a transmitter capable of 60 kW.

All this activity on the part of the pirate radio operators was in marked contrast to the silence of the authorities. Any statement by the Postmaster-General was conspicuous by its absence. The last that had been heard from him had been in May when he had enigmatically warned: 'The pirates have no future'. This prolonged silence in official quarters was widely interpreted as a sign of a climb-down on the legislation against the pirates promised almost weekly by Mr Bevins when they first came on the air. The *Daily Mail* asked in October: 'Are the pop radio pirates about to receive an official pardon and be given a licence to operate legitimately ashore?'

Throughout the year the pirates had been gaining more and more listeners. The most conservative estimate numbered the listeners who tuned in at some time during the day to a pirate to be between ten and fifteen million. Their popularity was undoubted and was increasing with each day of official silence. Many of those associated with the offshore radio stations, as they preferred to speak of them, hoped, and even suspected, that this lack of condemnation meant that a bill for legalised commercial radio on land was in the pipeline. In that case they certainly intended to be 'in on it'.

On the other hand, it seemed unlikely that the Labour Party Government would introduce a bill allowing hundreds of com-panies to set up local radio stations, in the finest tradition of private enterprise, and most probably reap large rewards.

Nor could they afford to ban the pirates, so popular were they – especially with a precarious majority of three and another General Election expected in the spring. There had been a curious result in the by-election at Leyton in January. There the ill-fated and unfortunate Mr Patrick Gordon Walker lost Labour a safe seat, dropping an 8,000 majority. A large number of reasons were advanced for this defeat, and one of them was that a pressure group with the slogan 'Don't vote Labour/they are going to kill Caroline' entered the campaign.

Thus Mr Wedgwood Benn was in something of a quandary as 1965 drew to a close. He could not, for ideological reasons, very well introduce commercial radio. But he could not ban the pirates for fear of the fury of the electorate, a fury which would be all the greater in the absence of any plans for an alternative 'pop' music service on land.

In December Mr Wedgwood Benn, finally stung into action, firmly rejected any idea of the pirates being licensed, or commercial radio being introduced. He hinted that he was ready to act, but that had been precisely the situation for eighteen months! This was unlikely to deter the pirates who had nothing to lose by carrying on, and who would, in fact, only lose by closing down. Radio Caroline was only just paying off its initial outlay. Radio London would not be in that position until 1966, and Radio 390 had just come on the air after an expenditure of £150,000.

Mr Benn clearly had not made up his mind on broadcasting policy. In this situation the pirates had flourished precisely because their activities went unchecked. They had been impeded neither by the Postmaster-General nor by the authors, composers, or musicians whose works they broadcast. The Musicians' Union had threatened to ban all recording in the country if the situation continued. But they did not. The British Copyright Council declared war, a war of words, against the pirates. Its members included the British Actors' Equity Association, British Copyright Protection Association, Composers' Guild of Great Britain, Mechanical Rights Society, Musicians' Union, Music Publishers' Association, National Union of Journalists, Performing Rights Society and the Society of Authors. A powerful body, one might suppose, but it failed to effect a spirited opposition to the pirates.

To check the pirates Mr Wedgwood Benn could have introduced national legislation to implement the European Convention which had been signed for precisely that purpose in January. On this charge his defence lay in 'lack of Parliamentary time'; or more probably the likelihood of lack of votes at the next Election.

One thing was clear as the year ended – Mr Wedgwood Benn had a problem. The *Sunday Express* offered him its advice, in its own inimitable style, in an Editorial headed 'Simple'.

The Postmaster-General, Mr Wedgwood Benn, sternly warns the operators of illegal radio transmitters that they may be prosecuted.

But there is a far simpler way of dealing with the pirates.

Radio Caroline and the others provide lively and gay music that millions of people want to hear.

Why, then, does not the BBC turn over the Light Programme to just this kind of entertainment instead of the pompous, pretentious pap it so often now purveys?

Then nobody would need to listen to the pirates.

3

'A Government which gets things done'

As the bells were ringing in the New Year another pirate came on the air – Radio Scotland. This was perhaps symbolic of the following months, which were to bring a veritable proliferation in the number of pirate radio stations. Scarcely a week was to go by without a new station being announced. Mr Bevin's prediction, that unless something were done to restrain Caroline we should have a fleet of pirates round our coasts, using unauthorised wavelengths and making confusion worse, gradually was to come true.

New stations came on the air, but the growth in number of listeners did not show a proportionate increase. Thus the mild competition of 1965 was to intensify almost literally to cutthroat level. Tragedy, sabotage, intimidation and bitter disputes were to be a direct result of this increase in competition for listeners and advertising, until things got out of hand and the death warrant for the pirates was finally produced in July.

In February the *Scottish Daily Express* described the latest pirate radio station in the following terms:

> Radio Scotland is the lusty infant of broadcasting piracy, as healthy a baby buccaneer as you might reasonably expect to find off the rugged, wrathful coast of East Lothian. And it has proved a point ... that a commercial radio station, spraying a relentless programme of beat music into Scotland's transistors, living room radio sets and car radios fills an entertainment gap.

'Radio Scotland, swinging to you on 242' soon established itself. Initial fears that the station would not be on the air by the New Year, after the Radio Scotland ship and tug, which was towing it north from being fitted out in the Channel Islands, met heavy weather, proved unfounded. In the Channel the Radio Scotland ship, the 500-ton ex-Irish lightship *Comet*, built at Whiteinch on the Clyde in 1904, actually broke free from her tow rope and went adrift, but by the end of December had safely reached her anchorage four miles off Dunbar, at the mouth of the Firth of Forth.

At ten minutes to midnight on New Year's Eve, the station came on the air. Paul Young, a young Edinburgh actor well-known for his Scottish stage and television appearances, made the opening announcement and then the managing director of City and County Commercial Radio (Scotland) Ltd, Mr T. V. Shields, made a brief statement of the company's aims.

Glaswegian Mr Shields had nurtured the idea of a Radio Scotland from the stage of a mere dream to reality. During a period as publicity manager for the millionaire. Lord Thomson of Fleet, he was preparing a. biography of his employer and found out that the Thomson empire was founded on commercial radio. When, several years later, he saw the development of offshore radio in Europe he began to plan a station which would serve Scotland. The task of raising capital, finding a ship and transmitting equipment was not easy. Mr Shields travelled hundreds of miles only to find that potential ships had sunk, had been claimed by people to whom the owners owed money, were too small or too large, or were dangerously rusty. Eventually he came upon the 90-foot ex-lightship *Comet* in Southern Ireland and set about converting it for its new role. The superstructure was stripped down, a 145-foot high aerial mast erected and two diesel generators and two transmitters, capable of developing a power of 20 kW, were installed. As the lightship had no engines she then had to be towed to her new position off the East coast of Scotland.

Within the first few days of commencing transmission, the £300,000 station came under official criticism – from H.M. Coastguard. Dunbar Coastguard Station was put on an emergency footing after a disc jockey announced over the air that an engineer on board, tuning a radio receiver, had heard a Mayday distress call. After investigation, however, this proved to be a false alarm, as were fears by listeners who 'phoned the Coastguard that the pirate radio ship was sinking after a disc jockey jokingly remarked on a leak in the control room.

It was not until January 16th that the station started transmitting on full power. For two weeks it used only 8 kW, but on the 15th a tiny valve arrived by air from New Jersey and enabled Radio Scotland to go out on a full, powerful 20 kW.

During the first six weeks of its transmission Radio Scotland was dogged by technical difficulties. First there was trouble with the aerials. When the station went off the air at the end of January for alterations to the mast, the switchboard of Radio Scotland's Glasgow office was jammed with hundreds of telephone calls from teenagers. There was also generator trouble, followed by signal trouble. At night the station's signal suffered from extreme interference, in the form of a whistle, in some part of its reception area. Eventually the station changed frequency from 1,241 to 1,2.60 kc/s, though retaining the familiar identification, 'Swinging to you on 242'. This trouble was then followed by transmitter trouble and the station went off the air for more than three days. This had the effect of not only disappointing listeners, but advertisers began to have second thoughts about their bookings.

Mr T. V. Shields said in an interview for the *Daily Express:* 'Principally we are in this business to make money and we are doing just that. We started with advance advertising orders worth more than £100,000 and though we had a pretty ropey start we have found our feet. Now I am sure we have the nucleus of a first class commercial station.'

Mr Shields might have thought this, but many listeners were disappointed in Radio Scotland. The music, many felt, relied to too great an extent on the Top Fifty best selling records. But it was the disc jockeys above all who came in for criticism. They were long-winded, brash, had affected American accents and chatted at length about nothing between records. One listener wrote to Mr Shields and called the station 'puerile and bumbling'.

These were some opinions. The station's mail approached a daily total of 1,000 letters, from as far apart as southern England, Newfoundland, Scandinavia, Germany and other countries on the Continent. Listeners in Scandinavia reported loud and clear reception of Radio Scotland, and thousands asked for record requests to be played over the air.

Mr Shields echoed what all the pirate radio station operators made no secret about. 'Of course, we started with the intention of breaking into commercial radio when it comes. With the experience we gain here we should be in an ideal position to make a bid for a commercial radio licence.'

Radio Scotland tried to provide a limited amount of programming with a Scottish flavour, and 15 per cent of its air time was at first given over to programmes like the evening 'Ceilidh' and 'Larry Marshall and the One O'clock Gang'.

When Radio Scotland went off the air on February 10th the reason for the silence highlighted the fact that not only was pirate radio lucrative, but also dangerous. With heavy seas breaking over her bows and into the chain locker, the 100-foot-long *Comet* started

The M.V. Comet, *the converted lightship from which Radio Scotland broadcast.*

taking in more water than her pumps could cope with. The radio ship went off the air and made a call for help which was heard at R.A.F. Leuchars. A plane took off for the ship, but turned back as a result of the bad weather. After nearly an hour, however, a boat from Dunbar, with a bilge pump on board, reached the *Comet* and Radio Scotland took the air again.

Only a fortnight later the radio ship sent out another dramatic call, for 'immediate medical assistance', on the international distress frequency. The motor vessel *Singularity* picked up the message and relayed it to Stonehaven Coastal Radio Station, which alerted the Dunbar Lifeboat. The lifeboat was launched and returned with a member of the crew who had been taken ill.

Meanwhile another pirate ship had fallen victim to the elements.

About 9 p.m. on the evening of January 19th coastguards at Walton-on-Naze noticed that the *Mi Amigo*, the 470 ton ship from which Radio Caroline was broadcasting, was dragging her anchors in the gale and rough seas. They tried without success to warn her crew by radio and lamp, but obviously the ship was not keeping a radio watch. In fact the crew did not realise that the ship was drifting; they were watching television! Walton Lifeboat was launched and the ship's own tender, *Offshore I*, left from Harwich. Caroline agent in Harwich, Bill Scadden, also chartered a tug and headed into the gale for the drifting ship. On board, however, the gravity of the situation was not realised. The anchor watch believed, from the angle of the cable, somewhat obscured by the blinding snow, that the anchor was holding. When the crew on board realised the situation the wind proved too strong for the ship's engines.

The crippled radio ship drifted further and further inshore, her progress followed closely by the Coastguard Station officer and his Rescue Company. At one point it looked as though the *Mi Amigo* would be impaled on a concrete groyne, but she miraculously passed over it and grounded shortly before midnight only fifty yards off Frinton beach.

The rescue operation presented a problem as the waves were too high for the lifeboat to get alongside. So parachute flares were fired and a breeches buoy set up by five coastguards and twenty auxiliaries, specially called out. By floodlight, in the early hours, five disc jockeys, two radio engineers and a steward were taken off in the hazardous rescue operation which was accomplished despite freezing wind and heavy seas.

One of the rescued disc jockeys, Tony Blackburn, told reporters: 'We were unaware of the danger until it was too late. The captain and crew did their best and the engines worked properly, but the wind was too strong for us. The ship drifted and could not be controlled. We all had a drenching as we were pulled ashore through the heavy seas.'

Left on board were the Dutch captain and six crew members, who were joined by two coastguards. On shore the coastguards and volunteer lifesaving crew stood by for thirty-six hours in freezing conditions to take off those on board the ship if necessary.

When morning came the ship was high and dry and listing slightly. On the noon tide she suffered a severe buffeting by heavy seas which threatened to smash her against the sea wall only a matter of yards away. During the afternoon a Dutch tug, the *Titan*, hove to 500 yards off shore. Although the wind dropped during the evening, there was still the possibility that the *Mi Amigo* might be driven on to the sea wall by the high tide. The *Titan* tried to pull the ship off on the midnight high tide but she stubbornly refused to budge.

On the next tide the Captain decided to attempt to free the ship on his own and an anchor was taken from her bows and dropped. Luckily it held, and by winching on the cable as the tide rose the ship came round until she was pointing out to sea.

The Captain then had the engines started, and as the ship lifted on a large wave the propeller bit into the water and the *Mi Amigo* moved out to sea. Walton-on-the-Naze Coastguards stood down from their long vigil. In May they were awarded the Board of Trade Shield for the Best Wreck Service of 1965-66 for rescuing the disc jockeys from the Radio Caroline ship.

The pirate radio ship was damaged as a result of the incident and it looked as if there would temporarily be no Radio Caroline for listeners in the south of England. But miraculously the Caroline organisation received an offer of another pirate radio ship, *Cheetah II*, better known as Radio Syd. Radio Syd had operated from off the Baltic coast of Sweden, near Gothenburg. Caroline accepted Radio Syd's offer, and on Sunday, February 13th Radio Caroline South was on the air again, although with a weaker signal than normal, from *Cheetah II*.

The owner of *Cheetah II* was Britt Wadner, 45, a former Swedish beauty queen who had run the first European pirate radio station in 1978. Since 1962 ownership of pirate radio stations had been

The Radio Caroline ship aground on Frinton beach.

illegal in Sweden, but despite a three month spell of imprisonment Mrs Wadner had continued her activities. That winter, however, due to Baltic ice the Radio Syd ship had had to be moved and it looked as though the station would be off the air for a few months. Therefore, Mrs Wadner suggested that Radio Caroline might like to use it - free of charge.

As two more potential pirates announced they were to go on the air, pressure on the Postmaster-General and the Government for some sort of statement on broadcasting policy built up during January and February.

'Radio 270' announced that it would commence transmissions on 270 metres in March from off Scarborough or Bridlington and 'Radio Mayflower' announced that in April it would transmit from the Wash near Boston, Lincolnshire.

In the House of Commons on January 26th Mr Paul Bryan, Opposition Spokesman on Broadcasting Topics, questioned the Prime Minister, Mr Wilson, on the pirate radio stations. He remarked that Mr Wedgwood Benn had announced many times 'in his most dynamic way' that legislation against the pirate radio stations would be introduced, yet there had been no result. If these 'pop' broadcasts were destroyed what would replace them ?

Mr Wilson replied that Mr Benn's Conservative predecessor, Mr Bevins, had also said 'in a much less dynamic way' that there would be legislation. This would be done because of the clash of wavelengths and the danger of interference with such important broadcasting channels as those for lifeboats. The pressure on Parliamentary time was very acute but, said Mr Wilson, 'discussions are going on to see what can be done to replace these programmes, which are very popular with a lot of people'.

Nearly a month later Mr Wedgwood Benn was the target for a spate of questions on the pirates, local sound radio, a fourth TV channel, colour TV, the licence fee and the future of broadcasting generally.

Mr Royle (Conservative M.P. for Richmond) complained about the delay in reaching a decision on local broadcasting. 'All you have done is to make empty threats against pirate radio stations.' Mr Benn replied, "You are linking local broadcasting with the pirates, which is what they hope for. It is not the Government's view that that issue should decide the allocation of licences for local broadcasting.'

The Postmaster-General was then asked to comment on reports that advertising was being considered for the BBC Light Programme. The harassed Mr Benn replied: 'It is tempting to deny but by denying you tend to confirm what you don't deny, and then by confirming and denying what you have announced before you have decided.' An incredible answer which took nobody any further forward in understanding the situation, least of all Mr Benn who revealed his utter lack of any grasp of the state of broadcasting. Asked why no steps had been taken against pirate radio stations, Mr Benn said his enquiries were not complete – sufficiently vague and non-committal an answer to ward off further attack.

The *Daily Telegraph* summed up the situation:

> So, for the time being, the pirates can feast and the BBC must continue in fasting and prayer. But for all his caution Mr Benn allowed a chilly wind to play on the pirates' long-term future. No news was not to be taken as good news.

From outside parliament also pressure was brought to bear on the unfortunate Mr Anthony Wedgwood Benn. During February a plan for establishing 285 local radio stations throughout the country was submitted to him, in time for his perusal before the publication of the promised White Paper on Broadcasting.

The plan was drawn up by a body known as The Local Radio Association. The Association represented eighty-six companies which had already been formed to take part in commercial broadcasting in the event of the Government legalising it. The LRA was formed in October 1964, 'as a result of a belief that the interests of potential radio companies could be served best through one agency acting as their spokesman'.

Outlining the Association's plan in January Mr John Gorst, secretary of the Association, said: 'We are not talking of something for tycoons, but for small organisations of local people in different areas.

'All the indications are that the Government is thinking in terms of licensing some form of local radio and many members of the Labour Party are now taking a sympathetic view. By introducing local radio we shall be applying the modernisation of communications at a local level.

'There is no doubt local newspapers will be affected but there are no grounds for inhibiting a new form of communication because it is a threat to an old one. Many local newspapers are in favour of local radio and between 30 and 40 per cent of our members have local newspaper connections.'

Mr Gorst thought that 50 to 100 stations could be operating within eighteen months of permission being given by the Government. The plan was to have one commercial radio station for a town of 50,000 inhabitants, two for 200,000 and ranging upwards to five for a city of a million. London would have twelve stations and Birmingham six. Only where a locality was entitled to more than one station would the BBC be allowed to operate to avoid their monopoly of radio.

Each station would have a radius of about ten miles broadcasting on very low power on a medium wave frequency during the day and VHF at night. Local boards to control the stations would be set up to act in the way in which the ITA controls the ITV companies.

Dr Harold Crowther, Chairman of a chemical company in Reading, and a member of the council of the Association said at the time: 'In our area we plan to have a station which will be of real service at an initial outlay of £50,000. Local people will be invited to take shares. It will definitely not be putting out endless pop music. In fact, a large part of the day's broadcast will be taken up with the spoken word such as local news, road conditions, local advertisements and anything of interest to people who live in and around Reading, with some sweet music in between.'

In February another pressure group was set up under the name of 'Track'. Its object was to get public discussion on the issue of local sound radio before a Government decision.

Mr Roy Shaw, Director of the Department of Extramural Studies at Keele, was the Chairman. As such he presided at an open meeting held at the end of the month in London. Speakers at the meeting included Mr John Gorst, of the Local Radio Association, and Mr Frank Gillard, of the BBC.

Track hoped, without success, to see a Government spokesman at the meeting 'to tell us what kinds of grounds will influence the course of their discussions'.

But, not unexpectedly, nothing was heard from the Government, after all there was a General Election looming up in March 1966. It remained unmoved by complaints from the Swedish Government that Radio 390, looked upon as one of the more agreeable pirates, was interfering with one of their Stockholm transmitters. The Swedes themselves had in the past taken vigorous action against the pirates and, naturally enough, expected Britain, as a fellow signatory of the Council of Europe agreement on the subject, to do likewise.

After Radio Caroline went aground on the Essex coast Swedish beauty queen Brit Wadner came to the rescue and loaned the Caroline organisation her vessel Cheetah II, shown here in Harwich harbour.

Worse than this, in February there came complaints from the Edinburgh and Dunbar areas that Radio Scotland was interfering with the Light Programme on 247 metres. Of its own accord, Radio Scotland changed from 243 metres to 240 to avoid this.

It is clear, however, that some of the charges levelled against the offshore broadcasters by the Government were exaggerated and even erroneous. Soon after Radio Caroline increased power to 50 kW it was claimed that complaints of interference had been received from Czechoslovakia. Shortly afterwards two journalists and a radio reporter from that country visited London to write a story and a programme on Radio Caroline; they knew nothing of any interference with a Czechoslovakian station caused by a pirate station.

In the pre-election atmosphere, with a broadcasting decision of some description obviously overdue, the Cabinet made a shrewd election move by choosing the relatively uncontroversial issue of colour TV, the introduction of which in 1967 was announced in a debate in the House of Commons. The pirates were dearly taboo, since housewives as well as teenagers enjoyed them. Local sound radio was an equally explosive subject. The matter of TV, revolving principally around colour TV, merely raised the question of whether it could be afforded.

A number of interesting statements, though, emerged in the debate on broadcasting in the House of Commons on March 3rd.

Mr Bryan, who opened the debate for the Opposition, started with a few home-truths for Mr Benn. He said the public, the broadcasting world and firms in the industry had reached the point of exasperation in waiting to hear what was broadcasting's future.

He continued by saying that what one heard about the Postmaster-General in the broadcasting world was: "This chap can't really decide anything.' He challenged Mr Benn to give one instance of an important broadcasting decision he had made while in office. (He in fact made his first important broadcasting decision, on colour TV, in that debate.)

Mr Benn, Mr Bryan said, had had many problems to deal with when he came into office. There was the fourth television channel, colour television, local sound broadcasting, radio pirates and the BBC's financial problems.

'Every decision has been given to another committee. I think this is poor treatment for a man of the calibre of the Postmaster-General.'

Commenting on the need for an early report from the committee considering the future of broadcasting, Mr Bryan said he did not believe the Postmaster-General understood the damage which this period of indecision was causing to the industry and to broadcasting generally.

Mr Deedes, Conservative M.P. for Ashford and an avowed opponent of the pirates, was a little more complimentary when he said that he did not think that Mr Benn lacked ideas, but he questioned whether his senior colleagues had the courage to implement them.

'The radio pirates had made the Government look an ass, and rather disreputable. He accepted some of the blame because they had been running for a considerable time, but the previous Government had at least been able to clothe its nakedness by saying that international agreement was needed. That was now achieved.

'The pirates are providing what people want. To some Members of this House that is sound democracy. It is not. It is pandering to populism. If the pirates are illegal, the House is compounding a felony. It is a very bad time for a Government to be seen compounding a felony.'

In reply to his critics, Mr Wedgwood Benn said that the central problem with which the House should concern itself was the problem of BBC finance (note, not pirate or local sound broadcasting).

On these more politically contentious topics he said the Government intended legislation against the pirate radio stations. Anybody who really thought they proved a demand for local radio of this kind was deceiving himself. (Which indicated that Mr Benn was deceiving himself.)

His brusque and scathing dismissal of pirate broadcasting, a business netting thousands of pounds every week and with millions of listeners, which then followed would be laughable if it had not come from the mouth of Her Majesty's Postmaster-General : 'Really what are the pirates but hulks with big masts, carrying microphones, gramophones and seasick disc jockeys. Anybody who thinks that by mooring Radio London in a berth in Barking you have pioneered local radio had better have another think.'

On the day of the broadcasting debate in the House of Commons the BBC published a pamphlet in favour of local public service broadcasting. Perhaps it was intended to be an oar for the sinking Postmaster-General, out of his depth, to grasp at.

The pamphlet stated that the BBC was ready to set up nine local radio stations throughout the country in a pilot scheme to test the reaction of the public. The scheme would give local broadcasting on community lines a trial run and would test its acceptability and usefulness. Each station would cost £1,000 a week to run and would have a permanent staff of about fifteen.

The BBC planned for the stations to broadcast up to six hours a day programmes of local interest. The remainder of their broadcasting time would be filled by programmes relayed from the Home, Light and Third.

The pamphlet re-stated the Corporation's opposition to daylong 'pop' music, despite the fact that the public had shown that it wanted it. The BBC's local stations would not be 'amplified juke boxes of the kind familiar to people who have travelled to some overseas countries'. The first impression that this makes is that it is typical of the pompous, smug, tyrannical, you'll-enjoy-what-you-get attitude of the BBC, which is financially supported by the British people who had no choice but to listen to its output, until the pirate radio stations come along and gave them what they wanted.

The pamphlet did highlight one of the genuine potential problems of local commercial radio when, noting the alarm of local newspaper interests, it pointed out: 'The new medium if it depended on advertising for its revenue, would necessarily be competing with local papers for the limited amount of advertising support available in each community.'

But with local radio in the hands of the BBC the paper forecast no difficulties. 'The contribution of the local newspaper is far too important for its existence to be put at risk and there is no reason at all why it should be.' But the BBC conveniently ignored the fact that many local newspapers, with ever rising costs nowadays, are finding it increasingly difficult to survive. The production of local papers is becoming increasingly less viable a proposition and, with the margin between profit and bankruptcy so small, the BBC's high-sounding local station could be the straw that breaks the camel's back. If, on the other hand, local commercial radio were to operate hand-in-hand with the local newspaper, and not in competition, it could mean a new lease of life for local journalism.

The assertion in the plan that the effect of BBC local stations would be more likely to cause the sales of local papers to increase rather than decrease would seem contrary to all rational expectations.

The nine experimental stations would involve no addition to the present licence fee (presumably the money would be spirited from somewhere) but if an extra 5s (the catch) could be obtained from each licence for the development of local broadcasting it would provide an annual revenue of nearly £4 million.

Not surprisingly, there was no reaction from the Government to the plan. It had other things on its mind.

As the General Election campaign opened the Welsh Nationalists announced they were planning to start pirate election broadcasts. A spokesman said that one of the moves under consideration involved breaking into BBC afternoon transmissions with a powerful transmitter moved around secret rendezvous in Wales . . . the skull and cross-bones seemed to be flying high indeed.

*

Returning successfully from a General Election which, if fought on broadcasting policy, or rather lack of it, it certainly would have deserved to lose, the Government found that developments had not waited for them on the pirate radio front.

Radio London's reply to Mr Wedgwood Benn's threat of legislation in the debate on March 3rd was four days later to increase its air time from fifteen to twenty hours per day. The station now broadcast from 6 a.m. to 2 a.m. instead of from 6 a.m. to 9 p.m. as before. The extra five hours included an additional thirty minutes of advertising time. After midnight more subdued music, as opposed to continuous pop, was to be broadcast. In the words of Mr Philip Birch, the Radio London chief: 'We know that the demand exists for all-night entertainment and we intend to fulfil it.'

At the end of March Radio Caroline, battered by Force 8 gales for three days, went off the air again when *Cheetah II* developed a cracked plate in her hull. The Swedish captain and crew managed to get the listing ship to port at Lowestoft where the leak was examined in dry dock. On May 1st *Cheetah II* ceased broadcasting for Caroline and was replaced by the *Mi Amigo* which returned to Frinton from Holland where repairs on her had been carried out.

It was expected that *Cheetah II* would return to the air in a different role. The ship was equipped with a powerful 625-line television transmitter and Mr Philip Solomon, of Radio Caroline, investigated the possibilities of commencing TV transmissions.

This plan, though, did not materialise.

A 'new look' in pirate broadcasting announced that it would take the air at the end of April. The projected station in question was to be called Radio Tower, and was to operate from Sunk Head Fort, fourteen miles South-east of Felixstowe. Instead of a continuous flow of 'pop' music the station proposed to operate primarily as a local radio station. Sixty per cent of the programmes planned were to be devoted to local news, current events, local fixtures, outside broadcasts, sport, farming and industrial news, education and politics. The Lady Edward Fitzroy, daughter-in-law of the deputy lieutenant of Suffolk, it was announced, had been persuaded to give readings aloud of children's stories, and the Council of Nature was to help with the programmes on natural history.

The station even set up its own advisory council, the members of which included county councillors and a canon of the Church of England. The council's function was to advise on the programmes about local affairs. Radio Tower had indeed taken steps to assume an aura of respectability.

Mr Peter Jeeves. joint managing director of the station, said of Radio Tower in March: 'We do not intend to become another floating juke-box. Our programme policy will be to interest and to entertain minority groups as well as to put on shows of broader appeal.'

He said that quality programmes with a strong local flavour would be the aim. Local businesses would be able to advertise, and births, deaths and marriages notices would also be broadcast. The station would cost £40,000 a year to run estimated Mr Jeeves, a former Southern Television official, who was backing it with a Colchester business man, Mr Eric Sullivan. Its potential audience of 4l/2 million homes was stated to be in East Anglia, London, Kent and Sussex.

The station was to go on the air on April 21st on a schedule of broadcasts from 7 a.m. to 7 p.m. on 236 metres. The Radio Tower enterprise, however, proved ill-fated and the station made only a few test transmissions. The fort was abandoned, supposedly after it was found impossible to supply in rough weather. Rumours of plans for a Television Tower' came to nothing, although it was reported in November 1966 that weak test transmissions had been received in East Anglia. But neither Radio Tower nor Television Tower ever became fully operational as broadcasting stations. Amid the mystery surrounding the two stations some people maintained that the Sunk Head Fort was being put to a more sinister use by a highly organised smuggling gang who were using the broadcasting activities as a front for their own operations.

Meanwhile, during March, as another pirate announced it was preparing to establish itself in a fort off the Essex coast, one man was carrying on a spirited fight against the fort-based pirates.

His name was Sir Alan Herbert, and he was carrying on his campaign against the pirate stations in his capacity as Chairman of the British Copyright Council. In March his campaign exploded across the correspondence columns of *The Daily Telegraph*. The main part of his attack was directed against those interlopers established on forts in the Thames.

On February 10th the Ministry of Defence had stated that it was 'too dangerous' to use force to remove pirate radio operators from disused Army forts in the Thames Estuary. It had been asked, with every justification, why no effort had been made to remove the operators of Radio 390 from Red Sands Fort and those of Radio City from Shivering Sands Fort – both of which it was suggested were within territorial limits. The Ministry said:

> The physical difficulty of removing these people is so extreme and so hazardous as to make it not a viable proposition at the moment.

The Ministry believed that the forts were approached by a narrow ladder to a trap-door which would allow only one man to approach at a time.

This clearly was a strange way of looking at the situation. The fort housing the Radio City operators was to be captured in the near future, though not by the authorities, and Radio Noordzee had been easily seized by Dutch police using the device of attack from the air. This would not appear to have occurred to the Ministry of Defence.

The Ministry did admit that the operators were occupying the forts 'without permission or right', but would not call them 'trespassers', a word which had been used of them by a Conservative Minister in the House of Commons. This was because the ownership of the forts had become uncertain. Apparently some Army lawyers had been suggesting that the Crown Estate Commissioners as owners of the sea-bed also owned the forts. The Commissioners hurriedly rejected this view, one suspects in case the responsibility for the forts was shunted on to them.

Sunk Head Fort off the Essex coast was commandeered by personnel of Tower Radio and television. Some test transmissions were made but regular broadcasts were never made. The fort was evacuated after widespread allegations of its use for drug smuggling and in 1967 it was blown up by the Ministry of Defence.

The Post Office, when asked why no prosecution had been launched on these pirates if they operated within territorial limits, came up with the excuse that illegal transmissions were not easy to prove in a court of law. The prosecution had to prove that a transmission took place at a certain time on a certain date from a certain place, and that 'this person' was concerned in it. It was 'a very difficult problem, even though the whole world might know that the accused person was guilty'.

Needless to say, this also smacked of official cowardice.

A very fair comment on the situation was made by *The Times*:

> It seems that if the forces of the Crown and the Post Office make such heavy weather of silencing pirate radios within the three-mile limit, those outside the limit have a long life before them.

This probably summed up the attitude of Sir Alan Herbert who was deeply rancoured by the pirates who seemed to flourish with impunity in defiance not only of international broadcasting regulations, but also copyright agreements. On March 9th he had a long letter published in *The Daily Telegraph* on the subject. He argued that the European Convention agreed on in January 1965 could have passed on to the Statute Book 'in a couple of days', citing Sweden as a country which had taken firm action to deal with the pirates. He then reminded Mr Wedgwood Benn of a threat he made on December 8th, 1965 to prosecute the tower broadcasters under the Wireless Telegraphy Act if they continued their illegal transmissions. Three months later nothing has happened.' Sir Alan suggested that the pirates be ejected forthwith simply as trespassers on Government property. 'This would not take precious Parliamentary time: and it would not mean tiresome prosecution or the heroic imprisonment of young 'pop' martyrs. . . . '

He then referred to the incredible Ministry of Defence statement:

> . . . The Ministry of Defence, I presume, has plans of the straggling forts it erected. Tide Tables can be purchased; suitable boarding vessels, hoses, even helicopters, can be borrowed if the Ministry is short. Warm clothing would be advisable. There are big tides coming and the thing could be done before the General Election, the last display of a Government which 'gets things done, and takes the steps that have to be taken without fear or favour' (Mr. Wilson).
>
> Or will he go to the country crying: "This great maritime State is defied and baffled by a few islands of desperate disc-jockeys ..." . . . Clear those forts, and clear them now; and as for the ships let us have the terms of the Bill and a rough date for its introduction. . . .

On the 11th, in the columns of the same newspaper, a reply to Sir Alan Herbert's letter was published. The reply was from Ted Allbeury, a former advertising agency executive, a Kent poultry farmer and managing director of Estuary Radio Ltd, the company owning Radio 390 on Red Sands Fort. Although he carried out the running of the station and was a well-known voice through his talks on the station, he never held any shares in Radio 390. His reply merits reproduction in full:

> Sir Alan Herbert's war against the offshore radio stations is being waged more as a matter of misguided principle than to the real benefit of the artists he champions.
>
> All the leading stations now pay a percentage of their revenue to the Performing Rights Society, and this will grow into a very large sum of money. The fees paid by our station are at the precise rate asked for by the Society.
>
> Although a few spokesmen in lofty places regularly claim that these broadcasts damage the interests of performers and composers, it is a little-known fact that all the offshore stations are continuously assailed by record companies, promoters and musicians with requests to broadcast their work. Free and unsolicited records arrive by almost every post.

This defence of the pirate radio stations in its turn provoked Sir Alan Herbert to reply, even more dangerous on the rebound, five days later:

> I can assure Mr T. E. Allbeury (March 11) that it is not 'Sir Alan Herbert's' war against the off-shore radio stations....

He assured Mr Allbeury and the readers of *The Daily Telegraph* that he was fully supported by the British Copyright Council which represented the interests of authors, composers, music publishers and artists.

> The payment of 'conscience money' by no means meets all their objections. For many reasons we are asking the Government to see that British laws are enforced and respected: if this is a 'misguided principle' I am sorry.

The battle was certainly hotting up. The next round came next day, the 17th, in the columns of the *Telegraph* again. This time it was the turn of Mr George Bonney of Bonney & David Ltd, a public relations firm which had been engaged by Mr Roy Bates for Radio Essex.

Surely Sir Alan Herbert must have some regard for the millions who prefer to tune their radios in to the so-called 'pirate' stations. That they do so is evidenced by letters received from all parts of Britain. The taste for 'pop' music is peculiar to a generation in which neither Sir Alan nor myself now belong. . . .

Mr Bonney also claimed that Radio Essex's twenty-four hour service had proved popular with night workers, relieving the monotony of the night-shift and increasing production. (This was a new argument, certainly, for pirate radio stations!) Mr Bonney quoted Mr Reginald Maudling as saying to Hampstead Conservatives at a House of Commons dinner: "They are providing a service which the public wants, and which it cannot get from the BBC.'

It was further claimed that Mr Roy Bates took expert advice before staking his claim on Knock John Tower. According to the advice he received, the fort, abandoned by the Army department and some seventeen miles offshore, belonged to the first person to take possession.

Mr Bonney concluded: '... Finally, I am assured by Mr Bates that artists are delighted that their material is broadcast; that many personally send in recordings, and others write "thank you" letters.'

Maybe Sir Alan was now overcome by sheer weight of numbers, but at least he had made a valiant attempt to unseat the pirates. The Government could not be interested, no doubt to Sir Alan's disgust. For the pirates offshore radio meant big business and they carried on, Sir Alan or no Sir Alan.

4

The pirates and their loot

For those involved in it, offshore commercial radio certainly was a very profitable business. They had discovered a new and largely untapped market, and had found a way of access to the big spenders of the sixties: the uninhibited, affluent teenage section of society.

Before Caroline came on the air on March 27th, 1964, there had been only one station prepared to provide the younger citizens of Britain with the sort of music they undoubtedly preferred. This station was not, of course, part of the BBC network. The Corporation had time and again disdainfully displayed its abhorrence of stations purveying such 'frivolity'. It did not occur to the BBC that a sizeable percentage of the population wanted to hear more than a few hours of 'pop' music a week. The only station to which they could tune was, of course, Radio Luxembourg, whose transmitter is outside British shores within the Grand Duchy of Luxembourg, and which has broadcast music to Europe on 208 metres since 1930.

As long as thirty years ago the BBC regarded itself as having a divine right to the ether. At that time commercial broadcasting to Britain from the continent was flourishing and gained millions of listeners. Not only Radio Luxembourg, but Radio Normandie, Poste Parisienne, Radio Toulouse and Radio Athlone were all very popular. A report published in 1938, *Survey of Listening to Sponsored Radio Programmes*, showed that these foreign entertainment programmes were popular, especially on Sunday when their audience ran into many millions while the BBC was off the air. In fact, about as many people were listening to stations such as Radio Luxembourg as were listening to the BBC. During week-days, the survey showed that 'about half the listening was to programmes broadcast when none of the Corporation's stations were transmitting'. When the BBC discovered that its more lively competitors were luring away its audience the reaction was typical. The BBC made no attempt to give the public the sort of programme it wanted but instead induced the International Broadcasting Union to pass a resolution declaring that:

> the systematic diffusion of programmes or messages which are specifically intended for listeners in another country and which have

been the object of the protest by the broadcasting organisation of that country, constitutes an 'inadmissible' act from the point of view of good international relations.

The Post Office was then asked to interfere with the stations in question. Even this, though, did not stifle competition for the BBC. A former BBC executive, Mr Stuart Hood, said of the episode in the magazine *Encounter* in April 1965:

> The parallel with the Corporation's attitude when Independent Television came into existence will be certainly inescapable – the same moral indignation, the same incredulity that the public might not wish to have an undiluted diet of BBC programmes.

Despite the BBC, Radio Luxembourg over the years has increased in popularity, providing music of the type wanted by young people. Radio Luxembourg, though, only broadcasts in the evening and there still was a lack of 'pop' music in the daytime until the pirates took the air. The pirate interlopers caused considerable chagrin to Luxembourg whose near monopoly was now broken, but the station set about making the best of the situation. Thus, by the beginning of 1966 extensive improvements had been completed, costing £300,000, on the 208 metre commercial station. Radio Luxembourg had always had a superior signal to any of the pirates and now it was even better.

In early 1966 the Sales Director of Radio Caroline, Brian Scudder, commissioned National Opinion Polls Ltd to carry out a survey of the commercial radio audience. The survey showed that 45 per cent of the population listened to an offshore station and/or Radio Luxembourg during the week of the survey.

Radio Luxembourg	8,818,000
Radio Caroline	8,818,000
Radio London	8,140,000
Radio 390	2,633,000
Radio England	2,274,000
Radio Scotland	2,195,000
Britain Radio	718,000

These figures clearly showed that Caroline had managed to capture a huge audience and was on an equal footing with the long-established Radio Luxembourg.

Tony Blackburn in his days as a Radio Caroline disc jockey.

The BBC exists on the handsome sum raised by the licence fee. (In the year 1965-66 the BBC received from the Post Office the sum of £64,314,769 to finance sound and TV broadcasts.)

Radio Luxembourg, as a commercial station, exists on advertising at rates varying from between £90 and £190 a minute. Although the entertainment provided by all commercial stations was free to the listening public, they were not, and there was no reason why they should be, philanthropic organisations. As Mr Shields of Radio Scotland said, 'We're in this business to make money'. Also, considerable costs had to be covered: both the cost of setting up the station, and running costs. The cost of getting Radio Caroline on the air was well over £250,000, with running costs estimated at £6,500 a week. Radio London's running costs were estimated as being as high as £50,000 a month. Where did the money come from?

Advertising was the answer. Every advertiser wants to get at people with money, and no section of society spends so freely as the younger generation. The pirate radio stations provided the perfect medium for contacting them. In April 1966, two years after their inception, it was reported that the pirate stations were being supported by revenue from advertisers amounting to nearly £2 million a year.

When Radio Caroline started most advertisers held off booking time for a few weeks in order to see what the station was like. When they did book time, and there was a big rush on May 13th when £30,000 worth poured in in one day, they found the advertising rates to be on the following scale:

Hours	Rate per 60 secs
6-7 a.m.	£70
7-9 a.m	£110
9-12 noon	£80
Noon-3 p.m.	£100
3-4.30 p.m.	£70
4-30-6 p.m.	£100

The rates, it can be seen, are based on the estimated number of listeners tuned in. At a peak time such as 7-9 a.m. when the radio is switched on for breakfast, and in the car for going to work, the highest rate is charged. These rates were based on a 100-mile radius coverage although actually the broadcasts from Caroline reached a larger audience than had been anticipated. As Caroline's success became increasingly apparent, so her advertising rates increased, reaching a peak of £190 for sixty seconds air time.

Two major agencies quickly booked time on Caroline for their clients: S. H. Benson, for a brand of lager, and J. Walter Thompson, for a packaged cheese. There was no lack of advertising, in fact, including a chain of restaurants, the Duke of Bedford's Woburn Abbey, furniture, and radio stores, Shell-Mex-BP, and the *News of the World* (which had a 2½ per cent increase in circulation in areas covered by Caroline). This newspaper was the first advertiser, with a fifty-two week contract. Six minutes per hour were given over to commercials (about the same as Luxembourg and ITV) and Caroline adhered to the codes agreed to by the advertising organisations; in October 1964 it turned down a political party which wanted to buy time, and in 1965 the station turned down an offer of advertising from the breakaway Rhodesian Government of Ian Smith. The sum involved was reported to be in the region of £50,000.

Caroline also ran sponsored programmes. Among them were a number of very successful competitions with large money prizes for listeners. The most successful, undoubtedly, was the Caroline Cash Casino which was introduced once an hour on the hour between 9 a.m. and noon by disc jockey Bill Hearne. Listeners were asked to deduce from clues, given in the form of rhyming couplets, the thing or person being described. A new clue was given every day and when a listener thought he knew the answer he wrote to Radio Caroline House with proof of purchase of a sponsor's product. The advertisers who took part in the competition were Findus Frozen Foods, Galaxy Chocolate, V.P. Wines, Nabisco, Shredded Wheat, Libbys, Brands Quality Foods, S.P.C. Fruit, Alberto Shampoo and Weetabix. The largest jackpot ever paid out to a listener was £4,070. In only the eleventh week of the game the millionth letter to contain an entry arrived at Caroline House!

Other competitions included the Caroline 'Free petrol' promotion and 'Partners in Profit', sponsored by Weetabix, and Lucky Birthday Bonanza.

Also there were American Evangelist broadcasts with the somewhat forbidding names of "The Voice of Prophecy', 'The Herald of Truth', 'The Hour of Decision' and 'The World Tomorrow'. Most pirate stations ran these programmes, as do literally hundreds of commercial stations throughout the whole world. These programmes emanated from two main sources: the Radio Church of God in Pasadena, California, and the Seventh Day Adventist Church 'Voice of Prophecy' Bible School. Both organisations have British branches in Hertfordshire and, although non-profit making, appeared to have vast financial resources, so heavily did they book time on the offshore stations.

The Radio Church of God was represented on six offshore stations by the *Hector*ing voice of Mr Garner Ted Armstrong 'bringing you news of The World Tomorrow'. In these half-hour broadcasts, recorded off the cuff in New York, the evangelistic rhetoric of Mr Armstrong warned of the perils of disobedience to God and the decline in moral standards and responsibility in the world. The organisation's business manager. American Mr Charles Hunting, has explained that most of the money for the broadcasts on offshore stations, who reputedly irreverently referred to the broadcasts as 'plastic bibles', came from America.

The Seventh Day Adventist Church's most widely distributed programme was the 'Voice of Prophecy' presented by American evangelist Dr H. M. S. Richards. They also produced a 'Time for Thought' short five minute broadcast, usually put on early in the morning. The offshore stations found, however, that when they transmitted such a broadcast at this time, their audience drastically dropped as radio dials were retained to a rival playing 'pop'.

The offshore broadcasters obviously made a great deal of money from such broadcasts and it has been said that some of them, especially the stations on the forts, would never have survived without such support.

This was not the case with Radio Caroline, though, for after eighteen months Caroline, it was announced, had grossed over £750,000 with the advertising still pouring in.

Radio London, with its powerful transmitters, quickly established itself and was not left out in the advertising stakes. Two months after coming on the air it announced that it had £200,000 worth of advertising in prospect with rates slightly higher than Caroline – between £110 and £150 a minute.

After eighteen months broadcasting the station had, according to a National Opinion Poll Survey in March 1966, no less than 10,330,000 listeners and its sales organisation, Radlon Sales Ltd, had booked advertising from such diverse sources as Pye, Crosse & Blackwell, 20th Century Fox, Maxwell House, Lever Bros., Wills,

The pirate radio operators: Philip Birch of Radio London

The pirate radio operators: Ronan O'Rahilly of Radio Caroline

Lyons, Warner Bros, and Rowntrees. In February 1967 the station booked its 1,000th advertiser, John West Foods.

Perhaps one of the greatest ironies in the whole pirate radio situation was when for a period in 1966 the National Coal Board used Radio 390 to advertise for staff! During 1965, similarly, the Egg Marketing Board had booked a four month campaign on Caroline. The reason? Their advertising was aimed at young people and housewives, and pirate radio stations presented the most effective means of communication! In all fairness it must be stated this advertising was later dropped for 'political reasons'. Pillar of the establishment, Royal Ascot, had no qualms about pirate advertising, though. Similarly, the police used Radio Caroline to advertise an athletics meeting at Portsmouth, despite warnings by the GPO that it was illegal to even listen to the unauthorised offshore stations.

Philip Birch, head of Radio London and an ex- J. Walter Thompson executive, claimed that 'practically every big advertiser in the country uses London, except Schweppes'.

Why most of the big agencies had quickly begun using the offshore stations was patently obvious. Commercial radio provided a coverage of the audience they were after at a time when people were not watching television or reading newspapers. Besides teenagers, and only one quarter of Radio London's listeners were reckoned to be in their teens, pirate radio was claimed to reach a large factory audience and a high proportion of car drivers. The rates also were attractive. The cost of reaching a television audience comes out at about £1 per thousand, compared with 6d to is for radio. The effectiveness of the offshore station as an advertising medium was quickly established. One advertiser with 10,000 pairs of nylons to sell planned a month-long campaign, but sold out in a week. He had orders for another 35,000 stacked!

In March 1966 Radio London's income was estimated at £600,000 a year, running at that time at £70 to £75,000 a month. Ninety per cent of the revenue was coming from national advertisers. At this time London was definitely ahead of Caroline for one main reason. The station was using a more powerful transmitter (50 kW as against Caroline's 10 kW), and thus reaching a larger number of listeners. Also, its wavelength was neatly positioned (266 metres) on the dial between the BBCs Light and Home Services as against Caroline's position at the very top end of the medium waveband on 199 metres.

The pirate radio operators: Tommy Shields of Radio Scotland

In May, however, Caroline obtained a new 50 kW transmitter and started transmissions on the new frequency of 259 metres, right next to London, in an effort to extend her popularity.

By May Caroline and London both were commanding in the region of £160 a minute and in that month a committee was set up by the Institute of Practitioners in Advertising, the Incorporated Society of British Advertisers and eight pirate stations, in order to examine the effectiveness and the future of such advertising.

Commander David Kinloch, chairman of the committee and a director of IPA, commented: 'We recognise they fulfil a need. We would be happier, though, if they were on-shore and permanent.' More support for the commercial radio lobby, and evidence of the success of the pirates.

Income not only came from advertising. As the success of the new stations was established they branched out into the whole field of pop-culture. A number of stations set up clubs. There was first of all the Radio Caroline club with a 5s membership fee. Radio London followed with the 'Big L Club' open to listeners for 5s 6d and started the Big L discotheque in London.

When Radio Scotland came on the air it announced the 'Radio Scotland 242 Clan'. For 5s a member received Radio Scotland car-stickers, a membership card and a badge. The club was run by an ex-beauty queen, Cathy Spence, who had her own programme on the station. Also, the station started its own glossy magazine '242' covering the Scottish beat scene and news of Radio Scotland. Listeners were offered over the air Radio Scotland T-shirts, beach-tops and biros, as the station took advantage of the profitable sidelines available through the control of a powerful advertising medium. Radio Scotland's 'Clan Balls' ran in most of Scotland's larger towns. These dances, at which 'Clan' members got reduced tickets, were attended by Radio Scotland disc jockeys and featured top beat groups. Most stations, like Scotland, distributed car window stickers advertising the station and its frequency. Radio London had a slightly more novel promotion gambit offering 'Big L' listeners an opportunity to become a racing driver. 'Know the thrill of driving a Lotus Elan round Brand's Hatch.'

Radio 270, when it came on the air in June 1966, relied less at first than its competitors on direct advertising and instead had 'bargain offers' for 270 listeners. 'It's incredible, you'll never believe it, three pairs of nylons for only 12s 6d.' Transistor radios, wristwatches and Radio 270 T-shirts, 'wear it where you feel it', were all among the wares offered. Radio 270, in common with other stations, distributed photographs of their disc jockeys, 'only one shilling each, anyone you want or a group photo'.

As the pirate stations expanded their business activities they found it necessary to try and assume a cloak of respectability. Mayfair became the venue for the headquarters of a number of the commercial radio organisations. Caroline, whose backers included Mr Jocelyn Stevens, the wealthy and supremely respectable publisher of *Queen* magazine, had opened offices in select Chesterfield Gardens in Mayfair. Radio London established headquarters in Curzon Street and in 1966 were joined by an American pirate radio organisation. Curzon Street became nicknamed 'Pirate Alley'!

The pirates brought success to other business enterprises besides their own. They gave a real chance to the smaller record companies, a chance which had been denied them before by the monopoly of the large and powerful EMI and Decca groups. The result of the offshore broadcasters taking the control of the record industry out of the hands of the giants was an increasingly more dispersed market as new label after label appeared.

Unrestricted by needle time agreements, the pirates launched hundreds of new groups, and gave them chances they would never have otherwise had, playing their records and promoting them in a way the national BBC network could not do.

Some of the stations, it is clear, made a great deal of money out of what is known as 'Payola' or payment for the playing of certain records. Such arrangements were made both by disc jockeys and by some of the companies operating the stations. At the beginning of 1967 it was reported that Radio Caroline was charging record companies £100 to have a disc broadcast thirty times in a week. One of the Caroline directors, Mr Philip Solomon, stated in answer to criticisms from NEMS Enterprises, the organisation which manages the affairs of a large number of artists, including the Beatles: 'We require a broadcasting fee only for those records not in the top 50.' When a record became a hit it was broadcast free.

Another version of this commercial bribery was the 'flip-side racket'. Most of the operators of the offshore stations also had interests in at least one music publishing company and, when approached to play a record, made a deal whereby they published the 'B' side and, since royalties are divided equally between the 'A'

The DJs at work: John Peel at the turntables of Radio London

The DJs at work: Mark West at Radio Essex (top left), Ed Stewart on London (left), and 'Daffy' Don Allen on Caroline North (above)

The DJs at work: a publicity shot of the Radio 270 men.

and 'B' sides, did very well financially out of the whole thing: even though, perhaps the 'A' side was a big hit and the 'B' side very poor.

These under-the-counter deals accounted for the strange looking hit parades put out by some of the pirate stations – charts which bore no resemblance to those in the musical papers. This tended to accentuate the cut-throat competition among the pirate radio organisations and often introduced rivalry among disc jockeys who, in a bid to project their own images, trampled on those of their rivals through derogatory jokes and remarks about them on the air. Some even removed their rival disc jockey's records from his stack or sabotaged his programme by ending with the same disc as he was starting his with. This inevitably led to bad relations on some offshore stations which tended to make life very trying when having to work, live and sleep in very cramped and difficult conditions.

The life of a disc jockey at sea was tough, exacting and far from glamorous. Although the first requirements were a good speaking voice and the ability to project oneself in sound, one of the essentials was to be able to get on with other people on what was virtually a small island for a fortnight at a time.

A man who became a disc jockey found himself cooped up on board a ship for days on end, working long hours, from early in the morning until late at night, and having to keep cheerful throughout. The normal cycle for a disc jockey was two weeks on, working seven days a week, and then one week off. Radio Caroline and Radio London offered salaries basically comparable with the BBC. Radio London men usually started at £135 a month and could, if they managed to reach the position of senior DJ, aspire to a salary double that. Radio Caroline was said to pay its DJs at sea in international waters, for services in international waters on board a Panamanian ship, and thus manage to evade income tax.

Disc jockey Simon Dee, who worked for Caroline for fifteen months, never earned more than £30 a week, but when he left pirate radio he was, four months later, taken on by the BBC. By the middle of 1966, he was a top BBC disc jockey and with advertising work and personal appearances was making more than £25,000 a year. A year later he had his own TV show which proved immensely popular.

'Caroline', he has said, 'was for a disc jockey comparable to repertory theatre for the actor.' As the days of the offshore stations became numbered in late 1966 and 1967 the BBC found itself having to prepare a 'pop' programme and, accordingly, approached the most obvious people – the pirate disc jockeys. As a result a few were lured away from pirate radio with its insecure future by fat BBC payrolls. Kenny Everett was among those who decamped to 'the other side'. Kenny Everett, indeed, was on record in a copy of *Beatwave* magazine as saying some very hard and rude things about the BBC:

> Our ad-libbing, as opposed to the BBCs scripted rubbish, sounds fantastic . . . after all the stilted gob which is scripted by the BBC it sounds quite human . . . we tend to regard it (the BBC) as a non-competitor. It's such a different thing you know; we are radio – they are, you name it ... something diabolical. They really provide a terrible service as far as radio goes. . . .

> Commercial radio on land would be a boot up the arse for the BBC ... we all have the same approach to the BBC – non-competitive, staid and aunty-ish.

Quite a different tune was played later by Mr Everett who would probably prefer not to have been reminded about this statement made in his swashbuckling days! Many disc jockeys did not stick the job for another, less commercial, reason. Simon Dee recalled that he had a strong stomach: 'A lot of the boys just couldn't stick it out. I managed but it wasn't easy to sit for three hours during a Force 10 gale at a panel over which the previous guy had been sick.'

Senior DJ on Radio Caroline South, Tom Lodge, gave his answer to seasickness as 'Eat a lot, and be happy, happy, happy'. The listening public obviously didn't want to know that the fellow supposed to be entertaining them was coughing his insides all over a wildly rocking studio.

Despite the rigours of life on board a pirate ship, when Radio Scotland advertised for disc jockeys it got 500 applicants for its six vacancies at £20 a week.

Life was no easier for the radio engineers and technical staff of a pirate radio ship. Radio Scotland advertised for an engineer 'who could handle a screwdriver and hold a bucket at the same time'. Working with aerial installations and high power transmitters in an extremely small area also presented technical problems. In such conditions it is difficult to get aerials working efficiently, and also metallic objects tend to charge up with what is known as R.F., a type of electrical charge. Alarming stories came out of Radio City and Radio Essex, especially, of unfortunate disc jockeys grasping door handles and being thrown the other side of the room!

The first and only marriage on board a pirate radio ship. This photograph shows Canadian DJ Mike Luvzit with his bride Janet Teret after their marriage on board Radio Caroline North. The ceremony was performed on board the Panamanian-registered ship by Dutch captain Martin Gips.

The disc jockeys often condemned as brash and over-loquacious certainly gained their stations a large following. Ronan O'Rahilly of Caroline summed them up: 'The announcers, unlike the BBC, are human. They come over as flesh and blood people who breathe fresh air and not by artificial respiration. They make human mistakes, and they can even be embarrassing. But at least they emerge as people, and not as slick BBC automatons.'

Not only could it merely be uncomfortable to be on board a pirate ship, but also dangerous as the Caroline disc jockeys found when they were hauled ashore by breeches buoy from their grounded ship. An earlier accident had ended in tragedy, at the end of 1964, when three men, including the station's owner, leaving the fort on which Radio Invicta was situated were drowned in mysterious circumstances.

Disc jockey Paul Beresford, of Radio 390, was, in his own words, 'a little shattered' when he was struck by lightning while on Red Sands Tower. Although it 'went right through' him the station's chief announcer survived, and a few hours later, carried on with his programme. When Radio London disc jockey Earl Richmond sprained his wrist moving a stack of Beatles records, however, his discomfort was somewhat alleviated by no less than 5,125 Get-Well cards and messages!

Life was far from boring for the pirate disc jockey and adventure sometimes came his way. When a U.S. jet crashed into the sea off Radio London, disc jockey Pete Brady saved the pilot by diving into the sea, and also gave Radio London a world scoop. Similarly, Britain Radio found itself first with the news when a hippopantic serving an offshore drilling rig capsized near the station and listeners were given a minute-by-minute account of the rescue operations.

On a number of occasions engineers, crew and disc jockeys had to be taken off the floating radio stations when they became ill. When Captain Van Liesnaut of Caroline North was bitten by the ship's dog the station put out an SOS and the Ramsey lifeboat was launched with a doctor on board.

In July 1967 the skipper of Radio 270 became ill and when the station appealed over the air for help to be sent, emergency services were flooded with calls from listeners all over the station's reception area.

On September 21st, 1960 two launches left Ramsey Harbour for Radio Caroline North, but their mission was for a much less serious purpose. They were loaded with wedding guests! Disc jockey Mike Luvzit had decided to get married on board the ship and the ceremony was conducted by Dutch Captain Martin Gips, and broadcast live over the station.

Disc jockeys tended to buildup a huge personal following which, many DJs have admitted, often led not only to letters of praise and adulation, but even to proposals of marriage! Mike Ahern, who sat in the hot-seat on Radio Caroline for the 9-12 morning show aimed at housewives, said once that he received four or five proposals a week from divorced women, widows and bored, frustrated housewives. Johnnie Walker of Radio Caroline enjoyed great popularity, especially with young female listeners to whom he affectionately bade goodnight at 11 p.m. every night, and started his own personal fan club run by his mother in Solihull. Offered by the club was a Johnnie Walker 'Kiss in the Car Licence' for couples who could kiss all the way through a record played every night at 11.30. That the offshore stations had become an integral part of many people's lives was indisputably shown by the vast amount of mail received by DJs on all the pirate stations.

On board Radio Scotland, bored disc jockeys, Tony Meehan, Mel Howard and Jack McLaughlin nearly brought a halt to their fan mail when they decided to take a swim from their ship, the *Comet*. Their swim was rudely interrupted when a school of basking sharks surfaced beside them. As the DJs struck out for a rope ladder thrown over the side by the crew of the ship two sharks left the school and pursued them! The men, fortunately, were unhurt but shaken.

It was the disc jockeys of Radio City, though, who were to be part of perhaps the most remarkable story associated with pirate radio. That, however, is another story. . . .

5

... and more pirates set sail

By April 1966 the competition among the offshore stations was noticeably intensifying. Radio London had a powerful 50 kW transmitter on the air and Radio Caroline, in order to keep pace with its principal rival, also pushed up its transmission power to this level. Both stations could be well heard in most parts of Britain. Radio Scotland was effectively covering most of Scotland and Northern England; as a result of researches into reception held in April the radio ship *Comet* changed position from the Firth of Forth to the Firth of Clyde, where she anchored three miles off Troon. From this position it was reckoned better reception would be achieved in Glasgow and the Central Belt, where the large proportion of Scotland's population is centred.

The Radio Scotland ship was towed round the North coast of Scotland, broadcasting as she went. The days of the station very nearly came to an end, though, early one morning. The *Comet* was passing Peterhead, on the Scottish coast, at about 5.30 a.m. when chief disc jockey Bob Spencer woke the crew and other DJs up with shouts of 'Fire!' Jumping out of bed, they found thick, black, oily smoke billowing from the generator room. Captain Fleming, who was in charge of the ship, and a crew member fought their way to the seat of the fire with wet handkerchiefs pressed to their faces and managed to put out the blaze with fire extinguishers. The crew member then collapsed, but was dragged on deck and revived. Disaster had only just been averted.

Radio City claimed to have increased power to 20 kW and was well heard in the South-east and East Anglia. Radio 390 now claimed to be running over 50 kW, and was proving a very popular station with housewives, who enjoyed its particular brand of sweet music. Radio Essex, the least powerful of the offshore broadcasters, claimed to have a large audience in East Anglia and the South-east where its broadcasts were quite well audible.

Against the background of these already existing stations, still more planned to commence transmitting. Radio 270 was due to start on April 2nd but suffered a number of setbacks, principally

The Radio Scotland ship under tow off the north coast of Scotland.

involving aerial trouble. At the end of April Pearl and Dean, the British advertising agency, announced that an American-backed pirate ship was due off the Essex coast 'within a few days'. This ship would be the base for two stations, 'Radio England' and 'Britain Radio'. A new station, 'Radio Channel', was reported to be nearing completion and would start transmitting from an anchorage off Bexhill, Sussex. During the month a mystery station, 'Radio Dynavision', was heard and was thought to be a projected station testing, but nothing more was heard. Another mystery station was heard at various times during May and the following months operating under the homely name of 'Radio Jim'.

At the end of May Radio England and Britain Radio came on the air with test transmissions, and by the beginning of June regular broadcasting had commenced. Both stations were located on an 186 foot-long, former American Liberty vessel. The ship, which was used in the Second World War, was originally called the *Olga Patricia*, but at a cost of £1,450,000 had been fitted out in Biscayne Harbour, Miama, Florida, for pirate broadcasting, and had been renamed the *Laissez Faire*. Although the two stations had completely separate studios they both shared the 210 foot-high aerial mast.

The station was financed by a group of American business men, but Pearl and Dean had a hand in the venture. Two of the Americans behind the venture were Mr William Vick, the managing director of the station, and Mr Jack Nixon, coordinator of the organisation. Mr Vick, a 40-year-old crew-cut Texan, had previous business experience in chemicals, oil and banking, and had been an early backer of Radio London but had pulled out. He maintained from the start that Britain Radio/ Radio England really wanted a licence to broadcast from on shore, and later a formal application was to be made to the Postmaster-General.

At the launching of the station in London Mr Nixon stated: 'We are doing nothing illegal, but we shall adjust our operations to comply with any legislation introduced by the Government. We shall pay royalties to the Performing Right Society, but not to record companies as we are not selling their records, just playing them.'

Mr Ernest Pearl, of Pearl and Dean, stated what was, undoubtedly, the hope of the pirates: 'Commercial radio must come to this country. There is ample evidence that people want these stations and no Government can stop people having what they want.'

The M.V. Laissez Faire *from which Britain Radio and Radio England broadcast. The station rapidly went bankrupt – less than a year after its champagne launching at the London Hilton..*

The *Laissez Faire* was anchored off Harwich, under the Panamanian flag, and when the two stations went on the air they were the most powerful of the offshore broadcasters. Radio England broadcast 24 hours a day on 227 metres with a power of 55 kW. Britain Radio was on the same power and schedule on 355 metres. The former station transmitted continuous 'pop' music with news every hour on the hour, and, in between, advertisements and offers of transistor radios and watches ('Do you know the date? You don't, well we have a watch here that not only tells you the time ...'). All this was liberally interspersed with announcements by slick, professional American disc jockeys that 'You are listening to 'Swinging Radio England'. Britain Radio, catered for a different type of audience, for those who preferred light, 'sweet' music, as its identification suggested: 'This is Britain Radio, the Hallmark of Quality.'

Initially, six disc jockeys were employed on the ship, but four more were engaged later. The station opened offices in Curzon Street, across the road from Radio London; in the words of Charles Greville of the *Daily Mail*, 'a very glossy pad'.

Within days of commencing transmission reception reports were not only received from more than 3,000 listeners all over Britain, but a much angrier one from the Italian Government which made an official protest to the Postmaster-General that Radio England was causing 'very harmful interference' at night with the radio station Roma Two, which broadcast on the same frequency, allocated to it under the Copenhagen Plan in 1948.

In May there had also been a complaint by Yugoslavia about interference with its transmissions from Zagreb on 264-7 metres. Yugoslavia complained to the European Broadcasting Union about the interference, from Radio London on 266 metres, and also in a broadcast:

> Zagreb is interfered with by a foreign broadcasting station which calls itself Radio London. Interference from this source is particularly strong between 6 and 9 p.m., when its constant intrusion makes it almost impossible for listeners in certain parts of the country to follow the programme.

The broadcast also revealed that 'an increasing number of letters' with complaints of bad reception were being received, and that listeners demanded that measures be taken to remove the interference as soon as possible.

The Radio England control panel on board the Laissez Faire.

Also 'pirate-hunting' was Sir Alan Herbert. In May, with his characteristic vigour, he pursued his campaign against the illegal broadcasters by producing the draft of a Law of Piracy (Extension) Bill. He did not believe that the measures agreed to by the Council of Europe in the Convention signed in January 1966 would be sufficient by themselves, if implemented by Britain, to dear the pirates from the seas. In fact, some of the promoters had already boasted that they could manage to get supplies and advertising revenue from other countries, principally from the United States. In Sir Alan's view the most direct remedy would be to deem the pirates actually pirates in law and 'simply bring them in'. This would avoid the tiresome necessity of chasing and prosecuting their various suppliers and advertisers.

This was not a bad idea, either. By the municipal laws of many countries some acts are deemed to be piratical, even though they are not reckoned to be so by international law. Slave-trading, a case in point, was deemed piratical by the Act of 1824.

As Sir Alan, Yugoslavia and the Italian Government complained. Mr Wedgwood Benn came under fire also in the House of Commons on May 18th. Mr Faulds, the bearded, ex-actor Labour M.P. for Smethwick, told Mr Benn that there was 'a new and sinister development' in the pirate radio field. Members gasped as Mr Faulds revealed that this was a political station called 'Radio Freedom', due to open in August, and which was going to pump political propaganda into Britain. Rumour had it that the station was to be on a ship chartered by the Rhodesian Smith Government, an advertising contract from which Radio Caroline had turned down. Mr Fauld's intervention came in a series of questions about pirate radios.

Mr Benn had earlier said: 'At present, there are four pirate stations broadcasting from ships to the country.' (There were, of course, seven pirate stations broadcasting to the country; the other three were from forts.)

The Postmaster-General had no official figures about the size of the audience, but 'the Government intend legislation as soon as the timetable permits and is considering how the demand for the more popular broadcast music can more rationally be met'.

Mr Deedes, Conservative M.P. for Ashford, reminded Mr Benn; 'The longer you delay action the harder it will be to take when the time comes.'

Mr Benn replied: 'I recognise this. The interference by these stations is creating mounting difficulties and this is a matter of international obligation.'

From these exchanges it appeared Mr Benn was experiencing difficulty in finding parliamentary time to fulfil 'international obligations' and to meet 'mounting difficulties': a poor situation indeed.

One man, however, was quite confident that the pirates would remain in business for quite some time yet, despite complaints and opposition. Mr Philip Birch, managing director of Radio London, told delegates at the British Radio and Television Retailers Association Annual Conference, in Brighton, on May 11th, that it would be a year to eighteen months before the Government would bring in legislation to try to stop the pirates. His prediction, though, turned out to be rather over-optimistic. He said the Government now recognised there was a demand for this type of broadcasting. 'Before they act', he declared, 'they will organise an independent radio service on the lines that we are running now.'

Wishful thinking on Mr Birch's part, although he did say that he expected legislation to be introduced to make it illegal to advertise on such stations as Radio London; most advertisers, though, were large international companies and could place their business from outside Britain. Mr Birch expected Radio London, which he claimed had an audience of ten million listeners in Britain and four million on the continent, still to be broadcasting in thirty years' time.

The BBC had earlier refused to allow its representative to the conference, Mr Leslie Turner, head of engineering information, to appear on the platform with Mr Birch. The telegram, from Sir Hugh Greene, the Director-General, wished the conference a success but confirmed the ban, adding: 'The BBC cannot accept that unlicensed broadcasts have any place in the discussion of broadcasting operations.'

Presumably, the BBC also found it could not accept the fact that recent polls had found the total pirate radio and Radio Luxembourg audience to exceed the number of listeners to the Home and Light programmes combined!

Mr Turner was, in fact, attending the conference, but did not enter the room while Mr Birch was speaking. A delegate to the conference later suggested that the Association should send a telegram to Sir Hugh telling him that they had 'plenty of offshore sand at Brighton in which he could bury his head if the BBC ran short'!

Clearly the British Radio and Retailers Association did not have the same opinion of the offshore stations as the BBC and the Postmaster-General, but it must be remembered that through the pirates, business had boomed for them, in the form of increased sales of transistor radios. Many transistors since 1964 had 'Caroline* and 'London' marked on the dial, while others had a special extra band for Caroline and Radio Luxembourg.

*

On June 9th Radio 270 started test transmissions from off Scarborough. The station was on board the 160-ton, 139-foot-long converted Dutch lugger *Oceaan 7*. The *Oceaan 7* was purchased in Holland and initial repairs were carried out there before she was fitted out as a radio ship, with transmitters and aerials, in the Channel Islands. The total cost was about £75,000 – quite cheap as pirates went!

The station was financed by about fifty shareholders and most of them were local North-east business men. Among the shareholders were three grocers, three farmers, three butchers, a fisherman, a knacker, an all-in wrestler promoter, and, from the world of show business, dance-band leader Cyril Stapleton.

Chief shareholder and Chairman of the Company, Ellambar Investments Ltd, was 50-year-old business man Mr Leonard Dale, a self-made man who started his own business at 19. As he ran a firm making diesel generators he supplied this equipment for 270. Another chief shareholder was business man Mr Wilf Proudfoot, who had been M.P. for Cleveland, but was defeated by Labour in the 1964 and 1966 General Elections.

The station had been due to go on the air on April 2nd but the *Oceaan 7* was driven from her anchorage a couple of days beforehand by rough seas, with a 100-foot section of her 154-foot radio mast broken off. Considerable trouble had been experienced with the aerial, which was originally made of soft copper wire which stretched in windy conditions, and so a stronger one had to be found.

Slightly more sensational, though, were rumours rife along the North-east coast explaining 270's aerial trouble. One rumour

*Pop pirate for Britain's north-east: Radio 270 which broadcast from
a converted Dutch fishing lugger off Scarborough.*

alleged that, while moored in Grimsby harbour, a rival organisation deliberately sabotaged the ship's aerials. This story had a far less sensational basis. Apparently a technician, described by a representative of the company as 'eccentric', stole some radio parts from the ship as he wanted to make sure he got his salary at the end of the month! The parts were returned to the station in the following morning's post.

During the following winter the anchorage of *Oceaan 7* was moved from off Scarborough to Bridlington Bay as this position gave better protection in bad weather. During one very severe Force 10 gale the small converted fishing vessel suffered a considerable amount of superficial damage and water even got into the transmitters. The position off Bridlington, however, not only gave the ship itself more protection, but it was found that it was easier to run the tender out to the ship from there. The station's owners always emphasised that the Captain exercised complete discretion as to what to do in bad weather; for example, whether or not to run for port or within the three mile limit for shelter, even though such action inevitably meant the loss of advertising revenue. Each day the Captain and his Dutch crew followed through an elaborate maintenance drill on board, involving testing the main engines, as opposed to the auxiliary engines running the station's generators, and checking the compressed air bottle and safety equipment. Before putting to sea as a radio ship the 270 vessel had been closely checked over by a Lloyds surveyor.

The station was equipped with a 10 kW R.C.A. transmitter which put out a very strong signal indeed in northern England and the Midlands, and one Lincolnshire newspaper reported two days after the transmissions started that 'a radio war is about to break over Lincolnshire'. Apparently the station's signal was so strong on 270 metres that teenagers complained they could not hear their favourite pirate station, Radio London on 266 metres!

Broadcasting from 7 a.m. until midnight the station quickly established itself in the North. The format consisted of continuous pop music with news and weather on the hour. At first this was liberally interspersed with offers and competitions '... to find Britain's best Mum. write in not more than 100 words . . .' or 'guess the combined weight of the seven 270 men', or 'time to play "scrambled names". The following is the scrambled name of one of the 270 men. Write on a postcard ...' The main value of these competitions was as a means of audience research, finding out where the 270 audience was.

In view of threatened legislation the precaution had been taken of registering the ship in Puerto Cortes in Honduras, whilst the British registered company, Ellambar Investments Ltd, was on paper as having loaned its capital of £50,000 to an obscure Panamanian company, Progresiva Compania Commercial SA. This company, again on paper, ran the radio station while another Panamanian company owned the ship. The agent for these two Panamanian companies was a 23-year-old Australian called Noel Miller, who became well-known to 270 listeners as disc jockey 'Neddy Noel' – the senior disc jockey on 270 and also the station's Programme Director. The principal shareholder in Progresiva was American citizen and film producer Jack Lament, who was an old friend of Wilf Proudfoot. Also, a number of Australians were originally among the eight disc jockeys, a useful factor in view of the threatened ban on British personnel working on offshore stations. Soon after the station went on the air its chief, Wilf Proudfoot, boasted that it had, from a legal point of view, 'the most watertight structure in the business'.

At one point during June it looked as though the British Government had learned something from the pirates. A number of newspapers reported that the British Government was to equip a pirate radio station on board an aircraft carrier, to be anchored off the Mozambique Coast, in order to beam programmes into Rhodesia following the unilateral declaration of independence.

The *Sunday Express*, below the headlines, 'Britain plans atom ship as radio voice in the Ocean', reported that both the broadcasting and propulsion would be supplied by a British-made nuclear reactor.

> Behind the scheme is a bid to ensure that the voice of Britain is heard loud and clear in the world's most troubled areas . . . Africa, Asia, and the Middle East.

The reason for this move was reported to be because Britain could thus regain her position in the world as an international broadcaster; in the war of words in which she had been overtaken by Russia and China, who daily saturate these areas with propaganda. From an anchorage in the Indian Ocean these, the most troubled areas in the world, would be effectively covered. The plan was denied in naval and government circles, but was reported to be confirmed in those of industry and diplomacy. It was reported that the 19,000 ton *Leviathan* had been chosen for the job, the aircraft carrier which was 80 per cent completed in 1946, when work on it was stopped. The *Leviathan* had never been to sea, but any pirate radio operator would assert that it would make a magnificent pirate radio station (even if a little expensive to run!).

Harland and Wolff, it was said, had already been asked to co-operate and it was likely conversion work would take place there. The cost was estimated at about £3 million, which was not a great deal when one considers Radio England/Britain Radio, with £1½ million cost. Nothing more, however, came of the story.

Another unusual story of a projected pirate station came at that time when it was reported that a group of businessmen in New Zealand were planning to set up a pirate radio station - Radio Hauraki. When this station appeared in December it gained immediate popularity. But at the end of January 1968, just over a year later, the life of Radio Hauraki came to an abrupt end when the 160-ton M.V. *Tiri*, from which the station broadcast, drifted on to the rocks of Great Barrier Island. Thousands of listeners listened to a running commentary of the drama given by the disc jockeys on board. The station then closed down to the sound of a grinding crunch, the wail of a siren and the words: "The rocks are within swimming distance. ... I love you Mum and Dad.' All the disc jockeys and crew were safely rescued, but the *Tiri* broke her back on the rocks and became a total loss.

*

Not only were pirates that June planned in the Indian Ocean and off New Zealand. Nearer home 'Radio 365' was preparing to take the air. This station planned to cover the North of England and to start VHF broadcasts. 'Radio Caesar' was reported to have started test transmissions. 'Radio Channel' was reported to have anchored off Bexhill. 'Radio Mayflower' was nearing completion, as was the threatened 'Radio Freedom'. 'Radio Manchester' was planned, as a sister ship to Radio London, to anchor off Fleetwood broadcasting to the North of England. Encouraged by its success, Radio 390 announced its intention of buying another pirate ship (actually *Cheetah II*, the Swedish ex-Radio Syd still off Harwich

New Zealand's pop pirate Radio Hauraki photographed at sea ....

... and hard aground.

although not broadcasting) and broadcasting from off the North of England as 'Radio 390 North'. Thus total coverage of England and Wales was hoped for. Also planned were 390 VHF transmissions for the London area.

Radio London, meanwhile, to meet the new competition, both from the projected pirates and more powerful Radio England, purchased a new 75 kW transmitter which would make it the most powerful offshore broadcaster.

Radio Caroline, not to be outdone, announced its intention of increasing the power of its northern station, off the Isle of Man, five times from 10 kW to 50 kW.

Clearly, even to the most enthusiastic supporter of the pirate stations, the situation was getting completely out of hand. If the June trend had continued, more than twenty radio ships would have been dotted around the British coasts by the end of the year.

Only two weeks after Radio Caroline came on the air in 1964 there was a cartoon by 'Jon' on the front page of the *Daily Mail*.

It was of a scene at the Ministry of Defence where an Admiral was giving instructions, his pointer on a map of the English coast around which were dotted, diagrammatically, ships. 'Not submarines, gentlemen – pop ships.' It was funny then, more than two years before. Nobody realised then that Radio Caroline would start such a tidal wave of pirate ships.

In this situation the chaos on the medium waveband would soon become unbearable. More than twenty unauthorised stations would use more than twenty frequencies, unallocated to them. They would interfere with authorised broadcasts in other countries, and this interference would increase as, in the cut-and-thrust of competition, they increased their transmitter powers. Who knows where it would all have stopped? Fifty stations, sixty stations, maybe even 100 with all the resulting chaos. Chaos for shipping to whom the pirates would be a danger to navigation. Chaos nearer home as interference was caused with the adjacent maritime and distress frequencies. Chaos as even the BBC eventually became jammed out.

Obviously a halt had to be called in order to avoid such chaos, and in order to honour international obligations. By the middle of June it was being reported that the Bill to deal with the pirates was drafted in all its major details. The Government had at long last woken up to the situation and to the fact that procrastination and vacillation would do no longer, even if it meant offending a considerable portion of the electorate and even larger numbers of potential electors. During June the Prime Minister himself admitted in the House of Commons: 'There have been a larger number of letters coming to me on the pirate radio Bill than on the question of the Prices Freeze.'

But the dramatic events of the next week, more than anything else, were to hasten the pirates' death warrant....

The Radio City fort in the Thames Estuary: this became the centre of violent drama and intrigue.

6

'The situation is getting dangerous'

Radio City – Drama and Tragedy

The events of that week were the most sensational to be associated with pirate radio and resembled more the days of pirates of old. There were all the ingredients of a good, rip-roaring pirate story: boarding parties, threats, hostages and shooting. There was also tragedy.

If not reminiscent of the days of the skull and crossbones, the events on and connected with Radio City, the station on Shivering Sands in the Thames Estuary, during that week in June had something of the essence of a first-class crime thriller. If one had read such a story, though, or seen it at the pictures, it would most probably have been dismissed as too far-fetched. It was certainly a most remarkable story, which captured the front pages of the daily press and held the mystified attention of millions for a whole week.

It was not until June 23rd that the story broke in the newspapers, but when it did it made the headlines. 'Police question boarding party on pirate station – Shivering Sands Inquiry after chiefs death.' The newspapers pieced together the evidence they had, but it did not fit.

The facts were: on June 19th Radio City was boarded and silenced by ten unknown people and a mysterious, unknown woman. On June 21st Reginald Calvert was shot dead at the home of Major Oliver Smedley, one of the founders of Radio Atlanta which merged with Radio Caroline. Why he was shot was anybody's guess, but Smedley was arrested and charged with his murder.

The sequence of events during that week went something like this. . . .

On Saturday, June 18th, the telephone rang in a council house in New House Lane, Gravesend. This was the home of 17-stone, 60-year-old Mr Alfred Bullen, known as 'Big Alf' to his mates. The telephone call was from his boss Mr J. Bradish, who hired out gangs for work on ships after crews have been paid off. He told 'Big Alf to collect ten of his men for a job the following day. Sunday. In 'Big Alf s' words: 'We all turned up at Gravesend Pier without knowing what was on. When we arrived we met a man who introduced himself. With him was a tall, thin woman of about 50 who said her name was Kitty Black, and that she was coming along as our cook.

'It seemed pretty clear to me that she was no perishing cook. But I didn't ask any questions. The rate was £2 10s a day for the job. We just got into the tug that was waiting for us. None of us knew where we were going so we got out the cards.

'Then the woman called me over and told us our job was to take over the Radio City fort. She said the equipment belonged to a certain man, and we were to prevent it from being used.

'It was about 3 a.m. when we arrived, and everyone was asleep. All of us, including the woman, climbed onto the fort. We found the Radio City party was seven strong. They got a bit of a shock when they saw us. But when we told them the score they realised that there was not much they could do.

'The man and the woman got hold of the crystals from the transmitter and climbed back into the tug with them. That was the last we saw of them.

'After that we all settled down to see what would happen.'

At 6 a.m. that morning Radio City, the Tower of Power', was silent. Listeners tuned the 299 metre spot on their dials in vain for the familiar identification. By this time 'the man and the woman' had reached the shore and were driving down the Kent coast. At 8.30 a.m. they met the British chief of Radio London, Philip Birch, on the lawn of his country house and arranged to meet him later that day in their office in Dean Street, Soho, that of a company named Project Atlanta. This was the company which had operated Radio Atlanta in 1964 for two months, and which had then become part of the Radio Caroline organisation.

The next day, Tuesday, the head of Radio City, 38-year-old Mr Reginald Calvert, went to the police and told them about the raid on his radio station, but there was considerable doubt whether or not the police had the power to investigate the complaint due to the fort's position. That evening Calvert decided to pay a call on Major Oliver Smedley, a 54-year-old director of a number of companies dealing with instruments, breweries, fruit farming, a distillery and the entertainment world. He had also been very active in the Liberal

Party as a former member of the Liberal Party Executive, and had fought four elections, two against Lord Butler, then Mr R. A. Butler. During the war he was wounded twice and awarded the Military Cross, having seen service in the Royal Artillery in Iraq, Egypt, Sicily and Europe.

At about 10 p.m. Calvert's car, a grey Ford Zodiac, was parked in a narrow lane next to Smedley's seventeenth-century thatched cottage in Duck Street, Wendens Ambo, near Saffron Walden, Essex. A friend, a Mr Arnold, who was a radio engineer, was driving because Mr Calvert's arm was sore after an injection for a holiday trip to Gibraltar. The two went up to the house and knocked on the door. A few minutes later a shot was heard.

Police were called shortly after 11 p.m. by Mr Neil Warden of Langley, Buckinghamshire, a sales representative of a chocolate firm, who was spending the evening at a friend's home adjoining Major Smedley's cottage. Mr Warden told the police that Major Smedley knocked on the door and asked him to ring for the police. He did so and they arrived about fifteen minutes later. Duck Street was sealed off and Det. Supt. George Brown, deputy head of Essex CID, went to the cottage. There Major Smedley, his housekeeper, Miss Pamela Thorburn, and Mr Arnold were interviewed.

Shortly after 4 a.m. Mr Calvert's wife, Mrs Dorothy Calvert, 38, mother of two daughters, was telephoned by the police and told of her husband's death. She was driven to Saffron Walden where she saw police officers, and spent the rest of the night in the lounge of a local hotel.

Later on the Wednesday morning a special court was held in Saffron Walden where Det. Supt. Brown gave evidence of his arrest of Major Smedley who was accused of murdering Calvert. Smedley wore an open-necked white shirt, grey suit and brown suede shoes and walked into court flanked by two senior detectives. During the hearing, which lasted only five minutes, he sat at the side of a large oak table.

Det. Supt. Brown told the court: 'At 2.40 this morning I went to the home of the accused at Wendens Ambo where I saw the body of a man, later identified as that of Mr Calvert. He had a gunshot wound in his chest. I was present at the postmortem, and at 10.40 this morning I saw the accused at Saffron Walden police station and told him the deceased had died of gunshot wounds which I understood he had inflicted.'

Reginald Calvert, owner of Radio City, pictured shortly before he was gunned down by Major Oliver Smedley after a row over the ownership of the pop radio station.

Det. Supt. Brown added that when Smedley was charged and cautioned, he replied: 'I don't think I had better say anything until I see my solicitor.'

Mr A. S. Tee, who appeared for Smedley, said: 'The only thing he has asked me to say is that he completely denies the charge.'

Mr Tee asked for bail but the magistrate, Lord Braybrooke, replied that he did not think the law allowed him to grant bail on that particular charge, and Smedley was remanded in custody for eight days. He was then driven in a police van to Brixton Prison.

By now the newspapers had scented a sensational story in the making and it broke the next day in the morning press. Mrs Jill Wildman, Mr Calvert's secretary, questioned by reporters, said that the Radio City staff had been instructed to stand by until they could start transmitting again. The boarding party, she added, had not stated their intentions; although she knew who they were she would not reveal their identity.

That afternoon six police officers, led by Det. Supt. Brown, went out to Shivering Sands by launch and visited the radio station. They questioned both the staff of seven men and the boarding party, and then left in the evening.

On the Thursday morning when the public first learned about the mysterious happenings connected with Radio City, it was mystified by the strange affair. Why was the boarding party on Radio City? Who were the boarding party? Who, above all, was the mysterious woman in it? Why was the chief of the station shot? All that, as yet, was unexplained, and was not to be explained fully until the preliminary court hearing nearly a month later.

In this atmosphere other rumours spread of strange happenings in the world of pirate radio. *The Daily Telegraph* headed one report, 'Spread of radio pirates led to bitter disputes'. In it ex-Caroline disc jockey Simon Dee was quoted as telling a reporter he could sense 'the dawn of war – that's why I got out while the going was good'. The intense competition was alleged to have sparked off the war and, according to the *Telegraph*:

> Men whose names are pronounced with ease in City circles offered to buy each other up, or off. There was talk of 'punch-ups' in normally quiet and respectable offices. There was even talk of blackmail.

Worried particularly about this latest development in the world of pirate radio were many M.Ps. Mr Quintin Hogg, Opposition

Drama at Radio City: a police launch approaches the radio station, (above) and the boarding party stands by to repel boarders (right).

Spokesman on Home Affairs, tried, unsuccessfully, to secure a Commons statement from Mr Jenkins, Home Secretary, about the police visit to Radio City. Backbenchers felt that the events highlighted the fact that legislation should be introduced immediately to deal with the pirates. In a 5; a.m. adjournment debate a Labour M.P. told the Commons that he hoped the Government 'would be jerked into action' by the extraordinary and tragic events which included the shooting of the head of Radio City.

Answering his appeal for higher priority for legislation to deal with such stations, Mr Wedgwood Benn asserted: 'Our Bill is ready. It will be introduced. We have to be very careful because some of the events of the last twenty-four hours may spill out into matters which may come into the courts. But every fresh example of what the meaning of unregulated broadcasting may be strengthens my own feeling of the need to legislate.'

Mr Jenkins, Labour M.P. for Putney, had opened the debate, which had in fact been arranged some days previously but which assumed a note of topicality with the events on Radio City. Referring to these events, Mr Jenkins said that they included the 'hi-jacking' of one of the ships of Radio City, and invasion and taking over of an illegally-occupied area by another group, equally illegally occupying it. The events had culminated apparently in 'the first mate of one of the pirate ships' being shot and 'the captain accused of murder'. People might have been more prepared if they had considered that piracy was an aspect of anarchy. When the Government condoned anarchy, as it had in effect been doing, gangsters soon took over.

When the circumstances of the financing and management of Radio Caroline and Radio City were investigated, Mr Jenkins thought it would be found that some respectable newspapers had been weaving a romantic web around some operations which would not look too well.

On the Thursday evening Mrs Dorothy Calvert, Mr Calvert's widow, appeared on television. She said that she hoped to have the station back on the air in two or three days. 'I do not intend to sell it but run it my way', said Mrs Calvert. Negotiations to sell the station, in progress before her husband's death, were now in abeyance. The next day, Friday, Mrs Calvert said that following her TV appearance she received a threat that she should not attempt to visit Radio City.

At 8.20 a.m. on Friday morning, though, others left Whitstable

The fort-based pirate radio stations were always threatened by physical takeover. Here a boarding party approaches Red Sands Fort (Radio 390)

with just that intention. Two boats, one full of journalists and TV men, the other full of Radio City relief staff, made the eight mile journey out to the wartime fort on Shivering Sands. A measure of the interest, even abroad, being shown in this affair was the presence of pressmen from magazines such as *Paris Match* and *Time*. As the journalists approached, in the boat of Whitstable fisherman Mr Alfred Downs, on contract to Radio City, 'Big Alf' Bullen, standing on the 60 foot-high platform of the winch house to the fort, waved at them to keep at a distance.

He allowed, however, two engineers in the leading boat, Mr Tony Pine and Mr Ian West, to be hauled aboard to begin a new tour of duty. Then the other engineers, Mr Paul Elvey and Mr Phil Perkins with a cook, Leslie Dunne, 17, were lowered to the boat for a break ashore. When pressmen shouted: 'Who says we can't come aboard?' 'Big Alf bellowed: 'I do.'

During this time the boarding party stood by to repel any 'raiders' with oxy-acetylene burners. They threatened, if any attempt was made to board the station, to wreck the 240 foot-high transmitting mast and sever the steel cables supporting the catwalks running between the forts.

Mr Elvey said, in answer to questions, that at first the invaders' attitude had been quite reasonable, but then it unaccountably became hostile after a motor barge delivered supplies to them the previous evening. He assumed some instructions may have been passed on from an unidentified group of people employing them. 'Big Alf' had called him from the Radio City living quarters after the barge's visit to warn him of what would happen if Mrs Calvert, or any of her officials, or any other 'unauthorised' callers set foot on the fort. If the situation arose they were ready to cut down the transmitting mast and sever the catwalks. With the catwalks demolished the seven Radio City crew members holding out would have been marooned in their sleeping quarters.

They have oxy-acetylene equipment with them', added Mr Elvey, 'so they are in a position to carry out their threat. If the mast went it would mean a loss of £2,000.' He also said that the invaders were keeping up a twenty-four hour watch, and patrolled the fort at night by torchlight. They were quartered in the sound studio and if any Radio City man went near it he was pushed away.

Asked how long he thought the invaders were likely to remain on the fort, he said: 'I have no idea except that I have heard rumours from the men themselves that three tugs of supplies are being sent to them. This, of course, would mean they could stay for a long time.'

Not surprisingly, Mrs Calvert had meanwhile cancelled her visit to the station and was considering what legal action, if any, could be taken against the boarding party.

Mr Timothy Hardacre, her lawyer, announced: 'Mrs Calvert has instructed her lawyers to issue proceedings against the persons who have forcibly taken possession of Radio City, and also against the persons who have aided and abetted them. She is to take steps to lay information for their arrest and committal to the Central Criminal Court.'

Commented Mrs Calvert: 'It is proving more difficult to get these men off the fort than we thought.'

Not surprising really, considering even Mr Wedgwood Benn and the Defence Department were experiencing great difficulty in finding a way of getting pirate radio operators, like her, to relinquish possession of the forts!

On the Saturday Sir Alan Herbert joined the fray, urging the Government to send the Navy at once to Shivering Sands.

'Ministers seem to be speechless as well as paralysed,' he angrily declared. '1 take it upon myself to send a friendly warning to the latest trespassers on the Shivering Sands Towers. It has been said that the fort is outside the territorial limits and that no court will take the case. This is a dangerous delusion. The Towers have been in territorial waters since September, 30th, 1964, under an Order in Council specially made for the purpose by the last government. Moreover, they are in the area of the Port of London, and all the criminal laws apply.'

Sir Alan added on a familiar theme: 'For many months the British Copyright Council have been urging the Government to turn the pirates off as trespassers on Government property. Now, with two hostile gangs aboard, the need is urgent. There may be violence, even a death, and Ministers will be responsible. They should send the Navy at once.'

Police inaction still prevailed, due to the issue of jurisdictional uncertainty, although on Saturday the Radio City boatman, Mr Fred Downs, was questioned about his trip out to the station and the threat to cut the mast down.

The Ministry of Defence, in answer to reporters, deftly passed the buck: 'I suppose you could call them abandoned war works,' said a spokeman. 'The Ministry has had nothing to do with them since the war, and it is understood they are Crown property.' Anything to avoid responsibility!

Then suddenly on Sunday evening, exactly a week after their mission started, the members of the boarding party left Radio City. At 9.30 p.m. the station started testing, and by 10 p.m. it was back on the air. The announcer explained that 'our guests have left', wished them a safe journey home and expressed the hope that they would not be returning.

'Big Alf' added a postscript to the week talking with pressmen: 'It was more exciting that watching "The Man from UNCLE". I wouldn't have missed being in on this. These days the nearest you can get to excitement and adventure is on the "telly".'

The focus of attention in the affair now switched to the House of Commons where a number of Ministers were questioned on various aspects of the events on Radio City.

On Monday, 27th June Mr Reynolds, Minister of Defence for the Army, rejected an M.Ps. suggestion that he should order an invasion of Defence Department towers used by pirate radios.

He cleverly excused himself from having to take such action by saying: There is no present or foreseeable defence purpose which would require me to exercise control over these forts.' A politician's answer if ever there was one.

A number of other Parliamentary Questions were put down. Mr Christopher Rowland, Labour M.P. for Meriden, put down a question to Mr Jenkins, Home Secretary, asking if he would call for a report by Chief Constables on police action taken concerning the boarding of Radio City, and 'action to be taken with regard to the boarding of towers within territorial waters from which broadcasts are being transmitted illegally.'

Mr Rowland, a former BBC producer, said: 'Now that it has been established, through events over the past week, that police can go aboard these forts, I hope they will feel free to board them and take action in respect of illegal broadcasting.'

Mr William Deedes, a well-known pirate 'persecutor', asked the Attorney-General, Sir Elwyn Jones, to introduce legislation which would bring the disused military towers 'within United Kingdom jurisdiction'.

Sir John Hobson, a former Attorney-General, also asked Sir Elwyn to refer 'recent events' at Shivering Sands to the Director of Public Prosecutions 'with a view to instituting criminal proceedings'.

On July 1st Mr Wedgwood Benn announced that legislation would be introduced before the Summer recess. Up until the end of June the Government line on the off-shore stations had been that a draft Bill was ready, but its introduction would be delayed by the pressure of other legislation. But, it was generally interpreted, following the boarding of Radio City, such had been the pressure from M.Ps. demanding the introduction of the Bill immediately, that the Government had decided to rearrange its timetable and rush it in. Only the week before Government sources had implied that there was little hope of its being introduced in the current session.

This change of mind was regarded as a victory for backbenchers like Mr Deedes and, in particular, for Mr Hugh Jenkins, a former assistant-secretary of Equity, who had announced that he would himself try to bring in a Bill to curb the pirates.

It was suggested that the Government might adopt what had come to be known as 'The Jenkins Plan'. This was that a new authority should be established to act as parent to publicly owned stations. The authority would produce a national popular radio programme and the stations would provide local news and features. The service would be financed by national and local advertising. This appeared to be, in the absence of commercial radio under private enterprise, vastly preferable to the extension of the BBC monopoly to local broadcasting.

The communications group of the Parliamentary Labour Party, under Mr Jenkins' chairmanship, discussed these proposals at length, and Mr Benn actually attended a number of meetings.

It was reported at this time that many Ministers wanted the BBC to run the 'pop and local service' but in considering this the problem of finance immediately arose. The Corporation is, and always has been, firmly against financing its operations by advertising, yet without it there would necessarily have to be a substantial increase in the licence fee.

Also reported as being examined were plans for the BBC to devote one programme to continuous light music, and this seemed the most likely one to be adopted.

The announcement of legislation on July 1st, all the evidence suggested, was made long before it was expected in official circles, as it was directly precipitated by the Radio City affair. Therefore the examination of these proposals was not very far advanced, and no preparations started.

All Mr Benn would add on July ist was: "The Government is completing its general review of broadcasting policy in the course of which serious consideration had been given to the better provision of more popular music on a national basis.

Tn addition, various proposals for the establishment of local public service radio stations have been under consideration. A statement on broadcasting policy will be made as soon as possible.'

In his statement he also revealed that there were four pirate stations operating within territorial limits. Three of them, including Radio City, were on abandoned forts in the Thames Estuary and the fourth was Radio Scotland, which, he said, was operating within the three-mile limit off Troon in the Firth of Clyde. No action was promised on these stations; they would be left until the Bill was passed.

On July 7th the Attorney-General, Sir Elwyn Jones, informed Sir John Hobson that the police had reported to the Director of Public Prosecutions about the recent events at Shivering Sands and that the Director, Sir Norman Skelhorn, was considering the report. In a supplementary question Sir John tried to pin the Attorney-General down on the matter of whether or not Radio City was within his jurisdiction. He asked if Sir Elwyn's answer meant that he took the view that Shivering Sands was in the territorial jurisdiction of the United Kingdom, and that law and order could be enforced there by the British Government.

'If so, why did you not advise the Postmaster-General about the possibility of a prosecution order under the Wireless Telegraphy Act?' He then asked for a definite ruling as to whether Shivering Sands would be within territorial jurisdiction under the proposed Bill.

The issue was neatly dodged though by the Attorney-General, 'whether you are right, or I am right on that, the position is that under the Territorial Waters Jurisdiction Act of 1873, indictable offences committed in territorial waters are within the jurisdiction of the courts of that country.

'As to summary jurisdiction that question will have to be decided if the Postmaster-General decides to institute summary proceedings under the Wireless Telegraphy Act, 1949.'

Sir John found himself unable to elicit any information that he did not already know.

Mr Hugh Jenkins joined the exchanges by asking: 'Are you saying in effect that it is in order for proceedings to take place and will you include, if you are going to take proceedings, Radio Scotland?'

The situation is getting dangerous

Sir Elwyn gave the stock answer: "These matters are being considered.'

Meanwhile, Major Smedley had been further remanded in custody, and appeared in court again on July 18th when the preliminary hearing on a charge of murder was heard.

The preliminary hearing at Saffron Walden brought its share of surprises. Not only were the mysteries of the events connected with Radio City revealed, but there were sensational new disclosures, laying bare a story of threats, shady financial deals and strong-arm men.

When the hearing opened at 10.30 a.m. Mr Peter Palmes, prosecuting, rose from his seat and outlined the prosecution's case. First of all, he said that some of the background to the case would have to be sketched in. This he did.

Smedley was concerned with a firm called Project Atlanta. This firm amalgamated with Radio Caroline and they were approached by Calvert. No financial agreement was made and the deal fell through, but nevertheless a transmitter worth some £10,000 was put on the fort on Shivering Sands.

It then came to the attention of the persons involved with Project Atlanta that a deal was going through between Calvert and an American group. Thus Smedley and those with him wondered about the property on Radio City. Their royalty for this property had not been paid for by Calvert and they wondered if this equipment was concerned in the deal.

The decision come to by the accused and by another person and other people involved was to protect their equipment by putting a party of men on board.

'On June 19th and 20th this happened. The accused, a Miss Black, and a band of some seventeen men boarded Radio City and the transmitter was put out of action. The accused and Miss Black came off the fort some time that morning. Arrangements were made for a third party to meet them at the headquarters of Project Atlanta in Dean Street, Soho. The meeting took place at 11.30.'

Mr Palmes continued by saying that at the meeting was Mr Philip Birch, head of Radio London and London representative of the American firm involved in the Radio City deal. Calvert also was present later. Smedley suggested that he and his friends should take part in the deal going through between Calvert and Mr Birch. Mr Birch, who subsequently disappeared from the case, and Calvert both turned this idea down independently.

'Calvert was obviously disturbed by the turn of events. He made threats, which perhaps no one took very seriously. In the course of these threats he said he had access to a number of strong-arm men. He also mentioned a nerve gas and, "when he really got going", he said that "all those on the fort would wish they had never gone out there in the first place".'

The final result was that he left the meeting.

On the morning of June 21st Mr Arnold, a radio engineer, who had installed an aerial mast on Radio City, came into the case. He was interested as to how the radio mast was working and listened to the programmes. That morning he noticed that the station had gone off the air and he telephoned Calvert. 'It could be assumed that Calvert put Mr Arnold into the picture as to what was happening', said Mr Palmes.

That night, about 9 p.m., Mr Arnold went round to Calvert's place and drove him to Saffron Walden. They went to Wendens Ambo and stopped in Duck Lane, near Smedley's cottage. Calvert knocked on the door, which was opened by Miss Pamela Thorburn, Smedley's secretary and housekeeper. The immediate reaction of Calvert was to thrust the door open, push her back, and to demand to know where Smedley was.

A scuffle then broke out in the hall with Calvert trying to get in and Miss Thorburn trying to stop him. Mr Arnold was hovering in the background meanwhile, but became concerned at the turn of events and rushed upstairs to see if he could find Smedley. The scuffle reached the sitting room where Miss Thorburn made a move to pick up the telephone. It was ripped out of the wall by Calvert.

Mr Palmes then picked up a heavy white marble bust of Napoleon from the table in front of him. He said that in the course of the struggle the bust, which was on a table by the hall, was thrown to the ground and cracked. There might be the suggestion that it was thrown at Miss Thorburn. It was an immensely heavy weapon to use and it was more than likely that it was knocked or thrown to the ground in a gesture of anger by Calvert.

Mr Palmes continued that while the struggle was still going on Mr Arnold thought the best thing he could do would be to get help, and he rushed out into the drive.

'No sooner was he outside than he heard a shot inside the house. He went straight back in and saw the accused standing in the dining room doorway holding a shotgun. He saw Calvert staggering from the sitting room door and collapsing in the hall, obviously badly wounded.'

Just before the shooting. Miss Thorburn would say, Calvert had held a statuette of Napoleon above her head. Miss Thorburn would also say that nothing was spoken between Smedley and Calvert at the time of the shooting. Calvert took a few steps forward, then he collapsed by the front door, and there he died.

When Calvert had arrived Smedley had apparently gone out at the back of the cottage to a neighbouring cottage. There, a Mr Warden was visiting the people who owned the cottage. Smedley asked him to ring the police because he had 'trouble'. While Mr Warden was on the telephone, after Smedley had gone out, Mr Arnold appeared in a state of excitement and said there had been a shooting.

When the police arrived, alleged Mr Palmes, Smedley told a constable: 'I shot him.'

Later he was alleged to have said: 'He had a tower in the Thames and the other day we took it from him', and in further explanation: 'He hammered on the door. I knew it must have been him. He had threatened to do me harm and kill me and all the others. ... I knew he came here to kill me, I could see he was mad, and I knew he carried arms. I had no choice but to fire. I did not think of aiming at his legs, I just fired.'

Mr Palmes then produced a thin pencil-shaped object with the appearance of a pocket pencil or torch: 'In fact it is a little gas gun which throws, one assumes, a small jet of tear gas. It was found when the body was searched.'

In his summing up of the case, Mr Palmes had revealed many of the mysteries of Radio City, and outlined the hearing. The depositions of witnesses were still to take place. They were no less melodramatic.

The first witness was Miss Dorothy Black, a theatrical impresario of Brunswick Gardens, London, who had been associated with Smedley in Project Atlanta. After explaining that Calvert had been given money and the transmitter by Smedley, while the former was in difficulties, she described the circumstances of the boarding, in which she took part. She then detailed the meeting in Dean Street at which she was present. Calvert said no deal or obligation any longer concerned him because he had already sold Radio City. Miss Black said that Calvert's immediate reaction to the boarding party was that he was 'very grateful he had been given some opportunity for some fun'. He had said: 'I will have them screaming to come off.'

There then followed the sensational disclosure that Calvert said that 'he had some knowledge of chemistry, and by accident had discovered a nerve gas'. He said that he would lob gas shells onto the Radio City tower.

'He said that so far he had only used it on animals and was keen to know what effects it would have on human beings.'

Calvert also said he was associated with dance halls and could call on the best fighters in the country to help him. He produced a pen-type object from his pocket which he said was a gas pistol which he always carried so he could look after himself.

Cross-examined by Mr John Cower, defending, Miss Black said that Calvert described himself as being an expert in explosives and poison gas. The gas he had discovered was a derivation of ammonia. 'It was heavier than air and could drift down so that it could be very valuable in attack on the fort', she said.

The next witness was also a shareholder in Project Atlanta, Mr Horace Leggett of Cobham, Kent. He was at the Dean Street meeting. 'Mr Birch', he said, 'conveyed the impression that the meeting did not really concern him, and that he had done his deal with Mr Calvert.' Mr Leggett said that Mr Birch 'got a little irate' and said the whole thing was 'high-handed'. 'He even referred to the whole thing as "blackmail".'

Asked what impression he formed of Calvert, Mr Leggett said: 'I was trying to assess the man. I had the difficulty of deciding whether the whole thing was a colossal bluff and just sheer boasting, or whether he was as ruthless as he made out to be.'

On the second day of the hearing, the court heard more about the struggle at Smedley's cottage from Miss Thorburn and Mr Arnold.

Miss Thorburn said: 'I literally thought I was within a split second of losing my life.' She said that at one stage Calvert threatened to take her away with him, or kill her. Seconds before the shot Calvert had held the 18-inch bronze statuette above her head. 'He looked like a raving maniac. I was petrified with fright.' When she had tried to dial '999' she had only dialled the first '9' when Calvert wrenched the 'phone away, pushed her and she fell through the bathroom door. 'I came rushing back and he hit me about the shoulder with the telephone handset.'

Miss Thorburn said that during the time Calvert was in the nouse he kept shouting: 'I'm a desperate man. I don't care what happens to me and I am going to get him (Smedley) alive or dead.'

She did not hear the shot, but saw Calvert stagger back and then saw Smedley with a shotgun in his hand.

In evidence, Mr Arnold said that he was 'flabbergasted' by what went on at the cottage, and too taken aback by the incident to take any part in it. He did not know that Calvert was carrying a gas gun and ammunition.

Mr John MacCafferty, senior experimental officer at the Metropolitan Police Laboratory, said that some gas cartridges which fitted a ballpoint pen he examined were only legally obtainable in Britain on a special permit from the Armed Forces. In his opinion Calvert could only have got them from illegal sources.

On the third, and last, day of the hearing the first witness, P.C. John Kearney, told of going to the cottage at about 11.30 p.m. In a later statement to P.C. Kearney Smedley was alleged to have said: 'This is a joke that turned sour. It started off as a very good story and you will be able to read about it in your newspapers tomorrow. It began as an excellent story. We went and took the tower in the Thames, but it all turned out wrong. He was a silly man to come the way he did. ... I feel morally right and I'm not worried, because he was a very violent man and I knew he came to kill me.'

Evidence of further alleged statements by Smedley was given by Police Sgt. George and Det. Supt. George Brown. Smedley was stated to have said: 'I probably saved the girl's life,' and to have turned to where Calvert was lying and said, 'Silly boy, silly boy. I was warned the situation was getting dangerous....'

Meanwhile, forty-five minutes before the last day of the hearing started, an Essex Z-car policeman had discovered a window ajar at Major Smedley's thatched country cottage. The court was informed that the cottage had been broken into during the night. Entry had been gained through the study window; drawers had been rifled, but it appeared that only small ornaments were missing.

After the police evidence, Mr Gower, for the defence, submitted that there was no evidence on which Smedley could be committed for trial. If any man killed in self-defence or in defending a member of his household, no offence was committed.

'It is abundantly clear that Smedley acted in self-defence of himself and Miss Thorburn. It may be old fashioned but it is the law of our country, that an Englishman's home is his castle.

'The law looks with great disfavour upon the activities of people who violate the sanctity and security of another man's home.

'If some person trespasses upon the property of another for the purpose of committing some violence or atrocious crime then the law of England justifies a householder in resisting to the utmost, even unto death and causing death to the person who had broken in.'

Mr Calvert had broken into Smedley's home and refused to leave, maintained Mr Gower. He was bereft of self-control and reason. It was against a background of a man in imminent personal danger that the case had to be judged.

Mr Peter Palmes, prosecuting, said that when a defence of self-defence was raised, the manner and degree of the intervention were matters which magistrates should leave for a jury to decide.

After listening for nearly two hours to submissions from prosecution and defence counsel the three magistrates retired to consider their decision. After a 50-minute retirement, the Chairman of the Magistrates, Mr J. H. Wiseman, announced: 'We have come to the conclusion that no reasonable jury would convict on a charge of murder.'

The magistrates committed Smedley to Chelmsford Assizes for trial on October 11th on a charge of manslaughter.

Smedley, when asked if he had anything to say, replied: 'I am innocent of this charge. I reserve my defence.'

The prosecution made no objection when Mr Gower made an application for bail. He said Smedley was a man of excellent character and was in a position to offer substantial surety. Bail was then granted in the sum of £500 with two sureties of £500 each.

The trial took place in October and only lasted two days. When the trial of Smedley for manslaughter started at Chelmsford Assizes, he pleaded not guilty. A surprise prosecution witness was Mrs Dorothy Calvert, widow of the shot former head of Radio City, and some new evidence emerged.

Mr Hugh Griffiths, Q.C. asked Mrs Calvert what explanation her husband had given her for the boarding party.

'He told me they wanted him to sign an agreement giving them half the profits of Radio City,' she replied. She said that the last time she saw her husband alive was when he left for Smedley's home on June 2ist; he was worried about the boarding party and for the safety of his men but, when he left, he was calm.

Mrs Calvert said that the transmitter provided by Smedley had never been used for broadcasting and was not serviceable. It was nearly 30 years old, components for it were not available and it would have cost thousands to make it serviceable.

Miss Black, who had taken part in the boarding, appeared once again in court and claimed that apart from providing the transmitter on Radio City, Smedley had also lent Mr Calvert money to meet salary bills. She also described again Calvert's remarkable and rather threatening behaviour at the meeting held in Soho the day after the boarding, repeating his threat to drop ammonia bombs on the fort and to use nerve gas.

Major Smedley's secretary and housekeeper, Miss Pamela Thorburn, also told of the threats, made by Calvert prior to the Soho meeting and after his visit to Scotland Yard.

She said that he rang Smedley's office: 'He was making a lot of threats and said he was going out personally to the fort and would tell the people there that the police had their photos, and that they would be arrested when they came oif. Mr Smedley would be charged with theft. ... He said he was going to kill them all.'

She then referred to a piece of paper on which she had written down a message from Mrs Wildman, Calvert's secretary, and sent on behalf of Calvert. It warned: 'The situation is getting dangerous'. Miss Thorburn said that she had discussed the message with Major Smedley but that they did not take it seriously. When she and Smedley returned that evening to Wendens Ambo, however, there was a loud knocking on the door at about 11 p.m. . . . .

After describing the assault on her by Calvert, and Smedley's shooting of him, she admitted under cross-examination that there was 'considerable attachment' between herself and Smedley. They 'sometimes' shared a bed, the pretty 23-year-old secretary told the court.

Little else that was new emerged at the trial, and on its second day the jury was addressed by counsel. Summing up the real issue at stake in the case, Mr Griffiths, Q.C. had either explained that Calvert had forced his way into Smedley's home.

'You may well come to the conclusion that this behaviour was outrageous. If a man breaks into your house and exhibits violence towards you, the law doesn't require you to be peaceful. You may stand your ground and meet violence with violence.

'In the submission of the Crown, the violence used must be proportionate to that which is offered to you. Outrageous though

Calvert's behaviour was, there was no warrant for the accused to go to the extreme of shooting and killing. It will be for the prosecution to satisfy you that the killing was not justified.'

In his summing up Mr Justice Stevenson told the jury that quite clearly Calvert and another man had forced their way into Smedley's house. 'It is not long before the man Calvert embarks on a sequence of acts which, you might think, is very much like the conduct of a lunatic. ... He was quite clearly a very angry and a very uncontrolled man.'

As the jury was about to leave the box to consider its verdict, one of its members asked the judge if it was necessary to retire. Told it was not necessary, the twelve men 'good and true' stood in a huddle in the jury box and after less than a minute, gave their verdict – Not Guilty.

Major William Oliver Smedley stepped from the dock a free man. Outside the court he said of his rival, who had frequently threatened his life: 'I feel no elation, and there will be no celebration. The whole affair has been such a tragedy. It is an appalling wastage of a brilliant man's life. Reg Calvert was the sort of man I regarded highly, who had found his way up through his own efforts.'

*

The Radio City affair, however, had had wider repercussions than the death of its chief.

The hearing at Saffron Walden had exposed pirate radio and destroyed something of its romantic aura. Behind the jovial disc jockeys and their popular programmes there lay a business of intrigue, threats, violence and intimidation, brought about by the increased competition in what had developed into a full scale pirate war. Too many pirates had spoiled the 'pops' and advertising had become scarcer.

Reports during the closing months of 1965 that the Caroline organisation was trying to take over Radio City were neither confirmed nor denied by either company. Commented the broadcasting correspondent of *The Daily Telegraph*:

> Nelson emphasised that a shore-based gun is much superior to one at sea and this applies with equal force to radio stations. I should therefore not be surprised if the Caroline move came about, despite the uncertainty of tenure.

Some newspapers at the time of the spectacular events on Radio City reported the station to be part of the Caroline organisation. This information, however, was stated to be false. Since Radio City was purchased by Mr Calvert from 'Lord' Sutch in 1964 for £5,000, it had been run by his King Music Publishing Company of 7, Denmark Street, London. Radio Caroline failed in its negotiations in 1966, when the station was valued at £150,000.

Radio Caroline, though, was not the only party interested in Radio City. Mr Philip Birch, the shrewd chief of Radio London who had made the most out of pirate radio, was also interested. Radio London, of course, was Caroline's chief rival.

Project Atlanta was the organisation formed to run Radio Atlanta in 1964 and Smedley was its Chairman. In June 1964 the Caroline and Atlanta organisations amalgamated and for a while were known, for business purposes, as Project Atlanta, but the name of the Caroline organisation was later changed to Planet Productions Ltd and the connection with Project Atlanta was severed; or at least so Radio Caroline has claimed. Was Smedley still connected with the Caroline organisation at the time of the events on Radio City, although Radio Caroline emphatically denied any connection with Radio City when the story broke in the newspapers? The fact remains that a company known as Project Atlanta lent Calvert money and gave him a £10,000 transmitter when he was in financial difficulties. When it heard that a deal over Radio City was going through between Mr Calvert and Mr Birch of Caroline's rival. Radio London, it used its 'hold' over Calvert, in the form of the transmitter, to get in on the deal. Project Atlanta, though, claimed that an agreement had been reached between it and Calvert, and that as soon as their £10,000 transmitter was shipped out Calvert set out to double-cross them by arranging a tie-up with Radio London instead. Calvert did not tell Philip Birch of Radio London that the transmitter was the property of Project Atlanta, and refused all demands for its return. The trouble and tragedy this precipitated has been described above. When Philip Birch met Smedley in his Soho office the day after the boarding of the fort, Project Atlanta offered to take their men off Radio City and restore the transmitter if they were let in on the deal. Birch refused to do this, and when Calvert arrived threatening to use 'nerve' gas on the fort the Radio London chief became very wary of the whole shady business and backed out.

If one of the rival organisations had succeeded in getting the Radio City station it would have been a valuable asset and would have represented a substantial victory over its rival. Project Atlanta realised the stakes and was prepared to play high; Mr Birch called it not only 'high-handed', but 'blackmail'.

When Radio London refused to do a deal, and with Calvert declining to co-operate, Smedley rang Radio 390 disc jockey Mike Raven, whom he had worked with on the Radio Atlanta enterprise, and asked him to arrange a meeting with Ted Allbeury. the chief of Radio 390, for the next day at the Special Services Club. Smedley's idea was that, since the Radio City and Radio 390 forts were barely five miles apart, they should combine and run two stations with one playing 'pop' and the other 'sweet' music. That plan was nipped in the bud, however, by the events at Wendens Ambo the following evening.

With the death of her husband, however, Mrs Dorothy Calvert stopped all negotiations and declared her intention of running the station herself.

It is only fair to say, in defence of the pirate operators, that in any highly competitive business tempers run high at times, intrigues develop and there are attempts to buy out rivals. Around pirate radio, though, there had been woven a romantic 'Robin Hood' image. In defiance of authority the modern pirates provided what a large section of the population wanted. The Radio City affair badly cracked this romantic image. It had the effect in some quarters of hardening opinion against the pirates where beforehand there might have been a more benevolent attitude. The rumours that started of threats and fights in offices in Soho and the City were even more harmful.

An important result of the Radio City affair was the speeding up of legislation to deal with the pirates. If the authorities had only acted earlier, actions which brought tragedy, and which made British law a laughing stock, could have been avoided. If the GPO, Defence Department and Crown Commissioners had met and hammered out the ownership of the Shivering Sands Fort, the law would not have been brought into disrespect, the police would not have been put in an embarrassing position, and those departments would not have had the loss of human life – death, to put it bluntly – on their collective consciences. The authorities, above all, must bear the blame for the events on and connected with Radio City that last, fateful week of June.

7

The Death Warrant is prepared

Realising the results of his inaction, Mr Wedgwood Benn was quick to try and make amends, or refurbish his tarnished reputation, whichever way one likes to look at it.

On the 1st of July he announced that legislation to curb the pirates would be introduced before the Summer recess. The next day he told an International Co-operative Day Rally at Bristol that he was determined broadcasting should serve the needs of the whole community, and should not be allowed to be regarded just as 'rich pickings for those who think they can make some money out of it'.

This was not so much in the nature of a threat to the pirates, who were pleasing a large part of the community previously left cold by the BBC's pious, pretentious offerings, as an indication of his opposition to the idea of commercial radio in general: a form of which many people were hoping would follow the closing down of the pirates.

The very next day, however, there was a notable and surprise development. In a Cabinet reshuffle provoked by the embarrassing resignation of Mr Frank Cousins, Minister of Technology, Mr Wedgwood Benn became the Minister of Technology. Mr Wilson probably regarded his resignation from the GPO as having a fortuitous side-effect in that Mr Benn, who had been a miserable failure as Postmaster-General, due more to the Government's policy than his own, could now be moved from that office, and a new look introduced in time to put the Bill to deal with the pirates through the House.

The new Postmaster-General was 53-year-old Mr Edward Watson Short, former Chief Whip. The day after his appointment *The Daily Telegraph* echoed the hopes of millions of listeners. While recognising that he would wipe the pirates off the wavelengths, an editorial asked:

> These stations supply a want which, if not noble, is at least legitimate. They supply it, moreover, at the expense not of the listener but of the advertiser. Why then put them out of business? Would it not suffice to force them to return to the mainland, to submit to the law in general and to the regulation of wavelengths in particular, and to pay proper performing fees?

If Mr Short moves along these lines, he will deserve applause. He may prefer, however, merely to suppress the pirates. This would be silly ...

But only three days after his appointment, on July 6th, Mr Short dashed all hopes of a change in Government policy on commercial radio, when he stated that the pirate stations would definitely not be replaced by local commercial radio stations. Broadcasting, he maintained, must remain under a public body.

On July 13th the new Postmaster-General answered a number of questions put to him in the Commons on pirate radio stations. He confirmed that the Bill to deal with the pirates would be introduced before the Summer recess, and that it would probably become law early in the New Year. The Bill would implement the agreement reached at the Council of Europe eighteen months previously, in January 1965. Under the terms of this agreement, states undertook to act against pirate radio stations, punishing as offences their establishment and operation as well as giving any form of assistance to such stations.

'These stations present a very squalid picture. It is no use talking about lawlessness in our cities if we are prepared to allow this to take place on the high seas.' Mr Short certainly seemed to mean business.

GPO lawyers were understood to be studying the legislation introduced in Sweden. The Swedish Government had taken firm action against the pirates operating off her shores many years before. This legislation made it illegal for firms, including advertisers, to trade with offshore radio stations. Thus their sources of vital supplies and advertising were cut off and they had to close down.

The pirate radio operators over the last two years had become accustomed to hollow threats by Postmaster-Generals of legislation against them, and had come to disregard them. This time, they realised, the Postmaster-General really was in earnest, and they began to channel their efforts into fighting the imminent attempts to wipe them off the air.

Listeners to Radio 390 became accustomed to hearing a recorded message from managing director of the station, Ted Allbeury, asking them to write to their Member of Parliament: 'It's the only way to save Radio 390'. Mr Allbeury also twice addressed the Conservative Broadcasting Committee. He announced that something like 100,000 listeners had responded to his request and written to their M.P. Replies from 70 Tory and Liberal M.P.s, he claimed, pledged support for free radio.

RADIO 390

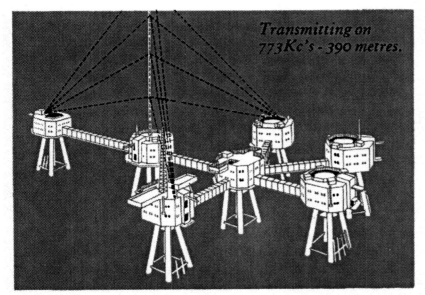

Transmitting on
773Kc's - 390 metres.

EVE

woman's magazine of the air

*The sweet music format of Radio 390 became an instant hit with
housewives in the English Home Counties*

Radio Caroline listeners were sent a car sticker bearing the plaintive legend, 'I love Radio Caroline'.

Mr William Vick, the Texan Managing Director of Radio England and Britain Radio, with what could only be described as unwarranted optimism, organised a champagne party in London for the end of the month.

'We will be celebrating massive public support in favour of licensing us, plus the support of the entertainment industry,' declared Mr Vick, who added that guests would be invited to 'set sail on a sea of champagne'.

At the same time, Mr Vick submitted to the Postmaster-General a request for a licence 'to install and operate two radio transmitting stations within the U.K. for the public benefit and at no public cost". Mr Vick's application for permission to come ashore was prepared by Sir Peter Rawlinson, Q.C.

Representatives of the offshore broadcasters, in particular Roger Braben, a public relations man active on Caroline's behalf, began meeting M.P.s. Even the most vociferous opponents of pirate radio were approached and regaled with the arguments for freedom of radio. One, Labour M.P. Christopher Rowland, admitted to being surprised by the snobberies of the pirates. 'They explained that they had nothing to do with those terrible people who ran the towers.'

Former Tory M.P. for Cleveland, Yorkshire, and chief of Radio 270, Wilf Proudfoot, contacted North-east M.P.s and even managed to induce Opposition spokesman on broadcasting. Paul Bryan, to board the *Oceaan 7* anchored off Scarborough.

On July 25th representatives and supporters of the pirate radio stations had a meeting with M.P.s at the House of Commons. They again stressed their object; that they should be legalised and allowed to establish themselves on land. If the Government, though, persisted in introducing legislation they would carry on, certain that they would be supplied from the Republic of Eire and get advertising through international agencies.

By now, however, they were too late.

On July 27th the Government introduced in the Commons its Bill to outlaw the pirate stations. That day it received its formal First Reading. Its object was described on the House of Commons Order Paper as 'to suppress broadcasting from ships, aircraft and certain other marine structures'.

The next day the Bill was published under the title of 'The Marine, Etc., Broadcasting (Offences) Bill'. Under the terms of the Bill nearly every British person who had anything to do with unauthorised radio stations faced prosecution. The only people not threatened by the Bill were the listeners, who should not be listening anyway to the unauthorised transmissions of the pirates under the terms of the 1947 Wireless Telegraphy Act.

The Government comprehensively covered in the Bill any structure fixed, floating or airborne, from which broadcasts could be made. Clauses provided that the master of the ship from which broadcasts were made, the owners and any British citizen who assisted in any way in the operation of die radio station would be guilty of an offence. The Bill also embraced anyone in the U.K. who got someone else outside the U.K. to do anything which was an offence under its terms.

Specifically, the terms of the Bill laid down that it would be unlawful to provide a ship or radio equipment for use in pirate broadcasting, to install or repair the equipment, to supply any goods or carry them to pirate stations, or to transport people to or from such stations.

On the passing of the Bill it would also be an offence to supply records, tapes or other recorded material for programmes, to take part in any of the broadcasts, to advertise goods or services on any of the stations directly or through an advertising agent, and to publish programme details, as many newspapers did.

Thus any British citizen connected in any way with a pirate station, whether a director, disc jockey, advertiser or ferryman, was covered by the Bill and was liable to a maximum penalty of £100 or three months' imprisonment, or both, on summary conviction in a Magistrate's Court. But an offender could be sent to prison for two years and fined an unspecified amount on conviction on indictment at a Quarter Sessions or Assizes. Responsible officers of companies, such as directors, managers or secretaries, could be proceeded against, as well as the company itself.

When the Bill was published at the end of July it was reckoned that the pirates had about nine months before it would reach the Statute Book. The reaction of the pirate radio operators was to fight the Bill tooth and nail. Mr Short was reported as being confident that the Bill would sound the death knell of the offshore stations, but there were loopholes in the Bill. It did not provide for the closing down of the stations by naval or police action, but merely the cutting off of their supply lines. The Bill tackled the pirate radio operators on the lines agreed by the Council of Europe, but not all contracting parties in the agreement had then, or still have, ratified it with legislation. From these countries supplies could still be obtained by the pirates.

Sweden and Denmark, in the middle of 1966, were the only countries to have ratified the agreement, with Britain intending to. Countries that had signed the agreement but had yet to legislate were Belgium, France, West Germany, Greece, Eire, Italy. Luxembourg, Holland and Norway. Whilst the Bill introduced in Britain would make operation for the pirates more difficult, it would need more countries to legislate on similar lines before becoming fully effective.

Upon introduction of the legislation Mr William Vick of Radio England and Britain Radio made it dear that his stations would have no difficulty remaining on the air. 'Our ship is American-owned and crewed, and the disc jockeys are American. I have already been approached by several continental businessmen about advertising.'

Radio Scotland said it had a master plan to beat the legislation. This was believed to involve supplying the ship from the Irish Republic at its anchorage, which would be moved 70 miles out into the Atlantic. The ship's Scottish crew and disc jockeys would be changed for foreign staff and a more powerful transmitter installed on board.

Other stations hoped to evade the restrictions by moving outside territorial waters and using more highly-powered transmitters. There was even talk of coastal waters around Spain and Portugal being used as anchorages for new highly-powered pirate ships, as neither Spain nor Portugal was a signatory of the Council of Europe agreement.

The owner of Radio Essex, Mr Roy Bates, said he would live abroad if it was necessary for the survival of the station.

Radio Caroline said they would concentrate on fighting the legislation when Parliament reassembled. They had engaged a public relations firm and were lobbying M.P.s with mixed success. A Caroline spokesman, the day the Bill was published, condemned it as 'spiteful, unimaginative and a negation of basic freedom that seeks to put an outright ban on the enjoyment of 25 million regular listeners to offshore radio, without submitting any alternative proposals for satisfying the legitimate demand'.

The pirate radio operators appeared determined to fight the Bill.

Mr Philip Birch of Radio London said: 'I believe that we will be still broadcasting in 30 years time. All we have to do is close down our offices in Mayfair and move the centre of operations out of the country. Our advertising can be handled from agencies in New York and Paris. The ship can be supplied with food and all other necessities from Spain or Holland.' Mr Birch also made the point that the Bill seemed to be designed to help foreign manufacturers to advertise their products to British markets. It would discriminate against the hundreds of British manufacturers who used Radio London to reach 12 million people. It also prevented British manufacturers and exporters from advertising their products to about 4 million people who listened to Radio London on the continent – thousands of letters were received from Holland, Belgium, Sweden and Finland.

Mr Proudfoot, managing director of Ellambar Investments Ltd, the company operating Radio 270, declared: 'This Bill does not worry us in the least. Parliament has given first readings to thousands of Bills which have never got onto the Statute Book. Even if it does get through there are ways of getting round these things, such as changing one's nationality.'

Radio 270 began perhaps the most concentrated campaign of all the pirate stations against the proposed legislation. All 270 listeners were invited to join the 'fight for free radio', and from the end of July disc jockeys continually asked listeners to write to their M.P. The response to this request was later said to have been very good; it was claimed that thousands of listeners had written to their Member. The centre-piece of the station's campaign was a half-crown booklet put out in conjunction with the Institute of Economic Affairs called *Competition in Radio*, by Denis Thomas. The booklet traced the development of commercial radio abroad and off Britain's shores, coming down firmly in favour of legalised commercial radio in Britain.

Mrs Dorothy Calvert, who had taken over the running of Radio City, said: 'I do not think the BBC could take over this kind of broadcasting. It has to be independent and not put on by people who do not understand the business. I am hoping that there are enough M.P.s in Parliament who realise that we are giving a public service. I hope they will throw the Bill out.'

Another spokesman for Radio City said they would wait for a prosecution before discontinuing broadcasts. They knew of no plan to prosecute them before the Bill became law.

But Radio 390, also inside territorial waters under the September 30th, 1964, Order in Council, said they thought the Government might well launch a prosecution against them in the near future. Mr John Ridley, station promotion manager of 390, said that if the Government did prosecute, the radio station would become seaborne in the vessel *Cheetah II* (ex-Radio Syd, ex-Radio Caroline, and the ship owned by former Swedish beauty queen Britt Wadner). *Cheetah II*, though, the week before had been towed into Harwich by tugs after dragging her anchor in heavy seas; the next day a writ of attachment had been nailed to her mast and the vessel impounded on a salvage claim. Mr Ridley said the claim would be met and that the ship would be leased. The destination would be Colwyn Bay, outside the three-mile limit. Meanwhile Radio 390 continued broadcasting appeals to listeners to 'save Radio 390' by writing to their M.P.s

July 28th not only saw the introduction of legislation against the pirates, but also the Britain Radio/Radio England champagne party! The party, which was held at the Hilton Hotel, was a costly publicity exercise designed to show that show-business supported the pirates, and to demonstrate their popularity generally. The evening, attended by 600 guests, in the Hilton ballroom cost about £10,000.

The pirates certainly seemed confident of their future. It looked as though legislation would probably squeeze out the smaller stations, and discourage the establishment of new stations. Advertising for the larger stations would be available from international agencies the supplies would come from countries who had not ratified the Council of Europe agreement with their own legislation. As more continental countries introduced legislation things would become tighter, but countries like Spain and Portugal, who are not signatories to Council of Europe agreements, having been refused entry to the Council, were not seen as being likely to act against the pirates. The idea of pirate radio ships off the Spanish and Portuguese coast with powerful transmitters beaming programmes to Britain was not so far-fetched, for the Bill did not encompass foreign radio pirates on foreign ships broadcasting material of foreign origin from outside British territorial waters. It only would make life more difficult for them.

When only one or two offshore stations were on the air back in 1964 there was no great urgency about acting against them. In fact, they were rather a pleasant change which, at least, in the eyes of the authorities, was keeping the public happy. To withdraw that pleasure would have been unwise in the election atmosphere which dominated British politics for two years from spring 1964 to spring 1966. But with a working majority the Government could now afford to act.

The growing number of stations, and the chaos and dispute involved, also precipitated legislation. By 1966 the pirate broadcasters were multiplying rapidly, and more and more wavelengths were being taken up. Interference was being caused to authorised transmissions from foreign broadcasting stations; Belgium. Yugoslavia. Sweden and Italy were among the countries who complained about this. The pirates were seizing wavelengths already in use in other countries and, occasionally preventing people in those countries from hearing their own broadcasting services.

On the other hand, the Copenhagen Plan of 1948 which allocated frequencies for medium-wave broadcasting, has never been strictly adhered to. A *Wireless World* editorial pointed out in May 1965:

> More than 50 per cent of long-wave and medium-wave broadcasting stations in Europe are at present operating on frequencies other than those allocated by the 1948 Copenhagen Plan. ... Let us go no further than to say that in the present free-for-all, some people have recently drawn attention to themselves by being a little more free than most.

The 1948 Copenhagen Convention, in fact, authorised only 208 stations to operate on the medium waveband. There were now 510 in existence, 302 of which were on unofficial wavelengths. The pirates represented a mere handful of stations using unauthorised frequencies. Among other offenders were the Vatican Radio, the Voice of America and Radio Luxembourg. To complicate the issue, many of the 208 authorised stations use unauthorised transmitting power. Thus, in all fairness, the pirate radio stations could not be castigated for causing confusion on the medium waveband, as the Government repeatedly alleged; only for making the already chaotic situation slightly worse.

Every year, as the winter evenings draw in, listeners to the BBC complain of foreign interference so bad that they could not at times listen to their own national broadcasting service. In 1948 seven countries, among them Austria, Sweden, Iceland, Luxembourg and Turkey, refused to agree to their allocations, went their own way and chose their own frequencies. The pirates were by no means the only guilty party in international broadcasting.

Another reason the Government advanced for the proposed closure of the pirate stations was that they interfered with radio services used for communication between ship and shore. This was true in the 'early' days of pirate radio when, it was, as one might say, in its 'experimental' stages. During the eighteen months before the legislation was introduced it had, though, been a rare occurrence.

The Government also claimed that the pirates evaded the copyright laws which authorised stations must observe. These laws compel broadcasters not only to pay for the copyright of authors and composers, which most pirates did, but limit their use of recorded material 'to protect the livelihoods of performers and record manufacturers'. This the pirates did not do. In international waters the pirates escaped the Copyright Act of 1956, and, therefore, the control of the 'needle-time' licensing body, Phonographic Performances Ltd, which laid down that the BBC should not broadcast more than 75 hours of music on record in any one week. Some pirates broadcast more than twice that amount of recorded music every week. Here they could be held to be in the wrong, although they countered this charge with evidence of thousands of letters from composers and artists thanking them for 'plugging' their work; and all the stations received with every post free issues from the record companies.

Whether the Government or Phonographic Performances Ltd liked it or not, the pirate radio operators had, on the credit side, brought pleasure to millions and filled a gap on the broadcasting scene in Britain. Many people have pompously condemned the wares of the pirate stations as synthesised musical drivel, or have described the pirate ships as merely amplified Juke Boxes. The fact remains that the pirates in two years had managed to capture between 15 and 25 million listeners (taking the lowest and the highest estimated figures to be absolutely fair). This size an audience cannot possibly be passed off as consisting solely of long-haired, transistor-touting, teenage layabouts. It must represent a fair cross-section of the listening public.

True, the stations proved immensely popular with many millions of teenagers. The BBC had refused to give them what they wanted and the gap had been filled by the pirates. Certain over-critical members of the older generation often appear to conveniently forget their youth, which undoubtedly was marked by its crazes, its distinctive attitudes, its own music and its dances.

But they condemned the pirate radio ships. Why? Nine times out of ten not on rationally-based grounds (i.e. interference with other stations on unallocated wavelengths), but merely because they supply something they did not want, and which they did not like – a selfish and unfair attitude.

The BBC was the arch-upholder of this attitude. 'They shall have what is good for them' (and like it) tended to be the Corporation's attitude. This also, to a large extent, was the Government's attitude. The pirate radio operators had a mass-communication medium over which it had no control. This could have its dangers, as was shown by the threatened Radio Freedom.

On the other hand, pirate radio produced not only 'pop' music stations but continuous all-day light music stations, such as Radio 390 and Britain Radio. The former was extremely successful, so successful that a 'Radio 390 North' was to be launched. This station was directed at housewives and businessmen in their cars, not at teenagers, and Radio 390 rapidly became one of the most popular offshore stations.

The day after the Marine etc. Broadcasting Offences Bill was published a letter appeared in *The Daily Telegraph*, the views expressed in which must have been typical of millions. The writer asked:

> Is there no other middle-class and middle-aged housewife like myself courageous enough to put in a word of praise for the pirate radio stations soon to be outlawed by our present government?
>
> I have to spend a lot of time at home doing household chores and find the BBC Light Programme music – 'old time dancing' and sentimental tunes from 20 and 30 years ago — really depressing. So I tune in to one of the less brash and Americanised pirate stations and I enjoy the background noise. . . .

One doubts whether Mrs Mann of Bromley, Kent, was indeed the only housewife with such feelings.

Thus the Government on July 28th not only threatened the pirates, but also the enjoyment of millions. Pirate radio had, for all its failings, highlighted the inadequacy of the BBC and existing broadcasting services. For no charge at all, in contrast to the far from small BBC licence fee, they had provided what a large proportion of the British people wanted, whether admirable or not. The question now arose – would the people in the future get what they wanted, or would they be condemned forever to suffer the tyranny of the British Broadcasting Corporation, now that pirates were no longer to rule the waves?

The Marine Broadcasting (Offences) Bill when introduced was, by its very nature, purely a means to suppress the pirate broadcasters. The problem facing the Government was the replacement of the pirate programmes with an acceptable alternative.

The attitude of the Conservative Party was immediately made clear when Mr Paul Bryan, Opposition spokesman on broadcasting, said that twenty million listeners would have every right to protest at the Government's banning of the pirate stations without any attempt to provide alternative programmes. The stations had uncovered a huge demand, not merely for a pop programme but also for a large variety of musical and other programmes.

'This demand,' he said, 'cannot be met by a single hastily set up all-music programme from the BBC. What is required is more local stations like Manx Radio.'

The next day Conservative M.P.s tabled two motions objecting to the Bill. Mr Iremonger (Ilford North) and Mr Gresham-Cooke (Twickenham) alleged that Mr Short's Bill 'will deprive millions of people of the sound of music they love and can at present get only from the pirate stations'. The other motion, tabled by Mr Eldon Griffiths (Bury St Edmunds) expressed the same complaint, and pointed out that the Opposition had persistently advocated the need for greater enterprise and a wider area of choice. In view of this, the House should call upon the Postmaster-General 'to make speedy provision for legitimate local broadcasting stations to meet the British people's evident desire for a wider range and greater variety of broadcasting than is at present available from the BBC'.

The Opposition had no doubt about its broadcasting policy. But at the beginning of August the Cabinet committee considering the future of broadcasting was reported to be in a state of deadlock, and the long promised White Paper on broadcasting was not expected to be ready until October.

What were the choices before the Cabinet committee in August?

(1) The institution of an all-day pop music channel. Rumours were rife that the Government would replace the existing Light Programme by a round-the-clock pop programme under the name of Radio 247.

An interesting variation on this was suggested in a paper published in January 1966 – *Possibilities for Local Radio,* by Rachel Powell, published by the Centre for Contemporary Cultural Studies of Birmingham University.

The writer of this paper pointed out that the Light Programme occupied three wavelengths; its 247 metre medium wavelength, its 1500 metre long wavelength and a VHF channel. The Droitwich 1500 metres channel can be heard throughout most of the country and much of the continent, and therefore may be regarded as a valuable potential export window for British ideas, art and entertainment. It would thus not be well advised to give it over to pop and it could continue to carry the Light Programme in more or less its present form. The medium wave frequency, though, could be given over to continuous popular music. Thus, those who like the Light Programme in its present form would not be deprived of it, and those who liked popular music would have their demand satisfied.

What upsets the applecart here, of course, is the problem of finance. Even if the Government was only to replace the Light entirely by pop and transmit it on the three channels (which would be a waste), the organisation of the new service would bring a rise in the licence fee. Many people who do not want 'pop' music all day inevitably would vigorously object. This led to suggestions that the Government would authorise advertising on the Light Programme.

This seemed unlikely to happen, so bitterly would the BBC fight it. The Corporation was also opposed to all-day 'pop'. It was argued that if it were to be forced upon the BBC, it almost certainly would wreak its vengeance on the public by pushing up the licence fee and by diluting the 'pop' content with 'palm court' music.

(2) The introduction of the 'Jenkins Plan' for local broadcasting. This plan, described above, was, briefly, that a new national authority should be established to act as parent to *publicly* owned local stations. The authority would produce a national popular radio programme, and the stations would provide local news and features. The service would be financed by national and local advertising.

This plan would retain control over radio in the hands of a national authority, with the consequent obvious disadvantages of over-centralisation. The 'Jenkins Plan', however, appeared to be vastly preferable to the next alternative, introducing as it would some new ideas at least into broadcasting.

(3) Acceptance of the BBC plan for Local Radio. This also has been described at length above. The main criticisms of this scheme were that it might have to be financed from licensed revenue, with a substantial rise in the licence fee, and that the stations would broadcast, according to the March 1966 plan, only up to six hours a day programmes of local interest. The remainder of their broadcasting time would be filled by programmes relayed from the Home, Light and Third. This would seem to be an utterly pointless exercise. More than 20 million people had shown they were not interested in the type of programme put out by the Home, Light and Third. They wanted continuous light and 'pop' music. In spite of this, the March BBC pamphlet had reiterated the Corporation's determination to provide anything but what the public wanted. It pointed out that the BBC's local stations would not be 'amplified juke boxes of the kind familiar to people who have travelled to some overseas countries'. Who pays the licence fee, anyway? The public, of course, and it may reasonably be argued that they have a right to hear what they want, especially when they are paying as much as the BBC demand. In 'some overseas countries' the truth is that the narrow-mindedness of the type displayed by the autocratic BBC has not prevailed. The people have got what they wanted; that is true democracy.

(4) The introduction into Britain of local commercial radio. The overseas countries so disdainfully referred to by the BBC no doubt were those countries, among the most prosperous and democratic in the world, which have a system of local commercial radio. They include the United States, Canada and Australia. The question many people were and still are asking is: why can not Britain have a similar system?

The pirate stations had proved a definite need for greater diversity in broadcasting. All the evidence suggested that the BBC could not, and would not, provide this greater diversity. In the report delivered by the Pilkington Committee on Broadcasting in 1962, there was a strong recommendation for the Government to introduce local broadcasting under the BBC. The Committee came out strongly in favour of local radio stations, and the BBC managed to convince it that it could run them. But if they ran them on the lines outlined above, they certainly would not be satisfying the public demand.

Even if the BBC could provide a more or less satisfactory service, is the perpetuation of its monopoly really in the public interest?

As long ago as 1946 a former Director-General of the BBC, no less, warned of the dangers of monopoly broadcasting in a letter to *The Times* of June 26th, 1946:

> ... monopoly broadcasting is inevitably a negation of freedom, no matter how efficiently it is run, or how wise and kindly the Board or Committees in charge of it. It denies freedom of choice to listeners. It denies freedom of employment to speakers, musicians, writers, actors, and all who seek their chance on the air. The dangers of monopoly have long been recognised in the film industry and the Press and the theatre, and active steps have been taken to prevent it. In tolerating monopoly of broadcasting we are alone among the democratic countries of the world.

Sir Frederick Ogilvy's words are still very largely true today. He also left behind at the BBC a significant memorandum:

> The evils of the monopoly and the gallant work of a very able and delightful executive staff in trying to overcome them – the BBC itself – good as it is, would gain vastly by the abolition of monopoly and the introduction of competition. So would all the millions of listeners who would still have the BBC to listen to but would have other programmes to enjoy as well.

The pirates, even, had proved Sir Frederick's point. Only after they had been broadcasting for some time, and luring listeners from the BBC, the Corporation made the counter-move of extending Light Programme hours until 2 a.m., playing recorded music. This pleased the public and was a welcome development, but was directly brought about by competition.

The BBC, in the last few years, has made a number of incursions into local programming on VHF; they have not been marked either by their originality or great success. The BBC is not exactly local. It is primarily a centralised monolith which experiences great difficulty in decentralisation. Of this centralised bureaucracy, Malcolm Muggeridge has said that it 'came to pass silently, invisibly; like a coral reef, cells multiplying, until it was a vast structure, a conglomeration of studios, offices, cool passages along which many passed to and fro; a society, with its Kings, lords and commoners, its laws and dossiers and revenue and easily suppressed insurrection'. The hierarchical structure of this vast organisation does not easily lend itself to the establishment of a medium flowing over with new, exciting and revolutionary ideas. Once such an idea has permeated all the levels of the hierarchy and gained its approval it has generally ceased to be either new or original.

The possibilities for local radio were enormous and exciting, but one doubted if the centralised monopoly that was the BBC could provide the necessary drive and imagination to make a success of them. It is far more likely that in the hands of enterprising local people the opportunities would be more fully exploited, and the local radio station would stand a better chance of becoming an integral part of the community.

The Beveridge Committee on Broadcasting (1949-51) rejected what it termed 'the assumption underlying the BBC's memorandum; namely "that the only alternative to monopoly is degrading competition for viewers and that in broadcasting a monopoly alone can have high standards and social purpose".'

The Pilkington Committee, which appeared to be deeply prejudiced against non-state broadcasting, pursued this assumption with reference to commercial competition which the report argued 'would be competition for audiences, and not competition in good broadcasting'. The idea, though, was not to have a selection of 'Third Network' or Home Service type programmes competing. Local broadcasting has not even been given a trial in Britain. There is no reason why it should be necessarily a carbon copy of what has happened in America, as Pilkington would seem to have expected. No doubt the committee suspected that any pretence to local broadcasting would quickly be discarded for the type of programme catering for a mass audience – continuous 'pop* being an example. The emphasis, they feared, would shift from local to commercial broadcasting.

The tendencies of its opponents are summed up in the following way by Mr Denis Thomas, in "*Competition in Radio*" (published by the Institute of Economic Affairs, May 1965):

> In business, as in a large section of British society as a whole, the energetic and inventive newcomer is commonly seen as an intruder, an upstart, an interloper, a disturber of the peace and of the 'done thing'.

> The national habit of closing the ranks extends through business and commerce and is still a force to be taken seriously in politics.

The arguments in favour of local commercial radio indeed appeared powerful, and the Government's long-promised White Paper on Broadcasting was eagerly awaited by the commercial radio lobby. They were to be disappointed.

8

Pirates brought to justice

While the pirates already on the air put a brave face on the ominous situation caused by the Government's bill, and continued broadcasting, it did have the immediate result of effectively stifling the plans for further offshore stations. Nothing more was heard of Radio 365, Radio Channel, Radio Mayflower, Radio Dynavision, Radio Caesar, or any of the other stations which had announced in the middle of the year that they would take the air.

Another blow was struck at the pirates on September 21st when summonses were served on the company operating Radio 390, Estuary Radio Ltd, and its Secretary, Mr David Lye. The summons alleged that on August 16th at Red Sands Tower 'situated 8½ miles off the coast but within the Thames Estuary, the company did unlawfully use apparatus for wireless telegraphy, namely a transmitter . . . contrary to Section One of the Wireless Telegraphy Act'.

The summons came just three days before the station was due to celebrate its first anniversary, and was served on Mr Lye when he visited the GPO Security Headquarters at Moorfields in the City to inquire about reports that the Tower was to be demolished.

The station's managing director, Ted Allbeury, remained defiant in the shadow of the hearing, due at Longport Magistrates Court, Canterbury on November 24th, and a possible fine of £100 and three months' imprisonment: 'Despite the summons we shall continue broadcasting and fight this to the highest tribunal in the land'. He added that there were over 300 'unauthorised stations (i.e. on unauthorised frequencies) on the medium waveband, including Vatican Radio, The Voice of America and the American Armed Forces Network. 'We are in very good company', claimed Mr Allbeury.

The next day the Postmaster-General, Mr Short, made a scathing attack on the pirate stations when speaking in Dundee. 'It is no good complaining about lawlessness in our cities and the murdering of policemen if you are prepared to tolerate this kind of thing. It is a breach of the law.' This equation of murder and violence with pirate radio immediately provoked Ted Allbeury to announce that he would consider suing the Postmaster-General for alleged slander.

Said Mr Allbeury: 'We are accused of an offence which, apart from the fact that it has not been proved, is not a criminal offence. It is completely wrong and defamatory to link this with the murder of policemen and other criminal acts'. After consulting his solicitors, he said, he would decide whether or not to take legal action against the Postmaster-General. Apart from the defamatory element in the statement, it might well have a prejudicial effect when the case against his company was held in court.

The same day Mr Allbeury received a summons himself alleging unlawful use of a transmitter at his offshore radio station. Listeners' protests flooded into Radio 390. Mr Allbeury said that there were, according to their letters, 70 Conservative and Liberal M.P.s willing to oppose the Government's bill in Parliament. Mr Emmanuel Shin well, chairman of the Parliamentary Labour Party, had also promised a month earlier, when speaking to a teenage audience, that he would see the pirates 'get a fair crack of the whip'. At the Liberal Party's Assembly on the 24th Mr Grimond, the Party Leader, chided the Government for being preoccupied with prosecuting pirate radio stations when there were thousands of more important things to do. Overall, he said, he regarded the stations as providing popular and harmless entertainment.

On the 29th the GPO struck again. At Southend Police Headquarters Mr Roy Bates, the head of Radio Essex, was served with a similar summons alleging use of a transmitter without a licence from Knock John Fort in the Thames. The summons stated that the fort was within the jurisdiction of Rochford Magistrates. This was strenuously refuted by Mr Bates, who claimed that the station was eighteen miles below Southend and at least nine miles from the nearest coastline at Foulness Island, Essex. At the same time, though, it was announced that the station had taken over another fort, on Tongue Sands nine miles off Margate, and plans for a new station, Radio Albatross, were going ahead; presumably so that another base would be available if it became impossible to continue broadcasting from Knock John.

One station on a fort in the Thames Estuary remained unsummonsed; Radio City, the property of Mrs Dorothy Calvert. Anticipating action against the station she declared: 'When my

Knock John Fort, a converted naval fort in the Thames Estuary, became the base for Radio Essex. Radio Essex owner Roy Bates was among the first to be prosecuted under the British Wireless Telegraphy Act for illegal broadcasting. After successful prosecution, he eventually had to give up broadcasting from the fort., but continued other activities from it.

husband went to Scotland Yard for police protection after our fort was seized in June, he was told the fort was outside British jurisdiction. I defy them, after all that has happened, to try to prosecute us.'

In the light of the Government bill and the summonses against Radio Essex and Radio 390, other stations began considering their future. The directors of Radio Scotland met in Glasgow early in October and decided to continue broadcasting 'in order to keep faith with the loyal audiences in Scotland and Northern Ireland'. Discussions had been held, it was stated, with visitors from overseas on the possibility of the station continuing without using British advertising.

Radio Caroline began organising meetings all over the country and asked listeners to sign a petition protesting against the Government's plans.

Britain Radio and Radio England also announced they would be broadcasting appeals to their listeners when Parliament reassembled.

With the pirates now generally regarded as being doomed, the debate temporarily switched to the subject of what was to replace them. As Parliament reassembled the BBC joined the fray with the claim that more than three quarters of the population over fifteen years old never or hardly ever listened to the offshore stations. The claim was based on the findings of a postal survey conducted by the BBC Audience Research Bureau among a sample of about 5,000 people. It was claimed to be a scientific sample chosen at random from the electoral roll, but it wildly conflicted with an independent survey conducted a few months before, and which showed that some 27 million people listened to pirate radio stations weekly. It was further claimed by the BBC that the Light Programme was listened to daily by four times as many people as tuned in to all the pirates together, and their findings indicated that the regular audience of over fifteen for the pirate stations was only just over 6½ million daily.

The pirate radio operators came under attack soon afterwards in the Corporation's annual report for 1965-66. It alleged they were spoiling reception for many listeners on the continent of their own stations. 'They are also stealing the legal property of British musicians, gramophone companies, and other copyright holders. The pirate stations, for the most part, pay no fees for the use of these rights. Those who do make payments limit them to derisory amounts.

'Although willing to do so, the BBC has not been free to provide such a service on its legally-allocated frequencies since it has to use its three networks to serve the community as a whole.'

Much heated discussion centred round the rumoured proposals to put out continuous light music on 247 metres, for the BBC was permitted only about five hours of 'needle time' daily, and the attitude of copyright holders, the gramophone companies and the Musicians Union suggested that it would not be easy to implement any Government instruction to broadcast a continuous stream of light music. Early in November representatives of the 35,000 strong Musicians Union met the Postmaster-General to discuss Government plans for the future of broadcasting. Mr Short was told at this meeting that many members of the Union were so strongly opposed to the plan for a new BBC service that the Union might be forced to ban musicians from making any more gramophone records or recordings for radio or television if it went through. The Union's strong opposition was based on the assumption that such a service would consist mainly of the playing of records. Musicians, of course, receive no additional payment beyond their fee for making a record, no matter how many times the record is broadcast. The Radio and Television Safeguard Committee, representing 16 trade unions for performers and production staff, later decided to endorse the Musicians Union's opposition to any new popular music programme.

On October 26th the Postmaster-General faced a barrage of questions in the House of Commons about the Government's radio plans. Mr O'Malley, Labour M.P. for Rotherham, urged Mr Short to say that the Government did not intend allowing private companies or individuals to run local sound broadcasting. Mr Short assured him, in reply, that the Labour Government would preserve the public service aspect of broadcasting in its proposals, but that he 'must wait for the broadcasting White Paper'.

Many Conservative M.P.s seized the chance to affirm their support for the pirate stations and for commercial radio. The Postmaster-General told Mr Buchanan Smith, Conservative M.P. for North Angus and Mearns, that a company describing itself as the selling agents for Radio Scotland had asked for authority for Radio Scotland to establish a commercial sound broadcasting station, or a chain of stations, on land. The company had been advised to await a Government policy statement. The Labour M.P.

for West Fife asked why this station had not been prosecuted for transmitting from within territorial waters, as it had been doing in the Firth of Clyde, but the Postmaster-General replied that this was a matter for the Procurator Fiscal. But Mr Michael Noble, a former Secretary of State for Scotland, declared his support for Radio Scotland, stating that it was the only broadcasting station audible in much of his remote West of Scotland constituency.

A few days later the *Sunday Times* Political Correspondent reported a clash between BBC chiefs and the Cabinet over a rumoured plan to set up a new authority to run a 'pop' programme service. Lord Normanbrook, Chairman of the BBC, and Sir Hugh Greene, Director-General, addressed an open Press Conference at which any questions on BBC plans for replacing the pop pirates' radio programmes were invited. The BBC's attitude was plain. It regarded any plans by the Government to set up a breakaway sound broadcasting authority as meaning a wasteful duplication of resources when the BBC had adequate staff, experience and technical facilities available. The timing of the Press Conference was significant; it was obvious the Cabinet Committee preparing the White Paper was running into difficulties. Both Lord Normanbrook and Sir Hugh Greene were both very guarded, however, in their references to the possibility of a BBC replacement for the pirates. Neither would say precisely how much 'pop' such a service would contain, but it was clear that it would not be an entirely new service; it would include large portions relayed from the Light, and Lord Normanbrook significantly talked about 'entertainment' rather than popular music.

*

As the BBC, Government and musicians argued about the future of broadcasting, the fight against the pirate stations continued, and the end of November saw the first GPO victory when the battle shifted from the sea to the courtroom.

On November 24th the GPO prosecution of Estuary Radio Ltd, the operators of Radio 390 which broadcast from Red Sands Fort in the Thames Estuary, began at St Augustine Magistrates Court, Canterbury. The company and its two officers, Mr Ted Allbeury, Managing Director, and Mr David Lye, Secretary, faced summonses alleging that they 'on August 16th at Red Sands Tower,

Red Sands Fort in the Thames estuary housed King Radio and, later, Radio 390. Owner Ted Allbeury was successfully prosecuted under the U.K. Wireless Telegraphy Act and was forced to abandon transmissions. After the bankruptcy of Britain Radio/Radio England he started a similar service from the M.V. Laissez Faire.

in the jurisdiction of Kent, did unlawfully use apparatus for wireless telegraphy, namely a transmitter, except under and in accordance with a licence in that behalf, granted by the Postmaster-General'. They pleaded not guilty.

The Post Office had little difficulty in proving that Radio 390 had broadcast on 773 Kc/s on August i6th, 1966, without a licence. Four Post Office engineers were called upon to give evidence; one substantiated the allegation that no licence had been allocated, though Estuary Radio Ltd had applied for a licence to operate on July l0th, 1965, but no licence was issued. The other three gave evidence of monitoring the station and making tape recordings of its transmissions from Shoeburyness in Essex, Morden Point on the Isle of Sheppey and Herne Bay in Kent.

Establishing whether or not the former anti-aircraft tower on Red Sands, from which the station operated, came under British jurisdiction was a much more complex matter. Sir Peter Rawlinson, Q.C., who represented the defendants, told the court that the tower was situated at least six nautical miles off the Kent coast and was thus well outside British territorial waters and, therefore, the jurisdiction of the court. Mr John Newey, prosecuting for the Post Office, did not agree and gave two main reasons to substantiate his claim.

Firstly, under the terms of the Geneva International Convention of the Sea, 1958, which was ratified in September 1964 by the British Government in an Order in Council, the Thames Estuary may be considered as a bay if the area of water within the bay exceeded that in a semi-circle drawn, with a 24-mile base-line, across the indentation in the coast.

Lieutenant-Commander P. B. Beasley, head of the Hydrographic Department in the Ministry of Defence, told the court that, in his capacity as a naval surveyor, he had calculated the area of water in the bay and found that there were 683 square miles in the bay and five less in the semi-circle. For this calculation he had drawn the base-line across the indentation from Walton-on-Naze to North Foreland, and had taken in water in the Thames up to Greenwich, and to Rochester Bridge in the Medway. Sir Peter Rawlinson was not satisfied that this was permissible, and there was laughter in court when he suggested using Greenwich-on-Sea as a holiday attraction for a town situated in Greater London.

The prosecution also based its claim that the tower was within the court's jurisdiction on the Geneva Convention concerning low-tide elevations, which includes all islands that are uncovered at normal low water. Mr Newey claimed that Middle Bank, one of the sandbanks off the Isle of Sheppey, was one and as such formed the inner limit of territorial waters. Mr V. Davis, however, Master of the *Mallard*, which supplied the forts in the Thames Estuary, stated in evidence that, although it was marked on Admiralty charts, he had not seen Middle Sands uncovered for at least twelve months, and then it was only uncovered after an abnormal tide.

Mr R. Stiff, a Customs and Excise officer based at Whitstable, Kent, appeared upon a subpoena to give evidence for Radio 390. He stated that his superiors had ordered the Master of the supply ship *Mallard* to report before and after visiting the forts in the Thames Estuary. This order, though, had been withdrawn in May, 1966, he told the court, under instructions from the Commissioners of Customs and Excise. Under examination he revealed that no duty was levied on the transmitting equipment taken to Red Sands Tower from Rotterdam.

Sir Peter Rawlinson, a former Solicitor-General, told the court that territorial waters could be extended by an Act of Parliament. The Territorial Waters Order in Council of 1964, however, had been made under the Queen's prerogative and was not an Act of Parliament. 'If you accept the Order in Council is not good law and is to be treated as if it were in the wastepaper basket, I suggest that you look at the International Convention which says the same thing.'

In his summing-up, Sir Peter said that it was a remarkable thing that a matter affecting the sovereignty of the realm should turn on the evidence of a distinguished officer, but who only held the rank of a Lieutenant-Commander in the Royal Navy. He also referred to the fact that no official map or chart indicated changes in territorial waters, concerning this case, and that under the terms of the Geneva Convention the general public must be informed of such changes. His most convincing defence, however, lay in his submission that the prosecution could only place the tower within territorial waters by taking into account stretches of the Thames up to Greenwich and the Medway up to Rochester. Only by doing this could the Thames Estuary be called a bay under the terms of the Geneva Convention, and thus be placed within territorial waters – by five out of 683 square miles.

Soon after adjourning, the Bench returned and took further technical evidence from Lieutenant-Commander Beasley. After a second adjournment of half-an-hour Mr Donald Andrews, Chairman of the Bench, announced: 'We find that Red Sands is situated in territorial water. The Wireless Telegraphy Act of 1949 is silent on the question of local jurisdiction, but the territorial waters in question join the coast of Kent and for that reason we are of the opinion that the Justices of the County of Kent have jurisdiction in this matter. On the evidence before us we find the case proved.'

After a third retirement the Bench passed sentence, fining Estuary Radio Ltd the maximum of £100 for using a transmitter without a licence. Mr Allbeury and Mr Lye were given absolute discharges. The Post Office made application to the court to confiscate the transmitting equipment, worth £12,000 and in use through a hire-purchase agreement, and also for costs, but the Bench refused these requests.

The station's managing director immediately gave notice that an appeal would be made, but after consultation with his lawyers Mr Allbeury announced that Radio 390 would have to go off the air. On the evening of Friday, November 25th, Mr Victor Davis took his 39-foot boat, *Mallard*, and sailed to Red Sands from Whitstable with a tape recording made by Mr Allbeury on the previous Wednesday, the eve of the hearing. On this he gave reasons for going off the air and added: 'I have never been so happy as when running Radio 390. I cannot believe this is the end'. Radio 390, the 'sweet music' station, which claimed an audience of over four million, then left the air.

The GPO had certainly scored a victory, but Sir Peter Rawlinson's claim that the case was one of the most complex to be heard in a Magistrates Court could not be denied, and the case was, in fact, to be debated many more times in the courts.

*

The following Wednesday another pirate found itself fighting for survival in court. Mr Roy Bates, the owner and operator of Radio Essex, had to face a similar summons at Rochford Magistrates Court, under the Wireless Telegraphy Act of 1949, for using a transmitter without a licence from Knock John Tower in the Thames Estuary.

Mr Bates appeared without council and pleaded that the station was outside the jurisdiction of the court, since it was more than three nautical miles off the coast of Essex. He said the new rules for setting the three mile limit flew in the face of everything he had learned in twenty-five years' work connected with the sea, including the running of a fishing fleet. 'It seems to me that certain factors are being bent to produce certain results,' he added.

Mr John Newey again prosecuted for the Post Office and followed the same arguments as used successfully five days earlier in the Radio 390 case, claiming the Thames Estuary to be a bay. He also again introduced low-tide elevations, claiming that West Barrow was one. This lay within three nautical miles of Knock John Tower and was marked as a low-tide elevation on Admiralty charts.

Two Assistant Executive Engineers in the Post Office, Mr R. H. Dalton and Mr J. F. Woods, and an Executive Engineer, Mr J. H. Ainley, gave evidence of monitoring Radio Essex on 222 metres and locating the station on August 16th from Herne Bay in Kent, Shoeburyness in Essex and Morden Point on the Isle of Sheppey respectively. Mr W. Goldsmith, a Higher Executive Officer in the Radio Service Department of the Post Office, stated that although application had been made for a licence, the request had not been granted.

Before the magistrate retired, Mr Bates told the court that he did not wish to make a statement. After he had been found guilty the Post Office made application to confiscate his equipment and for a portion of the costs. In reply to this Mr Bates stated that he wished to make an appeal against the decision, and that the question of forfeiture should not be considered until after the appeal. The court then imposed the maximum fine of £100, but, as in the case of Radio 390, made no order regarding costs or forfeiture.

Outside the court a still defiant Mr Bates declared: 'No war is won until the last battle is fought. This is my radio station. I have no board of directors to call me to answer. I am determined to stay on the air and fight.' He added that he did not accept that he was within territorial waters. 'I do not accept that anyone can be sent to stop me broadcasting and pending my appeal broadcasts will go on. There is going to be commercial radio in this country and I am going to be here to be part of it.'

He also stated his intention of going even further. Within the next month he intended to open a new and more powerful station on Tongue Tower Sands, nine miles from Margate and within territorial waters as defined before the magistrates. Meanwhile Radio Essex was to continue under a new name -BBMS (Britain's Better Music Station).

A point which did not pass unnoticed as a result of the findings of the Canterbury and Rochford Magistrates, was that another station, Radio City, would appear to be within territorial waters. Some speculation existed as to why Radio City had not been similarly prosecuted, something probably not unconnected with the dramatic events which had taken place on Radio City the previous June. At this time, only five months previously, the police found themselves in something of a dilemma over both the ownership of the fort on Shivering Sands, and whether or not it was in fact within their jurisdiction. They appeared to come to the conclusion that it was not, in fact, within their jurisdiction and, it will be remembered, failed to do anything about the boarding party which took it over. As a result of this incident the owner of the station was shot dead. Thus in the event of a court case it was likely that embarrassing questions would be asked about what looked like a sudden and dramatic change in attitude towards jurisdiction over the station. When the lives of those operating the station were in danger the authorities had appeared singularly uninterested, but the summons to be served a month later showed that the authorities were now extremely interested in the fort on Shivering Sands.

The arguments about the extent of territorial waters continued in the High Court on December 12th when Radio 390's appeal began. Estuary Radio Ltd sought orders from Lord Parker, the Lord Chief Justice, sitting with Lord Justice Salmon and Mr Justice Blain, quashing the conviction by the Canterbury Magistrates.

Sir Peter Rawlinson, Q.C. again represented the radio company and argued that the station on Red Sands Tower was outside territorial waters and, therefore, outside the jurisdiction of the local magistrates. 'If a murder took place on Radio 390 could any British court deal with it under its jurisdiction?' asked Sir Peter.

The next day, however, the High Court ruled by a majority decision that the station could not start broadcasting again. Lord Parker and Mr Justice Blain found that the station had been operating illegally within territorial waters, and that the September 1964 Order in Council brought the Tower inside territorial waters. Lord Justice Salmon, though, disagreed with them and consequently they agreed that the issue could be taken to the House of Lords to test their findings. But outside the court Mr Ted Allbeury said he thought 'it would be pointless' to go to the House of Lords. Radio 390 remained silent.

Another station also left the air in November amid rumours of financial difficulty and shortage of advertising. Radio England, the American-backed 'pop' station run by Texan oil millionaire William Vick, which had come on the air at the end of the previous May, closed down, but was replaced on November 14th bv 'Radio Dolphin' broadcasting in Dutch. Radio England's twin station on board the *Laissez Faire*, Britain Radio, continued broadcasting in English.

9

'A manifesto for monopolists.'

December 20th saw the long-promised, oft-delayed publication of the Government's White Paper on the future of broadcasting. Few State papers in recent years had been so long talked about, and so many times deferred. It had first been mentioned early in 1965. In July of that year it had been promised for the autumn. In October 'a comprehensive statement on broadcasting generally' was promised before the end of the year. This soon became 'early in 1966'. Then it was to precede the General Election. There were second thoughts about that. In July 1966 the Government was 'completing its general review'. The White Paper then became a firm undertaking for the autumn, then finally 'before the end of the year'. This time they had just made it!

On the other hand, the difficulties which must have faced both Mr Wedgwood Benn and Mr Short should not be minimised. Besides having to steer their own ideas through a committee of ministers, the Postmaster-General had to contend with powerful pressure groups on all sides: the BBC, the Musicians Union, the 'pop' pirates and the commercial radio lobby.

It was immediately apparent upon the White Paper's publication that it meant a double victory for the BBC. It stated that not only was the BBC to run a popular music service on 247 metres, but that the Corporation was also to operate nine local radio stations for an experimental period of about a year.

In the White Paper the Government made it clear that it recognised a need for a new service devoted to the provision of 'a continuous popular music programme'. The fact that there was an audience for this type of entertainment was not regarded as new, but 'what is new is that by appropriating wavelengths allotted to other countries and by largely disregarding copyright in gramophone records, the pirate stations have been able to exploit the fact'. Quite rightly the Paper made the point that the most economical way of broadcasting such a programme was in the medium waveband, but with the medium wavelengths available to this country already intensively used, then room for an extra service could only be found by redeploying them. The Government had therefore discussed with the BBC the rearrangement of their services which would be needed to find room for the additional service. In the past the BBC had considered that their various audiences could be best served by providing the Light Programme on both long and medium Wavelengths, but now that their long wave transmission of the Light Programme was reinforced by the BBC's VHF transmissions, which themselves had virtually attained complete population coverage, and now that portable VHF sets were available at reasonable cost, the BBC felt free to devote its medium wave channel of 247 metres to a popular music programme.

The Paper went on to report that the BBC had informed the Government that on weekdays the programme would broadcast popular music continuously from 5.30 a.m. to 7.30 p.m. and again from 10 p.m. to 2 a.m., and on Sunday for most of the day's broadcasting. Over 6 hours of music would be played each day on record. The rest would consist of either live broadcasts or BBC recordings specially made for the service.

Dealing with local sound radio, the White Paper said that no general service of local sound broadcasting, which would be available during hours of darkness as well as daylight, could be provided on the medium wavelengths allotted to the U.K. The only possibility for such a service lay in VHF. Proposals put to the Government for the provision of a service had included those for it to be provided by commercial companies, whilst others advocated that it should be provided by the BBC. The Government shared the view expressed by the Pilkington Committee in the White Paper of July, 1962, 'that the justification for local sound broadcasting would be the provision of a service genuinely "local" in character'. Whilst the Government did not in principle rule out advertising as a means of financing broadcasting stations in public ownership, it considered that the provision of a genuinely local service would prove incompatible with the commercial objectives of companies engaged in local sound broadcasting.

'It is of first importance to maintain public service principles in the further development of the broadcasting service, declared the White Paper, which added that the Government rejected the view that a service of local sound radio should be provided by commercial companies.

'Evidence of the expertise and professional enthusiasm which the BBC could bring to local sound broadcasting is to be found in the trial programmes they have prepared. They lend much support to the view that, properly organised, local radio would provide a valuable service to the local community and, by giving a new means of expression to its particular interests and aspirations, serve to reinforce its distinctive character and sense of identity'.

Most importantly the Paper pointed out: 'There is also the question whether it would command enough support, including financial support, to justify the development of a service on a widespread and permanent footing.'

Therefore, the Government considered that an experiment was needed which the BBC would conduct as a venture in cooperation with local interests. The BBC had been authorised to go ahead with a nine station project on VHF. The stations would come into operation in about a year and would offer a full scale local service. After a year or so they should provide the information on which to found the final solution. For each station there would be a local broadcasting council appointed by the Postmaster-General in consultation with the BBC. Each would be widely representative of the community and would play a full formative part in the development of the station, both as regards programme policy and content and as regards its finance. The Government attached great importance to the need to ensure that the stations were truly local in character and not all moulded to a common pattern imposed from the centre, according to the White Paper.

On the all important question of finance the Paper went on: 'Since the essential purpose of the local station is to give expression to local interests and aspirations it seems right that its income should derive so far as possible from local sources and not from a general licence fee. These would not include general subvention from the rates. However the local authority, particularly for its educational services for which it has responsibilities, could properly commend its support'.

An important part of the experiment would be to establish whether enough financial support would be forthcoming from bodies such as the local authority, the local university, where there was one, chambers of trade and commerce, local councils of churches, arts associations and other representative bodies active in the social and cultural life of the community.

'If the experiment showed that local sources, without recourse to advertising, were not enough, the Government would have to re-examine the alternative methods of financing the service', said the White Paper.

'The Government reserves until the conclusion of the experiment any decision on the question of whether a general and permanent service should be authorised arid, if so, how it should be constituted, organised and by whom provided, as well as how it should be financed'. The decision that the BBC should conduct the initial experiment implied 'no commitment' that it should provide the permanent service if it was decided to authorise one.

The White Paper rejected the possibility of a Government contribution as a means of financing the BBC as it 'would be liable to expose the Corporation to financial control in such detail as would prove incompatible with the BBC's independence'.

At a Press Conference on the day of its publication, Mr Short emphasised many of the points made in the White Paper. When asked, however, if he would consider handing the local radio stations over to local commercial interests if they were not successful he said: 'We have excluded this. We feel it is incompatible with the objective of a local radio station, which would be to contribute to the communal life of the town. I do not think you can reconcile this with commercial interests.'

It was estimated that each station would cost £35,000 to set up, £50,000 a year to run, and would have a radius of five miles. Mr Short said that he could not name the areas where the BBC would set up the stations. Different types of area would be selected after talks between the Government and the BBC. The BBC was holding talks with interested authorities.

Mr Short said that he had been influenced by the possible effect of local stations on newspapers. If there was a sizeable diversion of small advertising from local newspapers to the local radio station many newspapers, especially small weekly newspapers, would go out of business. He expressed the hope that local newspapers would be represented on the local radio councils.

Reactions to Mr Short's plans were very mixed. Radio Caroline dubbed the White Paper 'a manifesto for monopolists'. 'It does little but perpetuate the dreariness of British broadcasting which the public has clearly rejected in its enthusiasm for the offshore stations'.

The Conservative frontbench spokesman on broadcasting, Mr Paul Bryan, condemned the paper as 'restrictive and reactionary', while his Liberal counterpart, Dr Michael Winstanley, said the White Paper was evidence of the Government's 'total inability' to take decisions.

Mr John Gorst, Secretary of the Local Radio Association, said that he completely disagreed with the White Paper. The use of VHF for local radio would limit the service to 11 per cent of the population, and deny it to motorists and rural communities (due to the technical difficulties inherent in VHF transmission and reception).

Late in July the BBC revealed its plans for the other half of its 'broadcasting revolution'; those for its 'pop' programme on 247 metres, to be called 'Radio One'. It was clear that the new programme would be an unashamed copy of the type of format pioneered so successfully by the pirate stations. Mr Robin Scott, organising the new service, admitted: 'It would be foolish to deny that we will use some of the techniques of commercial radio. We have professional admiration for what the pirates have done with an American format for a British audience.' Many of the disc jockeys would even be from the offshore stations closed down by the Government's Marine Offences Act, he stated, and jingles and slogans similar to those used by the pirates would be used.

The first six months of 1967 had indeed seen furious activity on the part of the BBC in its drive to establish still further its monopoly in sound, but this same period had not been one of such promise for the offshore radio operators.

10

The battle for survival

The New Year saw the renewal of the pirate radio stations' battle for existence in the courts.

Shortly before midnight on December 31st Radio 390 came back on the air. Mr Ted Allbeury, managing director of Estuary Radio Ltd, announced: 'We shall stay on the air now. We have new evidence that Red Sands Fort is at least a mile and a half outside territorial waters.' He said that the new evidence showed that a sandbank known as Middle Sand was never exposed at low tide, but the Court of Appeal had held the exposure of this sandbank brought the towers within territorial waters. This decision was in accordance with a 1964 Order in Council which provided that any ground, such as a sandbank, which was inside the old three mile limit and was exposed at low tide could be used as a base for the new three mile limit.

Although Red Sands is situated 4-9 miles from the nearest land, the court held that as Middle Sands was exposed at low tide, and inside the old three mile limit, it could be used as a base for the new three mile limit, thus bringing Red Sands within territorial waters.

Mr Allbeury said that in the court case it had been assumed that the evidence given by the prosecution's hydrographer, Lieutenant-Commander Beasley, was based on up-to-date information. They had since found that the area had not been surveyed since 1959.

'We then executed a survey in accordance with Admiralty practice,' stated Mr Allbeury, 'and in particular basing the calculations on the same low tide water datum level. We are now satisfied that the highest level of the sandbank, contrary to what appeared on the chart produced to the Justices, is never above the low water datum.'

He alleged that the whole case against them turned on this point and he was now convinced that the station was outside territorial limits. It would be up to the GPO to summons them again if they felt they had a case. Meanwhile, GPO experts were reported to be looking into the new situation.

Whilst Radio 390's resumption of broadcasting did not amount to contempt of court, another successful prosecution would render the company and its officials liable to further fines and the confiscation of their equipment. The 1949 Wireless Telegraphy Act also provides that where a person continues to use apparatus for broadcasting after conviction he commits a separate offence on each subsequent day.

At the beginning of February, however, listeners to Radio 390 and all those who supported the station in its fight were surprised to learn that their station manager, Ted Allbeury, had decided to resign, amid rumours of disagreement with his shareholders. In an interview he stated that he was resigning because he believed that broadcasting from a ship had a better future than from a fort. 'The forts are constantly being harrassed by the Government. I have not been able to persuade my shareholders to take a ship and am therefore hamstrung to continue....'

On February 12th it was announced that Mr Allbeury was to take over the American-backed Britain Radio on board the *Laissez Faire* off Harwich. He stated that he intended to alter Britain Radio's more brash style of presentation to 390's sober style, and that he aimed to increase its audience of 1,400,000 through the use of more powerful transmitters.

'Britain Radio is a very professionally run outfit. They are determined to go on, despite difficulties they have been having. The 390 board, being amateur, do not see the thousands of letters I get here. They have very little contact with the actual broadcasting side and the result is that they lack this feeling towards the listener that I and my staff have, and that Britain Radio obviously has.'

An immediate clash occurred between the new managing director and Jack Curtis, Britain Radio's general manager, who resigned for 'both professional and personal reasons'. In the press Allbeury had referred to Britain Radio's sound as 'a lucky dip'. Curtis, in his turn, in his resignation referred to 390 as 'stone age radio' and added that he believed that 'we each hold the other's format in equal contempt'. He also referred to the new managing director's programme format as 'a series of segmented dirges stitched together by sterile announcements'.

The immediate question asked by 390 supporters, of course, was who would run the station now? This problem was rendered all the more acute by the fact that, on the same day as Ted Allbeury joined Britain Radio, 28 summonses were taken out against Radio 390 by the Postmaster-General at Southend, alleging that the station had broadcast without a licence on January 4th, 5th, 6th and 7th. There were four summonses each against Estuary Radio Ltd, Edward Allbeury, company secretary David Lye and four directors: John Henry la Trobe, Michael Mitcham, John Goetring and Chris Blackwell.

Estuary Radio Ltd immediately sought an order in the High Court stopping magistrates at Southend from hearing the summons. On February 17th Sir Peter Rawlinson, Q.C. accused the GPO in the High Court of 'shopping around' to find a court favourable to them in their prosecution against Radio 390. The Kent magistrates, said Sir Peter, convicted on the grounds that the station was within territorial waters. Since that case Estuary Radio Ltd had obtained evidence which led it to resume broadcasting, contending that it was outside territorial waters. The Post Office had now, though, launched new proceedings for a hearing at a different court, Southend. The judges, however, refused the application. Lord Justice Winn, Mr Justice Ashworth and Mr Justice Widgery ruled that they had no power to prevent the GPO prosecuting in any court.

At this point Mr David Lye, the company secretary, stepped in as acting managing director. He said that the station would continue to be run on the former managing director's principles.

On February 23rd, however, Estuary Radio Ltd and its six directors were found guilty by Rochford Magistrates sitting at Southend on each of the 28 summonses of broadcasting without a licence. The company was fined £200, but gave notice that it would appeal against this second conviction. Mr David Lye also announced that while he was waiting for the appeal to be heard he would continue broadcasting.

In an attempt to stop the station broadcasting, the GPO on March 10th issued a writ in the Queen's Bench Division of the High Court against Estuary Radio seeking an injunction to prevent it carrying on transmissions. Mr Lye declared, though, that he would only stop broadcasts if the High Court granted the injunction. He thought that the Post Office was trying to stop the station's appeal by issuing the writ.

As Radio 390 grappled with the GPO in the courts two other stations were also doing likewise with considerably less success.

On January 31st a summons was served on Mrs Dorothy Calvert, the owner and operator of Radio City in the Thames, alleging illegal use of a transmitter without a licence. At a four and a half hour hearing on February 8th, Rochford Magistrates rejected a defence submission that the station was outside their jurisdiction and held that the fort on Shivering Sands was within territorial waters. Mrs Calvert was fined £100, but no order was made for costs or confiscation of the radio equipment.

Shortly after the hearing Mrs Calvert pointed out what had struck many people: 'It is ironical that last June when I asked the police for help after a boarding party put my station off the air I was told I was outside its jurisdiction. Yet within a few months, and after my husband has been killed, this view has changed completely and I am prosecuted for being inside territorial waters.'

As a result of the successful prosecution it was reluctantly decided by Mrs Calvert to close Radio City down. Also in January, Radio Essex, or BBMS as it had become known, left the air after its appeal failed. Plans to open a second station on Tongue Fort, off Margate, were dropped, but Roy Bates was reported to be preparing to establish a new station on the Rough Sand Fort off Harwich. Rumours that rival 'pop' radio groups were battling for possession of the fort were denied, but later turned out to be only too true.

In February Radio 270 also hit trouble as managing director Wilf Proudfoot clashed with his shareholders, just as Ted Allbeury of 390 was experiencing the same difficulty. Shareholders of the company running the ship, Ellambar Investments Ltd, called a meeting in March with the object of removing from office, without compensation, Mr Proudfoot. A spokesman for the shareholders said: 'There has been a lot of unrest for a long time now and we have not liked a lot of things which have taken place. We have lost confidence in his ability to run a radio station.'

Mr Proudfoot quite unperturbably commented: 'This is the second time this has happened. I think it will fizzle out on its own at the meeting and common sense will prevail.'

Radio 270 had encountered difficulties common to most of the offshore stations located on board ships. Bad weather had entailed leaving the air and subsequent loss of advertising contracts and revenue. A high turnover of disc jockeys had also taken place due to the difficult conditions of working at sea. In the end of the day, however, Mr Proudfoot remained as managing director despite his critics. When the company meeting was convened to deal with the complaint, none of the shareholders would even propose the resolution and the actual result of the meeting was a unanimous vote of confidence in Mr Proudfoot and the other directors.

As the Second Reading of the Marine Broadcasting Offences Bill loomed up in February, the fight to retain the offshore stations mounted in intensity. In the middle of January a new four-page illustrated paper *Radio News* appeared, as a supplement to the *National Advertiser* published by Brittain Press Ltd. The paper ran for only nine issues, but each one represented a defence of the pirate stations, and it consistently urged the introduction of free, commercial radio in Britain. It was announced in March that *Radio News* would be transferred to *Time and Tide*, the long established British news magazine.

On January 29th the Commercial Radio Listeners Association was founded to combat the Government's plans to close down the offshore stations. On February 19th a meeting was held in London with a view to forming an association representing all listeners of commercial radio, and which would have the full support of all the offshore stations. Most of the stations were represented at the meeting at which it was agreed that they should help the listeners' association in every way they could, particularly by broadcasting announcements for it over the air. They would not, however, finance the Association, nor be represented on its committee. Immediately after this meeting, the Association was formed under the name of the Free Radio Supporters Association. Contact was then made with the Commercial Radio Listeners Association and the two amalgamated.

The following day Ronan O'Rahilly of Radio Caroline advised the Association that its announcements could only be broadcast if the word 'Supporters' was dropped from the title. This was agreed and the Free Radio Association was born.

Announcements inviting membership of the Association were then broadcast by Radio 270, Radio 390, Radio Caroline and Radio Scotland. Car stickers, leaflets, badges and strongly worded petition forms were distributed by the Association. The hard-hitting petition declared:

> The Free Radio Association is fighting for free speech, free enterprise and free choice. The Government is trying to crush all competition over the air by silencing the commercial stations – thereby preserving the monopoly of the BBC and depriving us of the freedom to listen to the stations of our choice. This is a step towards dictatorship. If the Marine, Etc., Broadcasting (Offences) Bill becomes law in its present form, free speech will be suppressed, and the Free Radio Association will be partially silenced. No doubt this

would please the Government. But the Government will never silence us completely. We have pledged that we will fight until we win.

This is more than a petition. It is a declaration that we, the British people, will fight for freedom of the air as we have fought before when our freedom has been threatened. It is a declaration that we the undersigned support the Free Radio Association in its fight for the right of the public to listen to independent radio stations. And it is a declaration that we the undersigned will use our votes to remove this Government from power at the first opportunity, and replace it with a Government which believes in free speech, free enterprise and free choice.

It was only too obvious, however, that the Association had arrived on the scene too late to exert any real or decisive pressure on events. In fact, by the time it was formed the most important reading of the Marine Broadcasting Offences Bill, the Second Reading in the House of Commons, had taken place and had been carried. By the beginning of June, the Association had opened 259 branches but had only 1,920 members; an insignificant number when compared with the claimed pirate radio audience of 25 million.

One of the difficulties experienced by the Association was its failure to gain publicity in the Press. The Chairman of the Association, Mr Geoffrey Pearl, alleged at a large rally held on May 28th in Trafalgar Square that the press was 'playing down' the efforts of the Association. The press, not surprisingly, saw commercial radio as competition for advertising revenue. The point newspapers were appearing to miss, though, in playing down the issue of commercial radio was that freedom of the press and freedom of radio were just as important, and even allied issues. What the Government was doing to free radio in many people's eyes was precisely the same in principle as closing down the free press and making people read only government-controlled newspapers.

All the offshore stations stepped up their campaigns for legal recognition, but they all became more and more futile as 1967 wore on, and as the Government legislation to wipe the pirates from the wavelengths made its passage through Parliament.

On February 15th the House of Commons debated the Marine, Etc., Broadcasting (Offences) Bill. Mr Short, the Postmaster-General, moved the Second Reading and the Conservative opposition moved the amendment:

That this House declines to give a Second Reading to the Bill until

KID JENSEN

NOEL EDMONDS

TONY PRINCE

PAUL BURNETT

DAVID CHRISTIAN

208 PEOPLE
YOUR LUXEMBOURG D.J.'s

Radio Luxembourg had been established back in the 1930s and had broadcast evening English language pop music programmes on 208 metres during evening hours. Before the pirates, it had no competition and enjoyed much popularity. The pirates effectively stole much of its thunder although it went on to poach popular djs like Tony Prince and Paul Burnett from the pirate ships.

'Admiral' Robbie Dale at the Free Radio Association Rally, August 1968, in Trafalgar Square, London. At the time of his speech, Robbie Dale was working for the Dutch pirate, Radio Veronica.

the Government has put into effect a comprehensive broadcasting policy which takes account of the proved desire of millions of people to enjoy the choice of a wide variety of radio programmes, the interests of the artistes, and copyright holders, and Great Britain's international obligations.

Mr Short made the predictable, time-worn charges against pirate radio which had 'infested' the shores of Britain for three years. He charged the pirate radio operators with seizing frequencies not allocated to them under carefully laid down international agreements, but failed to mention that the agreements were not adhered to by most of the contracting parties, and that widespread confusion existed on the medium waveband without the offshore stations. He complained that their broadcasts were of poor technical quality and that they 'spilled over' into neighbouring frequencies. The Government's proposed action would fall in with the Council of Europe agreement on such stations, and if enough countries enacted legislation to deprive the pirates of supplies they could be cleared from the seas, where they were a hazard to shipping.

The Bill, Mr Short said, would make it an offence for any Briton to operate broadcasting apparatus without permission on any ship, aircraft or any structure on the high seas, and for anyone in the United Kingdom to arrange for such broadcasting. The provisions were intended to make it so difficult for pirate broadcasters to obtain all the things they needed, including advertising revenue, that they would be unable to continue.

He stated that a great many 'ingenious arguments' had been advanced by the pirates to suggest that, far from being suppressed, they should be actively encouraged. Freedom of speech and human rights had been invoked. But the Postmaster-General declared: 'I shall resist the temptation to answer them'!

In an attempt at scoring party political points, he alleged that the Opposition in its amendment wished to gain some imagined popularity by opposing world opinion as it had done over Rhodesia. Opposition members were putting themselves on the side of lawlessness.

Mr Paul Bryan, the Opposition spokesman on broadcasting, in moving the amendment to the Bill, said that Mr Short had described 'with some relish' the plans by which he meant to sink the pirates, but seemed less conscious of the fact that at one blow he was to deprive twenty million people of the programmes they enjoyed. 'We are not in favour of breaking international agreements, nor do we believe that the most sensible place from which to broadcast a radio programme is a small boat in the North Sea. But when, for purely electoral reasons, the pirate radio system has been allowed over two-and-a-half years to build up a huge audience, now to be left high and dry without any reasonable replacement, we have a right to protest on their behalf.'

The lesson of the pirates, Mr Bryan maintained, was that people wanted a wider choice in addition to the BBC. The signs were that this addition was wanted in the commercial type of programme.

'When the BBC try to imitate this type of programme it is rather like the Postmaster-General or myself going to a teenage dance. We should either be too merry or too dull.'

The Conservatives proposed local radio on a wider scale than the Government had in mind. Cities like Leeds and Manchester could sustain six or seven programmes. Is it not time the BBC monopoly in broadcasting was broken? The case against monopoly in broadcasting is as strong as it ever was,' complained Mr Bryan.

In a long and spirited debate the widely conflicting attitudes of the Conservative and Labour Parties towards broadcasting became clear, as Labour M.P.s set themselves up as firm opponents of commercial radio, with its wicked profiteering, capitalist implications, and condemned the wares of the pirates. The Conservatives emerged as the champions of the young and fought with vigour for the pirate cause.

Mr Gilmour, Conservative M.P. for Norfolk Central, winding up for the Opposition, regretted the absence of Mr Emmanuel Shinwell: 'Last September in *The Sunday Telegraph*, under the headline "Manny Shinwell: Prop of the Pop Pirates" we were reading:

Speaking to tens of thousands of cheering teenagers, at a beauty contest in his constituency last Monday, Shinwell proclaimed: "If we had been living in the 17th and 18th centuries the people who run these stations would have been sailing the high seas with Francis Drake, but I will see they get a fair crack of the whip".'

Mr Gilmour thought it was a pity that Mr Shinwell had not turned his buccaneering talents on Mr Short, who would not have been sailing with Francis Drake, but 'stamping out the theatre and other sinful pleasures'. What the pirates had done was not unlawful; they had broken into certain well-entrenched restrictive practices.

At the end of the debate, despite all the Opposition's protestations, the Government managed to get a Second Reading for the Bill, defeating the pirate radio supporters by 300 votes to 213, a Government majority of 87.

Over the following month the Bill was considered by a Commons Standing Committee, the Conservative members of which proposed a number of amendments with a not altogether unexpected lack of success.

Mr Channon, Conservative member for Southend West, moved an amendment to exclude television from the Bill, asking whether the Government thought pirate television stations were likely to ring Britain in the future. But Mr Hugh Jenkins, Labour M.P. for Putney, an arch-opponent of the pirate stations, stated that it could be said with some certainty that pirate television would have been taking place in six months because, about nine months previously, an American company had been formed to bring television broadcasts to Britain.

The member for Cathcart, in Glasgow, moved an amendment to exempt Scotland from the Bill because, he claimed, large parts of Scotland could receive no other programmes except those transmitted by Radio Scotland. He asked for postponement of the operation of the Bill in respect of Scotland to allow Radio Scotland to continue until an alternative was provided, but the amendment was defeated by eleven votes to seven.

The Conservatives also proposed an amendment to delay operation of the Bill for two years after the Royal Assent, and then only with the approval of both Houses of Parliament, which action caused the Postmaster-General to accuse them of 'going through the motions of supporting law and order and at the same time coming down on the side of piracy'. He said that during the winter Radio 390 had been causing interference in Sweden. Britain Radio in Italy, Radio Scotland in Poland. Radio London in Jugoslavia and Belgium, and Radio Caroline North in Czechoslovakia and Belgium. He also, with all due seriousness, stated that 'it is not possible to assert firmly that no loss of life had been caused by the pirate radio stations'. A non-statement if ever there was one. This amendment was also defeated.

Mr Hugh Jenkins launched what the *Scottish Daily Express* headlined as an 'amazing attack' on Radio Scotland and its finances. He declared angrily in the Committee: 'We know very little about who finances Radio Scotland. Is it the Equitable Industrial Company of Scotland? Is that company controlled by Mr Leonard Jackson, who spent some time at Her Majesty's leisure, for the simple crime of carrying Conservative principles to their logical conclusion? Is he still behind Radio Scotland? Where does Mr Tim Holland fit into the picture?'

Radio Scotland promptly denied that its finances derived from the Equitable Industrial Society of Scotland, although they had a 'nominal' shareholding in the company. Mr T. V. Shields, the station's managing director, agreed, however, that Mr Stanley lackson, brother of Mr Leonard Jackson, the head of Equitable Industrial referred to by Mr Jenkins, was one of the three directors of Radio Scotland. The third man on the board was Mr Alan Carr, a London property owner with many interests in show business. A member of Equitable Industrial, Sir Andrew Murray, a former Lord Provost of Edinburgh, had also been on the board as Chairman of Radio Scotland, Mr Shields admitted. He had. however, left after only a few weeks.

Mr Jenkins also attacked the part that Radio Scotland was playing in the Glasgow Pollok by-election to be held in mid-March. Originally Mr Shields had announced over Radio Scotland that he intended to stand as an independent candidate in the Labour-held marginal seat. He said that one of the issues on which he intended to make a stand was the retention of a free, commercial radio service for Scotland. In February, though, he decided not to stand upon the advice of his directors, former parliamentary candidates and election agents, fearing that if he only attracted a few votes it would be held against independent radio stations when the Government made the final decision on their future. As the election approached the station did not remain silent, though, and advised listeners who believed in free, commercial radio like Radio Scotland to vote for the Conservative candidate. This, in its turn, led to Mr Jenkins' fierce attacks on the station.

Mr Shields then revealed that in September of the previous year the Government was given an opportunity to 'take full control of Radio Scotland – both financing and programming'. The only stipulation was that the station should be land-based in Scotland. The Postmaster-General, however, turned down the offer.

'When Mr Jenkins talks of irresponsibility he is completely wrong ... our books are open for all to see ... we are not associated in any way with the Equitable Industrial Company of Scotland.'

On March 15th, only a week later, Radio Scotland again found itself under attack from an English Labour M.P. in the House of

One of Radio London's top DJs, Keith Skues.

Commons. The Tory member for Glasgow, Cathcart, Mr Edward Taylor, had produced a sheaf of letters which, he said, had been written to Radio Scotland from the Regional Headquarters of the Argyll and Sutherland Highlanders, the Royal Air Force at Leuchars, the Sea Cadet Corps, and the Glasgow Corporation Health and Welfare Department.

Squadron-Leader H. B. Todd of RAF, Leuchars, wrote: 'My Commanding Officer has asked me to thank you and all concerned for your broadcasts, and to let you know that your generous contribution to the success of our "At Home" day is appreciated.'

Lieutenant-Colonel T. B. G. Slessor of the Argyll and Sutherland Highlanders wrote: 'It was most kind of you to provide so much publicity on Radio Scotland for the Argyll and Sutherland Highlanders beating Retreat in Glasgow. The Retreat went extremely well and we had a large crowd, entirely due to your efforts on our behalf.'

Mr William Frame, Glasgow's Health Education Officer, wrote: 'May I take this opportunity of thanking you for your valuable support in our present polio campaign. I have heard many favourable comments from the public about the messages you are transmitting and current attendance figures at our fixed and mobile clinics are most encouraging.'

Lieutenant Gilbert W. Baird of Glasgow Sea Cadet Corps wrote: 'I am writing on behalf of my unit committee and myself to say a very sincere thank you to you for being so generous as to give our advertisement two transmissions at no cost to the unit.'

As Mr Taylor produced these letters, Socialist members quivered with rage and shouted 'Let's see them.' Four were at once seized by Mr Brian O'Malley who read them and declared: 'It would appear that the RAF and the Army and Navy have been deliberately using pirate radio stations in the full knowledge of the Government's intentions about those stations.'

He said that it was 'disgraceful' that commanding officers under the Ministry of Defence should do this. 'What on earth do Squadron-Leader Todd, the Lieutenant-Colonel of the Argyll and Sutherland Highlanders, Commander Norris of H.M.S. Collingwood and Lieutenant Baird think they are up to?' exploded an enraged and indignant Mr O'Malley. 'What kind of instructions has the Ministry of Defence given to these people, who should have read the newspapers in any case? I hope that the Postmaster-General will make some very detailed inquiries.'

Mr Taylor replied that the people mentioned by Mr O'Malley had legally used the pirate stations to promote the interests and defence of the country by assisting recruiting. 'It would be scandalous if the Government used the information with which I have provided the committee so as to engage in a kind of witch-hunt about something which was legal and in the public interest'.

Equally furious over the attack were the officers in question. Commander Morris explained: 'We were trying to organise Christmas messages from parents and sweethearts at home to our men abroad. Radio Luxembourg mentioned us several times, and Radio Scotland, Radio London and other pirate stations quoted my name so that people would know who to get in touch with.'

Lieutenant-Colonel Slessor stated: 'We were to beat Retreat in George Square, Glasgow, with the Lord Provost taking the salute. I wanted to let as many old Argylls as possible know, so that they could turn out.'

During the reading Mr Short and the assistant Postmaster-General, Mr Joseph Slater, smiled when the Conservative member for Belfast North, pointing out one of the anomalies of the Bill, said: 'A pirate radio station might announce "Joe Slater will now play *Sweet Violets* for Ted Short". Under a sub-section of the Bill the Postmaster-General would be guilty unless he could prove that he had not written to the pirate station asking for the record *Sweet Violets* to be played.'

On April 5th the Report Stage of the Bill, the last before its entry into the House of Lords, came before the Commons and was duly passed, despite a plea from Mr Taylor to exempt Scotland from the Bill, and a request from the Conservative member for Southend West to exempt Very High Frequency transmissions as 'a final last desperate attempt to improve the Bill'.

Mr E. Griffiths, the Conservative member for Bury St Edmunds, complained that, in his constituency, it was frequently quite impossible to receive BBC programmes because the power of their broadcasts was quite inadequate. On one occasion, in his own cottage, his wife had found that the only BBC programme to be heard was a lesson in Chinese. She preferred Radio Caroline.

Mr Short, however, had little sympathy with Mr Griffiths' wife. He maintained that if the pirate stations were legalised or ignored they would proliferate and create chaos. He also dismissed an amendment designed to safeguard Press freedom. Under the terms of the Bill it would be an offence to publish details of programmes broadcast by the pirate stations. This, Mr Short again maintained, was necessary in order to deal with the pirates by penalising those who collaborated with them.

As the British House of Commons passed the Marine, Etc., Broadcasting (Offences) Bill, however, the Manx House of Keys rejected the same Bill. The immediate effect of this appeared to be to guarantee the continuance of the activities of Radio Caroline North, moored 3½ miles off Ramsey.

Radio Caroline had become very popular not so much as a result of the 'pop' music it pumped out, but as a result of the considerable amount of free publicity for the island's resorts which it broadcast. Such welcome publicity had been maintained during the preceding summer's seamen's strike, which had threatened disaster for the island's tourist industry.

The Dutch crew of ten, and the eight British disc jockeys received most of their food, water, mail and broadcasting material by motorboat from Ramsey, and the Bill sought to make such trading illegal. With it defeated, though, the menace to Radio Caroline's existence evaporated temporarily.

After the Bill had been defeated by nineteen votes to three Ronan O'Rahilly of Radio Caroline announced: 'I am in negotiations now with the Manx Government to put Radio Caroline on the Isle of Man. There are 50,000 people living on the island … it is pretty clear that they want a high-powered radio station on the island and I am willing to provide it.'

*

During the months of March and April the campaigns both for and against the offshore stations increased in intensity. Over the air the pirates protested more and more desperately of their impending doom as Parliament and the Courts brought it nearer and nearer.

In March, following upon the successful prosecutions of Radio 390, Radio Essex and Radio City, a summons was served upon Radio Scotland, which was operating in the Firth of Clyde. At Ayr Sheriff Court on March 13th, City and County Commercial Radio (Scotland) Ltd and its managing director, Mr T. V. Shields, were both charged that 'on September 14th, 1966, on a hulk moored in the Firth of Clyde near Lady Isle, in the parish of Dundonald,

Ayrshire, in territorial waters adjacent to the United Kingdom' they 'used for the purpose of wireless telegraphy a transmitter without a licence from the Postmaster-General'. The Company pleaded Guilty to the charge, but Mr Shields pleaded Not Guilty. Both pleas were accepted by the prosecution and Mr Shields was discharged from the case.

Mr R. J. Cruickshank, Procurator Fiscal, said the case was self-explanatory. On September 14th Post Office engineers had monitored a broadcast from three points on the Ayrshire coast which was found to be coming from a hulk (the Radio Scotland 'ship' had no engines) clearly within territorial waters. The hulk from which the transmitter was operating was in fact at least 35 miles inside territorial waters. It was in the Firth of Clyde which, in terms of the September 1964 Order in Council, was a bay.

Mr Hugh T. McCalman, a Glasgow solicitor, stated in the Company's defence that the station had been operated in the honest belief that it was outside territorial waters, and that the operation was perfectly legal. It had always been thought that territorial waters only extended to three miles from the shore. The complexities associated with the definition of territorial waters were stressed by Mr McCalman, who said the ship was moored 6 1/2 miles from the nearest coastline. The broadcasts of Radio Scotland, he added, were in no way offensive; indeed, they provided good, clean entertainment. The company had passed over hundreds of pounds to charitable organisations through free airtime being available for worthy causes.

As the Sheriff fined the operators of the station £80, it went off the air, but disc jockey Mel Howard announced: 'This is not goodbye, just "au revoir". We shall be back again, perhaps on Wednesday or Thursday.' The ship then weighed anchor and a Clyde tug prepared to tow the ex-lightship *Comet* round the North of Scotland to a new anchorage off St Abb's Head at the mouth of the Firth of Forth. The court case, however, marked the beginning of ten weeks of trouble for Radio Scotland.

The planned £5,000, four-day tow never began. At the last minute it was cancelled as gale warnings for the area were received which made it much too risky for the tow to start. Two weeks later the ship was still anchored, silent, off Troon as gales battered the north coast of Scotland. Most of the crew and staff had been withdrawn and only one disc jockey and a skeleton crew remained on board. A few days later a move was at last possible, but no sooner was the *Comet* out of the Clyde than gales bore down again on the wild West coast of Scotland and the ship had to seek shelter in Loch Ewe.

Shortly before this, the directors of City and County Commercial Radio met and arrived at a decision not to move to the new mooring off the East coast after all. The tug *Cruiser* then towed the *Comet* across the Irish Sea and headed for a new anchorage off Ballywater, County Down, but gales struck once again and forced the Radio Scotland ship to shelter in Belfast Lough. Finally, on April 9th, after 28 days of silence, at 12.31 p.m. from five miles off Ballywater the station came back on the air as 'Radio Scotland and Ireland'. She did not anchor, though, without drama. As the two and a half ton anchor was released it ran out of control and an engineer, who tried to halt the roaring metal links, was seriously injured as the chain jumped and gashed his hand. A call for assistance was immediately put out and an hour later he was taken off by lifeboat.

But even now Radio Scotland's troubles were not over, for the programmes beamed from her new anchorage, while audible in most of Ireland and the North of England, couldn't be heard in Scotland. Also, the station ran into difficulties with the Irish authorities. After trouble with the Customs and Excise the ship had to be provisioned from Belfast which was more than twenty miles away. Originally the *Comet*'s tender operated from Port Avochie, near Donaghadee, but the Customs and Excise insisted that the tender sail out of a Customs port, or pay £8 for every trip to cover the cost of Customs examination, which would have cost the station £50 a week.

Portavogie?

Complaints were also sent to the Postmaster-General that the station was causing severe interference to broadcasting services in Eire and to radio communications with New Island lighthouse at the entrance to Belfast Lough. The Irish Government warned any Irishmen who might be intending working for Radio Scotland and Ireland that their jobs would soon be in peril, as new laws would be passed making it unlawful for Irish citizens to be connected with such stations.

At the end of April the *Comet* upped anchor and, towed by the Clyde tug *Campaigner*, left her Irish anchorage; her destination this time was Fife Ness off the East coast of Scotland. After three weeks of fine weather, however, the tow was delayed again by gales off the North-west coast of Scotland. On May 8th Radio Scotland at last reached her destination to find that the boom defence vessel with her mooring anchor on board was fogbound in port, and so the *Campaigner* had to keep towing the ship around until the boom defence ship managed to reach her.

When the station eventually came back on the air its silence had incurred an estimated loss of about £15,000 in advertising revenue, not to mention the cost of the tow to Ireland and back round the North of Scotland.

At the end of May there came another big shock for the station when, after managing director T. V. Shields sacked the coordination controller, Mr Brian Holden, four members of the staff, including the head disc jockey, resigned. Sales and promotion man, Eddie White, who resigned, complained: 'The ship has been moved all over the place. As Mr Shields has already stated, this has cost thousands of pounds apart from the tremendous loss in advertising revenue when the station was off the air.'

Former disc jockey and advertising man Allen Mackenzie said that 'Brian was really Mr Radio Scotland. He ran the show lock, stock and barrel. We all feel that his sacking was a gross injustice. I have known him work for up to twenty hours a day, but he has been made a scapegoat. It is time the public knew the facts.' Sales co-ordinator Mrs Elizabeth Kearsley and senior disc jockey Bob Spencer also resigned. Bob Spencer, perhaps the station's most popular disc jockey, had been with Radio Scotland since the start in December 1965 and before that he was on Radio City.

He resigned amid rumours of dissatisfaction among the station's disc jockeys, and at a time when the turnover among them was very high. Bob Spencer resigned with three stitches above his lip after a disastrous Radio Scotland 'Clan Ball' in the Locarno Ballroom in notorious Sauchiehall Street in Glasgow. Many of those present claimed that the dance was shockingly mismanaged. In any event it ended in an epic Glasgow free-for-all with the station's top disc jockey and 17-year-old disc jockey Tony Allan rushed to hospital with head injuries after what was described as 'a white rain of beer glasses' when they went on the stage.

As the story began to circulate that the station was to close, its managing director made an appeal to listeners for an annual subscription of 10s. The money, he said, would be used to give subscribers holidays at reduced rates. There would also be raffles and lucky numbers draws similar to Premium Bonds. Although he claimed the station itself would make no profit, it was revealed that it still needed to operate another nine months in order to make up its initial cost of £175,000 and yearly running costs of £100,000; and no way had been found around the Government Bill to stop its operation. Radio Scotland indeed appeared to be in rough waters.

*

At the same time another projected Scottish pirate radio station was sunk by GPO action. This station, King's Radio, was to have operated from a converted fishing vessel off Aberdeen initially as part of Aberdeen University Charities Campaign. The station was to have run in this form for two weeks in April and had been organised over a five month period, but was suppressed at the very last minute by GPO action.

With only a few days to go, and all arrangements for broadcasting completed, pressures were brought to bear on the student organisers of the station. GPO Headquarters in London had, a month previously, stated that although they did not 'look kindly upon the station, there is nothing we can do about it until the Bill goes through'. But with only a few days to go, the GPO in London told the students that even though it might be unlikely that they would be prosecuted 'they should consider the future of their positions at the University'. This threat was backed up by a visit of the GPO Area Engineer to the University authorities.

As a direct result of the threats and pressures brought to bear by the GPO, the use of the fishing vessel from which the station was to broadcast was withdrawn by the skipper who, it was made clear, would also be subject to insidious and indirect pressures. With only a few days before broadcasts were due to start, the station was left without a ship. It looked as though five months of effort and expense would be wasted. Tapes were made, a studio had been set up on land, disc jockeys had been trained, an English electronics firm had offered to install an aerial system free and advertising contracts worth nearly £1,000 were signed. It looked as though revenue from the station would run into many thousands – all for charity. A last ditch attempt was made to put the station on the air, but due to the expense which would be involved it was decided to attempt it on a permanent basis.

Negotiations were begun to purchase a 300-ton coaster by the students and it was planned that King's Radio would become

Scotland's second pirate radio station, serving the East coast. A debate that week on the Marine (Offences) Bill in the House of Commons, however, at the last minute caused financial backing to fall through and with it the station.

In the words of the organisers of the station: 'The suppression was despicable for its pettiness. One can only conclude that we have been singled out for persecution as a result of political circumstances and bureaucratic intolerance. It is a sad reflection on the country that a station planning to broadcast for only a fortnight on behalf of charity should be suppressed in ways reminiscent of a police state.'

Mr James Davidson, M.P. for West Aberdeenshire, found the matter disturbing and asked the Postmaster-General about the insidious pressures brought to bear on the operators of the station. The Postmaster-General, not surprisingly, rejected the complaint, reminding any other would-be pirates that 'broadcasting on the high seas is forbidden by international law'.

Another pirate to strike trouble was the year-old Radio England/ Britain Radio, the company operating which went into liquidation in March. Creditors of the company, Peir Vick Ltd, were told that in the year it had operated it had lost more than £100,000. Its debts totalled £113,000 and its assets £5,004.

The company had been formed on March 11th, 1966, and it had an issued capital of only £2. The two stations, which were both operated from the converted American Liberty ship *Laissez Faire*, had experienced difficulty in gaining listeners and advertising. Radio England's 'pop' format offered nothing new against the well-established Radio Caroline and Radio London, while Britain Radio had to compete with the much longer established Radio 390. Six months after its inception Radio England was renamed Radio Dolphin and began transmissions in Dutch. In February 1967, Ted Allbeury, it will be remembered, left Radio 390 and joined Britain Radio intending to model it on Radio 390. Shortly after the winding up of Peir Vick Ltd in March, it was announced that Carstead Advertising Ltd, with Ted Allbeury as managing director, had taken over Britain Radio and that it was to be renamed Radio 355.

May saw a renewal of the troubles of that much persecuted station Radio 390, when Mr Justice O'Connor, in the Court of Appeal, decided that the Post Office was entitled to an injunction restraining Radio 390 from broadcasting from Red Sands Tower. As before, Estuary Radio maintained that the station was not operating illegally without a licence because its base was on the high seas, and not within United Kingdom territorial waters.

But the Judge upheld the argument of the Post Office that the station was in territorial waters and was broadcasting without a licence. He also dismissed a counter-claim by the station's owners that it was on the high seas and, therefore, did not need a broadcasting licence. The station was ordered by the Court to go off the air immediately, but after a plea by Sir Peter Rawlinson, Q.C., representing Radio 390, a nineteen day period of grace was allowed, which meant that the station could continue its activities for that period pending an appeal over the ruling.

Mr David Lye, acting managing director of Estuary Radio, said outside the courtroom: 'We have lost today, but our fight to keep the station on the air goes on. Our fight to do so is very much alive.' He added that the station would seek leave to appeal and meanwhile would carry on broadcasting

*

The increasingly pessimistic outlook for the offshore stations was somewhat relieved on May 1st in the House of Lords when the Government found itself defeated. Opposition peer Lord Denham proposed an amendment which would delay the operation of the Marine Broadcasting (Offences) Bill until the Postmaster-General had provided alternative programmes to the pirate broadcasts. Moving the amendment, he said that by delaying legislation the Government had allowed a situation to develop in which twenty million people listened to pirate radio.

'It is the Government's responsibility to fill the void left in the lives of their listeners by the planned demise of the pirate ships with a satisfactory alternative. If they don't, someone else will do it for them.'

He said that the new BBC programme would start in the autumn, and the purpose of his amendment was to fill the gap between the coming into operation of the Bill and the start of the new programme.

A decidedly unsympathetic Lord Sorenson stated, for the Government, that the gap would only be six or seven weeks. 'We have to assume that 10 million young people, or people pretending to be young, are going to feel desolation in their hearts that they never felt before. One is tempted to ask what they were doing before the pirate stations started. Does Lord Denham propose that if this alternative service is not available we should connive at continued illegality? I cannot think that Lords, respecting law and order, will justify that.'

Lord Sorenson then asked the astonishing question: 'Surely one is not all the time to be dictated to by the tastes of one small section of the community? If ever we became subordinated to the transient tastes of one-sixth of the community that will be a bad day for the country.'

These last few remarks prompted Lord Carrington to spring to his feet and declare that Lord Sorenson's speech was one of the most superior things he had ever heard. 'It was just the man on the Front Bench knows best'.

Contrary to the noble Lord's expectations the House did, however, 'connive at illegality' by passing Lord Denham's amendment by 65 votes to 44. Immediately after the vote there were angry exchanges. Lord Sorenson announced that, so there would be 'no dubiety in the minds of those operating the pirate radio stations', if the Bill was enacted with the amendment included the Government intended to bring in an Order in Council bringing the Act into operation one day after the expiry of one month.

At this Lord Denham rose angrily and declared: 'This is treating the House with contempt. I have never heard anything so ... words fail me.'

The Earl of Longford, the Lord Privy Seal, intervened accusing Lord Denham of speaking in a 'very wild fashion'. Amid cries of 'Shame' from Conservatives, he said that he hoped he did not use the word contempt 'just because he finds he has not succeeded in being quite so clever as he thought'.

It was thus quickly made clear that the Opposition amendment represented but a hollow victory for the pirates. The Government made only one concession on the Bill, when Lord Sorenson gave an undertaking at the end of May to consider again the question of defining 'advertisement'.

Viscount Colville of Culross had said that he understood that certain items in newspapers which might ordinarily be thought to be editorial matter might be considered offensive under the Bill. Another peer, Lord Drumalbyn, accused: 'There is, I believe, no satisfactory definition of an advertisement in general. The Government appears to be leaving the whole matter vague in that hope that everybody will be careful what they say.'

Lord Sorenson, for the Government, said that it did not intend to penalise the publication of editorial comment or genuine news items concerning the pirates. He agreed, though, that the meaning of 'advertisement' was not clear.

It was obvious by the end of May that the Marine Broadcasting (Offences) Bill would probably be passed by Parliament before the Summer recess. The pirates themselves began to realise that they were doomed and that all the invocations of democracy and freedom would do no good. This sense of the hopelessness of their struggle led to an expression of attitudes, and to actions which, in many cases, were calculated to enrage authority. For the first time pirate stations played politics with the obvious intention of causing as much discomfiture to the Government as possible.

During March and April Radio London ran a survey among candidates for the Greater London Council to find out who was for or against free radio and obtained the following result:

	For	Against
Labour	4	23
Liberal	28	6
Conservative	38	0

1 Labour candidate didn't know

The station also broadcast the findings of an opinion poll it made among M.P.s, which showed that while 65 per cent of Conservative M.P.s were in favour of the offshore broadcasters, the majority of Labour Members wanted them closed down. Officials at Transport House were reported as becoming very alarmed at the revelation of these findings. They well understood both the popularity of these stations and the fact that the wrath of the public at their being closed down would show in the impending elections.

For several weeks the station failed to tire of reminding listeners of the result of their polls. Radio Caroline and Radio 270 also made attempts to influence the outcome of the nationwide May local elections. One Member of Parliament alleged in the Commons that the pirate stations were trying to influence 'improperly' the results of the Greater London Council Elections. Mr Crossman, Leader of the House, replied confidently, however : 'I do not know what they are doing, but if they are doing what I suspect let us hope they will provoke all good men to vote the right way.'

The Postmaster-General appeared to take a much more serious view in mid-April, perhaps to be justified by the following month's election results which were to prove disastrous for Labour. In York he warned that legal aspects of intervention by pirate radios in political elections were being examined. At the same time Wilf Proudfoot of Radio 270 announced that the station would carry 'paid political advertisements' to be submitted by local political parties. Candidates for the local council would be allowed twenty words each advertisement and a maximum number of five announcements for each candidate. Not surprisingly, the only party to take up the station's offer was the Conservative party. Mr Proudfoot announced also that the first political broadcast from an offshore station would be transmitted on May 1st.

The broadcast in question was on behalf of the Conservative Party and featured Mr Patrick Wall, M.P. and members of York University Conservative Association. During the broadcast Mr Wall spoke about future relations with Rhodesia, urging that talks be resumed with Mr Smith's Government. Mr Andrew Faulds, Labour M.P. for Smethwick, heard of the broadcast beforehand and immediately put down a question about it, but when the question came up on May nth his criticism proved premature. The tape containing the broadcast had arrived on the ship the previous weekend, but was found to be recorded at the wrong speed and only high-pitched squeaks emerged from it. It, therefore, had to be sent ashore again where it was rerecorded and transmitted later. Mr Faulds, in his zeal to protest, failed to find this out and asked the Postmaster-General whether 'in view of the fact that an illegal broadcast was made from Radio 270 last Saturday by the Hon. Member for Haltemprice, he would have the results of the previous day's York municipal elections declared invalid?' There was much laughter in the Commons at this, but Mr Short replied seriously: That question is one for the Home Secretary. I do not underestimate the seriousness of this. I hope that no one will underestimate the seriousness of it, the unwholesomeness of it. This is the first time in peace time that this country has been subjected to a stream of misleading propaganda from outside territorial waters. It is an extremely serious matter.'

Mr Wall was not present as the attack was made on him, but he later explained that the broadcast was not illegal and that he hoped Mr Faulds would 'use the normal conventions of the House to apologise for making an attack on a member who was not present'. He also announced that he would continue making such broadcasts until it was proved illegal. 'If you write a letter to a newspaper on a political subject it is a proper and perfectly acceptable thing to do. If that is all right, why is it not all right to broadcast? Free speech is the same whether written or spoken.'

Mr Proudfoot, of Radio 270, emphasised that Mr A. W. Lyon, Labour M.P. for York, had been offered similar facilities, but had turned them down. Using a now popular equation of offshore radio with free speech he declared: 'I believe in free speech and I will broadcast a Communist point of view if they send it to us.'

In June it was announced that York University Conservative Association's Monday Club had prepared another broadcast featuring two M.P.s, Mr Patrick Wall, again, and Mr John Biggs-Davidson. The broadcast went out over Radio 270 at the end of June and Mr Faulds was sent a full transcript of the programme 'to make sure he doesn't make any mistakes in the House of Commons this time', in the words of the club's chairman. Mr Wall's talk was again on Rhodesia. Mr Biggs-Davidson spoke on the situation in the Middle East and Israel. The programme was described as 'a direct attack on the Government both in its handling of foreign and domestic affairs'.

Both Radio 270 and the students intimated that they would continue such broadcasts as long as they were legal.

By May 1967 Radio 270 was just a year old, but during that year it had established itself as an offshore station with a local flavour as well as national coverage. Listeners in the North-east found a number of services available. A novel idea was that of the 270 'Swop Shop', through which listeners could write in, say what they had and what they wanted to swop it for and the announcement would be broadcast, free of charge, over the air. Traffic reports, 'Kiddies Corner' and frequent charity announcements were also broadcast, widening the scope of the station beyond the confines of mere 'pop' music. 270 probably gave more time to charities than any other offshore station benefiting the RNLI, Oxfam, the Salvation Army, Rotary Clubs, Lifeline and children's homes and orphanages, among many other good causes. Sales of 270 Fight for Free Radio' car stickers at 1d each raised over £500 for the Wireless for the Blind Fund.

*

At the end of May a curious incident occurred. The Prime Minister, Mr Wilson, was leaving a conference of Labour women at Southend-on-Sea when a boy, Nigel Fell, of Thundersley, Essex, who had a tape recorder, stepped forward and asked him what was his attitude to commercial radio. Since the beginning of independent radio in Britain Mr Wilson had never made a full statement giving his own opinion on the offshore stations.

Mr Wilson started to answer the boy's question and had spoken on the subject for about half a minute when the microphone was noticed. Three burly detectives immediately rushed forward, seized the microphone and erased the tape.

It appeared that Mr Wilson's views on the issue were never to be recorded for posterity. The incident may be regarded as more than curious, it may even be found disturbing that in a so-called democracy such a thing should occur. Freedom and democracy seemed to mean little to the Government, though, as the Bill to suppress the enjoyment of over twenty million people was forced through Parliament.

11

The Pirates are sunk

On Friday June 31st 1967 the Marine Broadcasting (Offences) Bill completed its tortuous passage through Parliament and needed only the Royal Assent to become the Marine Broadcasting (Offences) Act. The offshore broadcasters had already begun intensive activity with a view to beating it.

As early as January, evidence of such preparations had come to light when Radio Caroline engineers went out to the Rough Sands Fort, eight miles off Felixstowe in international waters, and began work on it. Dozens of bottles of acetylene were delivered to the fort by sea and coastguards reported signs of burning from the wartime fort. Much of the superstructure and the gun mountings from the platform of the tower, perched on two narrow legs, were cut away and tipped into the sea. By March, a large flat area had been cleared on the platform and yellow lines marked out a square helicopter landing area.

The Caroline organisation then put under contract L'Aero-naute Ltd as aviation consultants to provide 'a varied helicopter and fixed wing support for the future requirements, both exploitation and servicing, of Radio Caroline and Ronan O'Rahilly personally'. The fort was dearly to be used as a heliport – probably for flying in and stockpiling supplies when the British supply routes were cut off by the Government's anti-pirate Bill. Holland was tipped as the likely source of supplies and equipment.

Rough Sands Fort without a doubt lay outside territorial waters, unlike its counterparts in the Thames. In January, though, squatters had been manning the tower for two years, and not all of them were from Radio Caroline either. Radio Essex had also claimed the fort and the station's owner, Roy Bates, had at various times put his men on board the fort. After the successful prosecution of Radio Essex, operating from Knock John Fort in the Thames, Mr Bates intended transferring his radio equipment on to Roughs Tower and the two rival pirate organisations came into conflict. After rumours of violent battles over the fort, a temporary agreement was reached about sharing it, and each station put two men on board.

The Caroline men, however, went ashore when one of them needed medical treatment, leaving the fort in possession of the Radio Essex men, and the agreement fell through in April. Amidst great secrecy Caroline made many attempts to regain the fort, but the nature of this fiercely contested battle only burst into the open at the end of June when the newspaper headlines once again blared out that the 'pop' pirates were at war, and that Roughs Fort, this time, was the scene of violence and rivalry.

On the evening of Tuesday, June 27th the Caroline tender *Offshore II* left Harwich. On board was Mr Percy Scadden, ex-police inspector and local agent for Caroline, and with him a boarding party. Their aim was to take over the fort, which they later claimed they thought to be deserted. If so, when they arrived at Roughs Tower a shock awaited them.

As four men tried to board the tower, the night sky was lit up by flaming petrol bombs and oxygen cylinders which rained down on them and the tender from the platform. Thirty-six year-old ship's carpenter John Hoiles was half-way up the rope ladder when, in his own words, 'all hell was let loose'. Mr Scadden's clothing caught fire and the boarders took cover on the boat which, on fire and carrying five tons of oil, retreated – minus Mr Hoiles who was left clinging to the swaying ladder twenty feet above the water as he tried to avoid gunfire and Molotov cocktails.

As the tender made for Harwich it sent out a distress call and the Walton lifeboat was launched. Meanwhile, John Hoiles was lowered a wooden crate with blankets, and food and coffee was also sent down. It was nearly three hours before he was rescued by the lifeboat just as, at the end of his strength, he was 'about ready' to fall into the sea.

On shore, the tender and lifeboat were met by Essex police who began enquiries into the incident as pressmen arrived attracted by a good story.

The owner of Radio Caroline, Ronan O'Rahilly, said he was staggered by the incident and expected the police to act 'within 48 hours'. He added that he had plans for the fort which were 'nothing to do with broadcasting'. He claimed that he intended to establish a health centre and holiday hotel, complete with heliport, on the tower, and that he had spent £15,000 on developing it.

'My men left two months ago after it was taken over by force. I don't know what I am going to do now.'

Mr Bates also claimed that the fort was his the next day when he went out to Rough Sands to deliver food and water to its defenders: 15-year-old Michael Bates, his public schoolboy son, and 25-year-old disc jockey David Barron.

'This is the eighth time we have been attacked on the fort,' he complained, 'and now I have decided to build an electric fence to make it impregnable. We have all the materials aboard and will go ahead immediately.'

Reporters who boarded the station, under the barrel of a twelve-bore shotgun, spoke to the fort's defenders and were shown a veritable armoury of weapons which included six shotguns, a flame thrower, two air-rifles and a stack of petrol bombs. David Barron said that he had been told that the fort was worth £1 million to a radio station as a long-term enterprise and that he was being paid £10 a week to hold it indefinitely against rival groups.

'We intend to stay here against all comers. Six times boarders have tried to take it from us, but now we have a complete security system working.' When questioned about the attack he admitted: 'I'm afraid we overdid it a bit. When one of the men got half-way up the ladder we let the boat have it with petrol bombs made by filling old bottles with petrol. We tried to hit everyone we could and the whole boat went up.'

All the equipment from Radio Essex was on board the fort but Mr Bates said that he did not intend to set up a radio station. The name 'Roy Bates' could be clearly seen painted over the fort and its helipad in large white letters, but his purpose remained obscure. The fact remained that the fort was one of the only two outside the three mile limit and, therefore, potentially extremely valuable to a broadcaster.

It therefore appeared to be outwith the jurisdiction of the police, and two days later it was reported that top level Home Office and Ministry of Defence talks were going on about its future. Statements taken from the men on *Offshore II* were collected by police cars and taken to London to be studied, but the problem seemed so complex that it was even conjectured that a Cabinet decision might be taken.

The following week the Home Secretary stated in the House of Commons, in answer to a question asking what action he was taking 'to end gang warfare on pirate radio stations', that the Chief Constable of Essex was considering what action was called for following the incident at Rough Sands Tower.

The problems faced by the police were highlighted again the same day as the Home Secretary answered the question in Parliament. That evening the 480-ton *Laissez Faire*, from which Radio 355, the station which succeeded Britain Radio, broadcast sent out a distress call which was picked up by coastguards at Walton-on-the-Naze saying: 'We have a man on board who is threatening murder. He has already assaulted the captain.' The radio operator, who was locked in his radio shack, asked for police to be sent out in Walton lifeboat to take the man ashore. The English captain said a fight was raging on board the ship between English and Dutch factions of the crew and that men were in danger of their lives.

Deputy Superintendent Brown of the Essex police, who had investigated the incident at Roughs Tower a week before, instructed the lifeboat to stand by while senior police officers discussed the matter at Clacton. A statement was then issued: 'It is a matter in which, it would appear, the police have no jurisdiction.' The lifeboat was instructed not to launch and the problem was referred to the Royal Navy at Portsmouth who, in their turn, referred it to the Ministry of Defence. The Ministry decided to take no action immediately, but asked the coastguards to keep them informed about the situation on board the Honduras-registered ship, anchored half-a-mile outside territorial waters.

Those on board the *Laissez Faire* had deliberately placed themselves outside the reach of the law and they found themselves without its protection when they needed it.

By July the plans of the pirate radio operators once the Act became law were emerging from the barrage of rumour and mystery which had previously surrounded them.

Rumours had been many and various. One was that two commercial stations were being planned in the Pyrenees. A wilder version of this was that an organisation of British and American businessmen were financing a station in Spain, which would broadcast to Britain via satellite. Radio Andorra in the Pyrenees, however, which had broadcast to Spain and France since 1939, began plans to broadcast an English service during the night in an attempt to fill the gap which would be left by the demise of the pirates. Another rumour was that an American religious organisation was preparing to finance a 'pop' music programme once the operations of the existing stations had been curtailed.

*Ex-Radio Essex man Roy Bates occupies the Rough Tower Fort off
the Essex coast and declares the Independent Republic of Sealand.*

The oldest and most experienced broadcaster, Radio Caroline, had begun plans to survive earliest of all. In March an ultimatum was issued to the twenty British members of the Radio Caroline staff. They were told that if they wished to continue with the organisation, they would have to give up their British citizenship.

Said Irish managing director Ronan O'Rahilly: 'It wasn't easy asking these people to make up their minds on an issue as important as this, but we must look to the future. We have already taken on six or seven new staff, mainly American and Canadian, and we will probably be employing more.'

Two British members of the staff, a disc jockey and a newscaster, stated that they were 'almost certain' to become stateless persons until they could become nationals of another country. They had decided to give up their British passports and, according to Mr O'Rahilly, 'one of them, who has lots of jobs open to him, has said he would not want to remain a citizen of a country which would bring in laws like these.'

It was stated at the same time that an office was to be opened in Holland, and that in conjunction with a French agency in Paris foreign advertising contracts were being built up. Mr O'Rahilly optimistically forecast that in a year's time the station would be 'choc-a-bloc' with advertisements for transistors from Japan, oranges from South Africa and other goods that 'have nothing to do with Britain'.

On March 1st Radio 355 and Radio 227, the stations operated from on board the *Laissez Faire* by Ted Allbeury's Carstead Advertising, opened an office in the Berthelostraat in Amsterdam East. From this office Australian John Withers started the search for foreign advertising to support the two stations.

At the end of May the Dutch-owned tender *Offshore I* left Felixstowe with three transmitting valves manufactured by the English Electric Valve Company of Chelmsford. These were delivered to the 10,000 ton M.V. *Galaxy*, from which Radio London broadcast. As a result the station became independent of British supplied transmitting valves for the foreseeable future – the life of each valve being between nine months and two years.

Mr Philip Birch, the station's managing director, and a man with eleven years advertising experience in the United States, made it plain that Radio London would rely almost entirely on American advertising revenue. Holland would be the source of the station's supplies, and in May one of the station's directors, Mr Dennis Maitland, set up a shipping office there.

Radio Caroline also opened offices in May in Holland – with a South African, Basil van Rensburg, in charge. The organisation announced that a Dutch language programme, with Dutch disc jockeys, would be started after the installation of a second transmitter on board Radio Caroline South. After the Bill became law music would come from Dutch and United States record companies and from the Dutch agents of British record companies.

Mr van Rensburg told reporters that there would be a task force of five men moving around European and North American cities seeking advertising from non-British firms who export goods to Britain. The station was experiencing no difficulty in finding non-British disc jockeys, and these would be based in Amsterdam.

Meanwhile, Ronan O'Rahilly had been touring Europe in a bid to draw advertising. In France he met representatives of Services et Methodes, the public relations firm that numbers General de Gaulle among its clients. In Canada, Caroline sought advertising through Masirah Associates, a Toronto-based firm run by Terry Bate whose face became well known at Caroline House in London. In August 1966 Ronan O'Rahilly had persuaded this 33-year-old Englishman to leave the Canadian Broadcasting Service and to join Radio Caroline as a consultant on a seven year contract; proof indeed of the Caroline organisation's belief in its capacity to survive.

Most of the pirate stations used the tenders *Offshore I*, *Offshore II* and *Offshore III* for their supplies of food, water and equipment. Their owners, the Dutch Wijsmuller salvage firm, before the Marine Offences Bill became law, let it be known that their services would still be available. This meant that the pirates could not be starved out of existence, as the British Government planned. The stations off the South-east coast could be quite easily supplied from Holland, while *Offshore III* could, if necessary, make the longer journey to Caroline's northern station off the Isle of Man.

At the beginning of July details of a spectacular campaign by Radio Caroline in reply to the Marine Offences Act were made known. On the first day the Act became law, the station would break it by using a newscaster, a disc jockey and a religious broadcaster; all English subjects who under the terms of the Act are liable to both a fine and imprisonment for working for a pirate station.

In the words of O'Rahilly: 'Each broadcaster breaking the law will have to be prosecuted under the Act. I want this to happen because I am going to take each case to the Court of Human Rights, whose jurisdiction Britain accepts.

'They will have made broadcasts knowing them to be for the use of Caroline and they will have to be arrested. I am morally right in this. Harold Wilson is morally wrong. What are people going to think if ordinary British people are put in prison for working for a legal radio station?'

The poet and dramatist, Ronald Duncan, founder of the English Stage Company, stated in *The Daily Telegraph* in June that he would write scripts for the pirate stations once they became illegal.

'If freedom of speech means anything it means to say what you like, to whom you like, so long as you do not incite to crime or violence.

'I hope many writers will join me in offering to write for any pirate station once it becomes illegal. I am prepared to do so for 6d because I value very highly my freedom to write for whom I like.'

For other offshore stations the outlook was bleaker. In June Mr David Lye, acting managing director of Radio 390, agreed that the Act would mean the end of his station, and efforts to find a landbased location in France or Spain were not meeting with much success.

The end came for Radio 390 just over two weeks before the Act became law, on July 28th. That day three Court of Appeal judges, Lord Justice Sellars, Lord Justice Diplock and Lord Justice Winn, ruled that the Red Sands Fort was within the internal waters of the United Kingdom, upholding the ruling of Mr Justice O'Connor made in the High Court in May. Mr J. P. Harris, junior counsel to Sir Peter Rawlinson, Q.C., who had represented Estuary Radio throughout its legal battle, asked for the station to be allowed to stay on the air until the Marine Broadcasting (Offences) Act became law. He told the judges: 'Your Lordships may think that people in hospitals and on the beaches should not be deprived of listening to Radio 390.'

An unmoved Lord Justice Sellers, however, refused this application: 'You may break our hearts with talking about the hospitals, but certainly not over people on the beaches.... All you have to do is cease broadcasting eighteen days earlier than you would have done.'

After the hearing Mr David Lye said that the company had lost money in the two years that it broadcast. The protracted legal battle had cost over £10,000 and Estuary Radio would lie dormant as a company 'so that it will have an opportunity to use its experience by going back into business if the law about commercial radio is changed'.

A boat then left Whitstable Harbour to let those on Red Sands Fort know the result of the station's appeal. To the strains of the National Anthem, Radio 390, the sweet music station with an estimated audience of as many as eight million, left the air at 5.10 p.m.

The company, however, had succeeded in its object of keeping a complex legal battle of trial, appeal and counter-appeal going for nearly a year, and thus had managed to stay on the air, while its less well organised counterparts, Radio Essex and Radio City, had allowed themselves to succumb in the first rounds.

Although the days of broadcasting from Red Sands Fort had been brought to an end, its days of drama had not. Ten days after ceasing transmission, four 390 men left on the fort to guard the valuable transmitting equipment were woken up as five men armed with sledgehammers, piping and spanners made a dramatic commando-style raid on the Red Sands Towers.

At 6 a.m. the men had boarded the Canvey fishing boat *Shemali* and asked its owner if he would make a trip to the fort 'to pick up some equipment'. When they reached the fort one of the boarding party climbed up the metal ladder and then shinned up a fifteen-foot metal upright onto the narrow catwalk surrounding the tower, surprising a Radio 390 man on watch who was warned: 'If you want trouble you can have it.' He then released the bolts on the trapdoor through which the fort was entered and let the other boarders through from the ladder.

The boarders then crashed into the living quarters, waking up one of the station's announcers, Graham Gill, who later described how he sat up in bed to find a man threatening him with a sledge-hammer. The gang began stripping the fort of its fixtures, smashing brass fittings off radiators, seizing copper wire and collecting navigation lights. They warned the 390 men: 'Don't cause any trouble or you'll get hurt.'

Unknown to the boarders, however, one of the station's engineers, Douglas Seymour, was sending out an S.O.S. on a transmitter he had hidden under a pile of rags. His message was picked up by his wife at their home in Whitstable and she immediately contacted Mr David Lye. It was also picked up by the Southend fishing boat *Kestrel*, whose crew passed it on to the tug *Avenger* which called the coastguards, who in turn contacted the police. Shortly afterwards an RAF Air-Sea Rescue helicopter left Mansion, Kent, with a police officer and doctor. The policeman was winched down to the fort when the helicopter reached Red Sands, but left when he found no one was injured.

Meanwhile, Mr Lye had borrowed a light aircraft from a friend and flew over the Thames Estuary searching for the fishing boat referred to by Mr Seymour in his message. Eventually, he located it and buzzed it for about 45 minutes, taking photographs. As the *Shemali* approached Southend she was met by a Port of London Authority launch which took her in tow to Canvey Island, after putting two men on board who told the boarding party that they were under arrest, and that their cargo would be confiscated. As the boat berthed at Hole Haven the boarders found police waiting on the quay who took them to Benfleet police station, where they were questioned for three hours while Customs and War Office officials examined articles found on board the fishing vessel.

Mr Lye later said that metal, wire and equipment worth £1,000 had been removed by the raiders, and appealed for police protection for his men on Red Sands. He added that his company would abandon the fort once all the valuable radio equipment had been removed. The £40,000 worth of broadcasting equipment was to be put into store as, in Mr Lye's words: 'the chance of us doing anything with it in the near future are pretty well out.'

On board another fort, however, its occupants made it clear as the Marine Broadcasting (Offences) Act approached that the last thing they intended was to abandon it. Mr Roy Bates, former owner of Radio Essex, warned that he would 'fight to the death' anyone who tried to take Roughs Tower, eight miles off Felixstowe. The six-foot, ex-Desert Rat warned that he had the fort booby-trapped and surrounded by an electric fence, and said that members of his family and two employees were taking turns in guarding it. 'I will try and get them off if trouble starts, but if I cannot they will stay and fight. I am prepared to die for it.'

Mr Bates not only had his eyes on the Radio Caroline organisation, whom he had fought eight times for possession of the tower, but he revealed that the Ministry of Defence had offered him £5,000 for the fort if he would return it to the Crown. He had refused the offer but did not believe the Ministry's promises that force would not be used against him. A Ministry of Defence spokesman admitted that a detachment of Royal Marines and two helicopters were standing by to invade the fort 'in case negotiations are successful'. The Ministry explained: 'We wanted to get rid of this present situation in view of the Act which comes into operation soon.' But Mr Bates plainly did not believe that force would not be used: 'You don't have that lot standing by for nothing.' The Ministry's reason for its preparations to board the fort were obvious. If negotiations were successful and Mr Bates moved out it was very likely that Radio Caroline, who had spent £15,000 developing its helipad and other facilities, would attempt to move in again once there were no occupants in possession. Despite the Marine Offences Act which made it illegal for a British person to be connected with a pirate radio station, Mr Bates still seemed determined to hang on to the fort.

What was interpreted as a spectacular attempt to weaken his resolve took place shortly after the Act came into operation in August when twenty men of the Royal Engineers reoccupied the only other disused wartime fort off the Essex Coast in international waters. Observers who flew over the fort, Sunk Head Tower, eleven miles off Felixstowe, saw soldiers fitting wires and detonators around the gun emplacements. The Sunk Head fort had been used for a short time, it will be remembered, by the short-lived Radio Tower, and a number of pirate stations were reported as having considered it as a base for supplies. The Defence Department announced that it had ordered the destruction of the fort to 'prevent its use by anyone other than the department'.

Three days later a flash of orange flame, a cloud of light grey smoke changing to dark grey, and a loud explosion marked the end of the fort, built in 1940 as part of the country's naval defence system. As the fort was blown up Mr Roy Bates watched from his own, Roughs Tower, only six miles away. The Ministry of Defence denied that it had similar plans for the fort which Mr Bates was holding with an armoury of flamethrowers, petrol bombs, rifles and 4,000 volts of electricity, but a Royal Engineer's spokesman said: 'The operation was obviously intended as a warning to Bates to give up Roughs Tower without a fight.'

On July 14th the Postmaster-General had announced in the House of Commons that the Marine Broadcasting (Offences)

An artist's impression of the projected propoganda station Radio Freedom. It was rumoured that finance for the station would come from 'rebel' Ian Smith's Rhodesian Government.

Act would come into operation on August 14th after the Royal Assent had been given. He reminded the House that after that date anyone rendering assistance to the pirate stations would be guilty of a criminal offence. When asked how quickly the stations which were trying to evade the Bill by setting up facilities abroad could be silenced, Mr Short admitted that it depended 'on our European colleagues'.

The owners of the stations reacted gloomily to the news. Mr T. V. Shields, managing director of the itinerant Radio Scotland, admitted that 'it would seem we have lost the battle'.

Radio 355 and Radio 227 appeared to have scrapped all plans for continuing from a base in Holland, and Ted Allbeury said that both stations would leave the air before the Act came into operation. It was widely believed that the company had experienced difficulties in gaining sufficient advertising from foreign sources to keep the station going. The Dutch language station, Radio 227, left the air on July 23rd and was followed two weeks later by its twin, when at 10 p.m. on Saturday, August 5th, the programme director of Radio 355, Tony Windsor, took the chair and officiated on the last programme broadcast from the station. All the disc jockeys took part in the programme and in turn wished their many listeners farewell. The moving and nostalgic programme approached its end at midnight. The last commercial was played – for Silexene Paint – and Tony Windsor made a quiet and sincere farewell speech thanking all those who had helped the station, including the Walton lifeboat and coastguard. Managing director, Ted Allbeury, then made an earnest plea for freedom and stated briefly the case for commercial radio. Pointing out the restrictions on personal liberty inherent in the Government's Bill, he reminded listeners that from August 15th, for the first time since the Middle Ages, there would be such a thing as an illegal sermon and that the only subject on which newspapers would not be allowed to write would be offshore radio. He ended with the words 'Good night and God bless'.

After a chorus of Auld Lang Syne the station closed down at 21 minutes past midnight to the sound of the National Anthem. As Radio 355 faded from the air many listeners undoubtedly felt that a very large piece had been cut out of their lives. They felt both sad and deprived at the same time. At 8 a.m. that Sunday morning the offshore tender left the *Laissez Faire* for the last time, with the Radio 355 disc jockeys and engineers aboard. For them, also, a way of life had ended.

August 14th, 1967: last day of transmitting on Radio Scotland and DJs throw the record library overboard. Stevi Merike (extreme left, later to join Caroline and North Sea International) and Tony Allan, also to join Caroline and North Sea, as well as the Peace Ship in the Mediterranean and Edinburgh's Radio Forth.

Wilf Proudfoot of Radio 270 announced in Scarborough: 'We close down at 23.59 hours on August 14th. We have not broken the law up to now, and we don't intend to in the future.' He also disclosed that there had been two offers to buy the ship from which the station broadcast. The prospective purchasers had plans to convert the *Oceaan 7* into a floating night club or discotheque which they hoped to tie up in seaside resorts. Although Radio 270 was closing down, Mr Proudfoot asserted that the battle for commercial radio would continue. 'BBC plans for local radio are illfounded', he alleged.

Radio London and Radio Caroline appeared to be the only stations preparing to defy the Government. Radio London urged the Postmaster-General to 'comply with the spirit of the law, which carries an amendment agreed by both Houses of Parliament that the law should be delayed until a satisfactory land-based alternative has been provided, so as to continue supplying twenty-five million listeners with a popular music service which they have been enjoying for the past three years'. Mr Philip Birch announced that Radio London would continue broadcasting. On the July 28th, however, as Radio 390 left the air, a shock announcement came for Radio London listeners. Mr Birch announced that the station would in fact leave the air on August 15th.

In his statement he said: 'We have repeatedly pointed out that the British public would benefit from independent radio stations operating under licence on land, but the Government has said 'No'. We have received hundreds of thousands of letters from listeners asking us to continue, but we would be operating too close to the law. As we have never yet broken the law, not even to the extent of getting a parking ticket, we have decided to cease broadcasting. Our ship will be up for sale.'

The real reason for the decision to close down the station, the largest in operation and with a claimed audience of nearly twelve million, was widely suspected to be the difficulty experienced by the company in getting foreign advertising. Up until a few days before the announcement the station had hoped to continue, but it discovered that the cumulative effects of the new law would be too great a handicap in selling advertising time to international firms.

Radio Caroline reaffirmed its intention of challenging the Government over the Act by taking any prosecution to the International Court of Human Rights in Strasbourg. In August its administrative headquarters would be removed to Holland and offices opened in Paris, Toronto and Dublin. The Caroline organisation revealed that in June a British director, Mr Philip Solomon, had become an Irish citizen. All the other British members of the Caroline board, including Mr Jocelyn Stevens, owner of *Queen* magazine, had resigned.

At the end of July disc jockeys began announcing that a broadcast would soon be made exposing 'The Private Life of Harold Wilson'. A spokesman for the station would not reveal the contents of the programme but stated that tapes containing 'the truth' about the life of the Prime Minister were being kept in bank vaults in Amsterdam and Dublin ready for broadcasting before August 15th. Ronan O'Rahilly declared: 'I don't have any rule book.' As it happened the tapes were never broadcast. They would most probably have done the station more harm than good in the eyes of the listening public and, wisely, the temptation to tarnish the reputation of its persecutor was resisted by Caroline.

Among other tapes prepared by the station were 'dummy' advertisements that had not been placed or paid for, but which would be broadcast after August 15th, thus making it very difficult for the authorities to prosecute British companies actually using the station, as the genuine advertisements would be concealed among fake ones.

American, Australian, Canadian and South African disc jockeys were standing by to man Caroline's turntables after the 15th, when her British personnel would be forced to go ashore. Two British disc jockeys, Johnnie Walker and 'Admiral' Robbie Dale, however, had decided to stay with the station and risk imprisonment if they ever returned to Britain. If either returned and was arrested, Ronan O'Rahilly declared that he would fight their case to the International Court of Human Rights.

Legal experts, however, doubted seriously the likelihood of a successful appeal to the International Court on the validity of the Act. Unlike America or a country which has a written constitution where the constitutionality of an Act passed by the Legislature can be challenged in the Courts, on the grounds that it is unconstitutional, there is no such procedure in Britain since by definition if an Act is passed by Parliament it must be valid. Even though it may be a bad law it must be valid since we have no written constitution against which to check it. British courts are subject to the overriding authority of Parliament not, as is the United States Supreme Court, the other way round. The sovereignty of Parliament is absolute. The Government is also bound by treaty to outlaw pirate broadcasters and the measures in the Marine Offences Bill had in fact been laid down by international treaty some three years previously.

On the other hand, legislation by a British Parliament for people of British nationality outside the United Kingdom has in the past been governed by the 1931 Statute of Westminister which, in theory, gives Parliament the right to legislate for her overseas dominions only. International waters hardly constitute British overseas dominions. Up until 1967 the law has only assumed jurisdiction over British subjects outside the three-mile limit in the most severe of cases, such as when a murder occurs on board a British ship or when real piracy takes place. In cases of violence which have occurred on board the pirate radio ships the police have firmly rejected any responsibility or jurisdiction. With the Marine Broadcasting (Offences) Act it would appear that on August 15th the police and law courts overnight acquired jurisdiction over British citizens, outwith British territory and on the high seas, on board the ship of another country. In this way it would appear that broadcasting has been categorised with murder and piracy on the high seas; not only a dangerous precedent but a threat to the freedom of British subjects.

Mr Ronald Duncan, the writer who had declared he intended to support offshore stations, stated in the middle of July that he had advised the Director of Public Prosecutions that he would be writing scripts for Radio Caroline. He declared: 'I maintain the Government has no right to tell me I should not write for someone if I wish to. The new law is a dangerous precedent. Heaven knows where it may lead. I hope I will be prosecuted as I think that the Government has to be tested on this matter.'

Ronan O'Rahilly of Radio Caroline put this vital and basic issue of freedom in a somewhat different way in the magazine *Time and Tide*: 'Most of the thinking people in Britain are unaware what the Bill will do. It will make Radio Caroline international; internationally recognised and legal. For the public it does this: if a British shopkeeper sells cigarettes to a Radio Caroline announcer he becomes a criminal. If the Archbishop of Canterbury or Cardinal Heenan or the Chief Rabbi gave a sermon on Radio Caroline, they would become criminals.

'If a journalist writes a newscast or talks on Radio Caroline, he becomes a criminal. If a British advertiser advertises on Radio Caroline, he becomes a criminal. If, on the other hand, the Pope was to write a sermon for Radio Caroline he would not be a criminal, nor would any foreign international figure who wanted to use the medium to voice publicly something he wanted to say. In other words, it is stifling the freedom of the British subject to speak where he likes about what he likes.'

At the beginning of August, with the Marine Broadcasting Offences Act only two weeks away, support for Radio Caroline appeared from an unexpected quarter as the Manx Government, Tynwald, rebelled against the British Government, which had stated that it would extend the Act to the island by an Order in Council. In April the lower house, the House of Keys, had rejected the Bill by an overwhelming majority. The British Government had since replied that, in order to silence Radio Caroline North, the Bill would be extended to the island, against its government's wishes, by an Order signed by the Queen. When it became clear at the beginning of August that this was to be done, indignant Manxmen, jealous of the island's independence, took action.

Principal among them was Mr Roy Macdonald, Chairman of the Manx Broadcasting Commission and Independent Member for Peel, who tabled a resolution rejecting the enforcement by Order in Council of Britain's domestic policies on the people of the island as 'incompatible with the freedom of a self-governing democracy'. The resolution demanded that, if necessary, the United Kingdom Government's decision should be sent for consideration to the United Nations Committee of 24 responsible for looking after the interests of colonial and subject peoples. More than half the members of the House of Keys supported the resolution and the island's Lieutenant-Governor, Sir Peter Stallard, was forced to recall Tynwald to consider it.

Mr Macdonald stated, as news of the impending revolt broke, that the issue was not particularly that of Radio Caroline, but that another Government should try to enforce its domestic policies on the island. The extension of the Marine Offences Act to the Isle of Man, though, clearly would mean a great loss to the islanders. Local businessmen thrived on supplying the ship with stores, and Caroline had not been forgotten for her broadcasting of free advertisements for the island during the long 1966 seamen's strike, which hit the tourist trade very badly. These free advertisements had then been continued by the station and many Manxmen regarded Caroline as an invaluable asset to the island. Any chance of their meekly accepting the British Government's action against the pirate ship had been shattered in July, when the Postmaster-General rejected a plea by the Manx Broadcasting Commission for more power for the land-based Manx Radio. It had been hinted by the Manx Government that if a more powerful Manx Radio were to be allowed, then it would acquiesce in the plans to silence Radio Caroline. Manx Radio could then take the place of the pirate in projecting the island beyond its shores.

Many Manxmen did feel the issue to be a wider one and regarded the extension of the Marine Offences Act to the island as merely the 'thin end of the wedge', fearing that the British Government would then proceed to impose more of its internal laws. With income tax at half the rate on the mainland, no surtax, no stamp duties and not even a dog licence, the Isle would indeed have a great deal to lose if the British Government were to start meddling with its internal affairs. Although closely linked to Britain, the island is supposedly completely independent in the handling of its domestic affairs, while international matters are in the hands of the British Government. For this reason an appeal to the United Nations by the island is not really feasible as, if Britain is responsible for its foreign affairs, then the British Foreign Secretary would have to go to the U.N. to complain about Britain's behaviour!

Ronan O'Rahilly, the head of Radio Caroline, who had made many visits to the island to discuss the station's future with members of the Tynwald and the local people, was jubilant about the turn of events: 'It seems that the courageous little Isle of Man intends to stand up for itself against what amounts to aggression by the British Government. We have warned for months that basic freedoms are at stake in this Bill. It now seems that it is going to be the Isle of Man that is going to be the David who is going te step into the ring against Harold Wilson's Goliath.'

As Tynwald prepared to reassemble to discuss the situation, it was announced on August 3rd that the island's petition, to the Committee of the Privy Council considering the extension of the Marine Offences Act to the island, had been rejected. Accordingly the Order in Council was to be submitted to the Queen for her approval. This only served to heighten the militant mood of the

Radio Caroline North continued broadcasting after the introduction of the Marine Broadcasting Offences Act. She was serviced st her anchorage off the Isle of Man by chartered vessels of the Dutch Wijsmuller tug and salvage company.

indignant island. The Isle of Man Government revealed that it was considering a takeover of the GPO in the island, and tourist board chief Mr Bill Quayle announced that Manx passports would soon be issued for the first time. They would have the title 'British Isles and Islands', but would bear the stamp of the Manx Governor, Sir Peter Stallard. Plans were also submitted to the Manx Government for the creation of a Manx Army by officers of the island's disbanded Territorial Army unit. Some commentators even began to wonder if the break up of the British Commonwealth was to be followed by the break up of the British Isles itself, as the moves for greater freedom and independence intensified.

Such fears, however, proved unjustified when the two Houses of the Manx Parliament met on August 8th. Not altogether unexpectedly, the threat of Manx allegations of Whitehall interference in the island's domestic affairs being dealt with by the United Nations faded after seven hours of stormy and emotional debate in Tynwald. After a day-long joint session the House of Keys and the Legislative Council, the Upper House of the Manx Parliament, could not agree, despite the fact that the leader of the Manx revolt, Mr Roy Macdonald, agreed to drop the clause in his resolution advocating the reference of the problem to the United Nations, and in its place moved that the matter be referred to the Commonwealth Secretariat. The House of Keys voted sixteen to eight in favour of this action, but the ten-strong Legislative Council, comprised mainly of Crown appointed members, voted unanimously against it. It was immediately moved that the House of Keys adjourn to its own chamber, which it did, and there voted to go it alone.

During the fiercely nationalistic debate, speaker after speaker deprecated the British Government's intrusion into the domestic affairs of the island. Mr Macdonald condemned it as 'an arrogant act of aggression. The British Government has no right whatsoever to force on our people criminal legislation which we do not want'.

Referring to Premier Wilson, the Independent Member for Rushen, Mr Howard Simcocks, after complaining how the 'paternalism' of Whitehall had changed into a 'dictatorship' pointed out: 'It is in practice the dictatorship of a single man, and experience has taught us that this is a man whose word most certainly is not his bond.'

One man who had flown in specially to watch the debate had not gone unnoticed by the pressmen, TV commentators and reporters from all over the world who had invaded the island. He

Teenage supporters of the pop ships riot at London's Liverpool Street railway station .....

was the man who had caused all the trouble, Ronan O'Rahilly. Before and after the debate he emphatically declared that Radio Caroline would stay put in Ramsey Bay whether or not the Manx Government was forced to accept the British Legislation. If he was forced to, he intended to challenge the Marine Offences Act by continuing transmissions using British personnel, and any prosecutions would be fought all the way to the Court of Human Rights in Strasbourg.

While on the island he also took the opportunity of visiting the sixteen-strong crew of disc jockeys and seamen on board *Caroline*. A number of them, however, were reported as being less than enthusiastic about being prosecuted, and a request for 'danger money' was turned down by O'Rahilly. Even the Canadians on the ship had their doubts. Disc jockey Jerry King explained: 'We all have our careers to think about'. In the ship's messroom, however, taped to one side of the television set was the optimistic message to the crew and disc jockeys from their boss: 'In 1970 we shall still be broadcasting. Long live Caroline'.

Ronan O'Rahilly still maintained his air of optimistic defiance as August 14th dawned, and the remaining pirate stations, with the exception of Caroline, prepared to leave the air. It was a sad day for dozens of unemployed disc jockeys, for the owners of the stations and, above all, for the millions of listeners who by the next day would be deprived of what had clearly been shown to be their favourite radio programmes.

Radio London was the first to go when it closed down at 3 p.m. in the afternoon. All day long the station broadcast farewell messages from stars, including Ringo Starr of the Beatles, Dusty Springfield, Lulu, Dave Clark and the Animals. In the final broadcast, Mr Philip Birch, the station's managing director, reviewed the three years' history of the station and thanked all those who had helped the station: listeners, disc jockeys, lifeboatmen, coastguards and its 1,027 advertisers. He said: 'I feel that Radio London has done very little harm and an awful lot of good. It has helped Oxfam, the blind, the lifeboat service and other worthwhile causes.' Disc jockey Paul Kaye ended broadcasting very simply: 'The time is 3 p.m. and Radio London is now closing down.' The Big 'L' jingle played for the last time and 266 metres went dead.

As the green-painted former minesweeper was towed away to dry dock in Hamburg, a fantastic welcome awaited the Radio

... as Radio London disc jockeys return home for the last time.

London disc jockeys returning to London from the ship for the last time. Announcements on the station that the disc jockeys would be arriving at Liverpool Street Station at 6.40 p.m. led to thousands of fans congregating there during the afternoon. For almost two hours they took over the station screaming, shouting and chanting 'Big L, Big L', 'Hang Harold' and '266 London – bring it back'.

At 6.40, when diesel locomotive 1768 arrived at Platform 11 from Ipswich, the crowd of teenagers ran riot as they leapt aboard trolleys and climbed piles of parcels to get a better view of the train. When some of the Radio London staff already in the city arrived to greet their colleagues they were immediately chased and beseiged. One, Ian Damon, was quickly recognised and admitted 'We never expected anything like this' as teenage girls pressed their faces against the windows of the station bar in which he was marooned. Keith Skues, one of the station's disc jockeys who had accepted employment with the BBC, was mobbed and pushed to the ground as he left a car to welcome his colleagues. Pursued by a screaming mob he hid in a women's toilet with policemen barring the door.

Meanwhile, disc jockeys Mark Roman, John Peel, Ed Stewart. Paul Kaye, Mike Lennox, Willy Walker and Chuck Blair found themselves beseiged in the train as it was surrounded by thousands of fans who had broken through the barriers set up by the police and station staff. As the mob surged forward girls were trampled, policemen were knocked down and the train windows were smashed. Hundreds boarded the train and raced up and down the corridors searching for the disc jockeys as the Radio London men tried to make their escape to a waiting taxi. As the taxi forced its way slowly through the crowd towards the disc jockeys people banged on the windows and tried to sit on the bonnet. The disc jockeys reached it only with difficulty as girls tore at their hair and clothes, and Mike Lennox was trampled underfoot.

On another part of the platform an angry mob furiously chased a policeman who had confiscated a banner proclaiming: 'Freedom went with Radio London'. One girl summed up the feelings of the crowd: 'This will give that horrible little man Wilson something to think about. All of us prefer the pirates to the BBC.'

The two other stations which left the air shortly before midnight, Radio 270 and Radio Scotland, did so a little more quietly.

Unlike Radio London, when Radio Scotland played itself off the air at midnight with a bagpipe lament it could not show a £100,000 profit, but instead showed a £100,000 loss. Its managing director, Mr T. V. Shields, claimed: 'If the station had been able to continue until the end of the year it would have come out of the red with a little bit to spare. It is a great shame that we have lost the battle – but it was a great adventure.' Similar feelings were expressed by the Radio Scotland disc jockeys. Senior disc jockey Ben Healey, who had taken over from Don Spencer after his resignation, said: 'We have all enjoyed being a pirate team. Life at sea had some drawbacks but was a great experience.'

The day before the station left the air, the disc jockeys boarded the tender leaving one colleague and an engineer to play out the station with the closing shows, tape-recorded in their Glasgow studios. The disc jockeys then joined 2,000 fans on the black night of the 14th at a close-down ball in Glasgow's Locarno Ballroom. There the teenagers, many of them wearing black armbands, gathered to hear the last show relayed from the ship.

Mr Shields declared: "This is the saddest day of my life. I tried everything to keep the station on the air.' He revealed that he had even offered the Government a controlling interest in Radio Scotland in his appeal for a trial licence to broadcast from land. He had not given up hope that Radio Scotland would come on the air again some time and for that reason he intended to keep his organisation together as much as possible.

But for the disc jockeys and the radio ship *Comet* it meant the end. As the ex-lightship was towed to the Fife port of Methil to be stripped of her aerial mast and put up for sale, the disc jockeys found themselves looking for work. Ben Healey started preparing a touring pop show, Jack McLaughlin went to see his agent ... at the Labour Exchange, and Stevi Merike fixed up a job playing records in a club in the South of England. A few weeks later, however, he got a job on Caroline. For all of them it meant starting a new life. This was a chance Mr Tommy Shields was never to have. Those close to him say he never recovered from the closing down of his dream, and six months afterwards he was to die in a Glasgow nursing home aged only 49.

Midnight on Monday the 14th also meant the end for Radio 270 off Bridlington. The previous Saturday three Conservative M.P.s had taken part in a political broadcast from the station which amounted to a searing attack on the Government for closing down the pirates. In the broadcast, the third and last sponsored by the

University of York Conservative Monday Club, Mr John Biggs-Davidson, M.P. for Chigwell, said he did not believe all Labour supporters would be glad about the closing of the pirates. 'Concern for freedom is not confined to one party,' he declared, 'and a voice of freedom will have been silenced when Radio 270 goes off the air.'

Mr Patrick Wall, M.P. for Haltemprice, was equally indignant; 'I think it is monstrous that private enterprise radio stations are being closed, and even more monstrous that the Government are not setting up an adequate alternative to cater for the amusement which many people want to hear. Indeed, I have had more letters on this subject than on any other in the thirteen years I have been M.P. for Haltemprice.'

The next day it looked as though Radio 270 was to be prematurely forced off the air, not by the Postmaster-General but by jellyfish! Transmissions became distorted and the station went off the air a number of times as giant jellyfish were sucked into the intakes, which provided water to cool the generators. The battle against the jellyfish was won, however, but not the one against the Postmaster-General; 24 hours later at 90 seconds to midnight Radio 270 left the air.

On the North-east coast the 14th dawned wet, windy and miserable with a Force 8 gale whipping the sea into foam around the 270 ship *Oceaan 7*, which plunged and rolled at anchor. The storm meant that the station's off-duty disc jockeys, who had planned to join their colleagues on board the ship for the last day's broadcasting, were left kicking their heels in Scarborough as it was impossible to board the small converted herring drifter in the heavy seas. Despite the weather, seventy eight-shilling-a-trip holiday-makers boarded the 250-ton pleasure ship *Coronia* for a mid-morning trip out to the Radio 270 ship. Adults and children alike leaned over the rail of the pleasure boat and stared fascinated at the death throes of the tossing pirate ship.

The success of Radio 270 spoke for itself. According to a National Opinion Poll taken in June, a year after transmissions commenced, the station had captured 4¾ million listeners, more than half of whom were over the age of 24. In fourteen months it had taken in £100,000 worth of advertising which had paid off the initial expenditure of nearly £75,000 plus the running expenses of £750 a week. Although the station had no outstanding debts, it had made no profit, no salaries had been paid to its directors and no dividends to its shareholders. Given another year the station would really have paid dividends to those who had so bravely pioneered it.

As the last evening's transmissions went out over the air the disc jockeys on board the radio ship were surprised to see an RAF Air-Sea Rescue helicopter hover overhead, and at 9.15 p.m. disc jockey Ross Randell announced over the air that the helicopter had just dropped recorded farewell messages from three of the disc jockeys shorebound in Scarborough. Unfortunately the tapes, wrapped in a plastic bag, had fallen in the sea, but he thanked the RAF and invited the crew of the helicopter out for a drink. Unknown to those on the ship, Mike Hayes, deputy programme director, had arranged the drop with a friend who was a pilot at RAF Leconfield and he had enclosed with the tapes a note saying: 'Do not (repeat not) mention the drop'. As the note finished up in the sea with the tapes, though, the announcement was made and did, in fact, have unfortunate consequences for the helicopter's crew. An RAF inquiry into the 25-mile flight to the *Oceaan 7* was instituted, and it was said that the Prime Minister himself had demanded to know its results. Mr Wilson, on holiday in the Scilly Isles, was reliably reported to be furious that a Government agency should appear to have assisted a pirate radio ship less than three hours before Government legislation to put it off the air came into force.

The station's last programme from 10 p.m. until midnight brought back many memories for millions of listeners. All the disc jockeys took part as well as the captain, crew and technicians who talked about themselves and their time on the offshore stations. Programme director Vince 'Rusty' Allen, who had been with 270 for nine months after leaving Radio Essex, sat in on the final programme playing all the 270 theme tunes and jingles. As the midnight deadline drew near a farewell message was played from the chairman of the company, Mr Leonard Dale, who said he hoped to serve the listeners again from a land-based station. In his thanks he included the Air-Sea Rescue team at Leconfield for their help when the captain fell ill and when a crew member had an accident. He ended with the heartfelt words: 'It is my sorry duty to say goodbye.'

A telegram from the managing director, Mr Wilf Proudfoot, on holiday in Spain, was read: To all 270 listeners and staff -we will return.' Vince Allen then said: 'Oh, dear, there are only five minutes left – I don't know whether I'm coming or going. I guess I must be cracking up or something.'

He then played the last record of Vera Lynn singing 'Land of Hope and Glory' and closed down the station. 'I'm sure going to miss you one helluva lot. I hope some day soon we'll meet again on the air.... God bless and goodbye.' After the National Anthem the transistors clutched in the hands of teenagers in the streets of Bridlington crackled vacantly. Radio 270 had gone – and an integral part of their lives for over a year had gone with it.

At 1.15 a.m. a small fishing boat drew into the quay at Bridlington and disembarked its cargo of disc jockeys and technicians from Radio 270. A great shout went up from the 600 teenagers assembled there as Vince Allen stepped ashore carrying two suitcases, and police had to grapple with girls who rushed the disc jockeys.

The next day the radio ship berthed at Whitby watched by large crowds, and Mr Dennis Tuckley, a local estate agent, received one of his strangest commissions. He announced 'We are offering the ship lock, stock, barrel and aerial.' The advertisement which appeared in papers in the North-east read: We are instructed by the pirates to offer a useful ship known as *Oceaan 7*. It is fully equipped with radio transmitting equipment with 10 Kilowatt output, extensive crew and disc jockey accommodation. Would make an ideal floating home. Everyone would hear your hi-fi. The price is £12,500 o.n.o. Many records included.

At one minute past midnight on August 15th two pirate radio ships, however, were still flying the Jolly Roger in defiance of the British Government. Radio Caroline North off Ramsey, Isle of Man and Radio Caroline South, off the East coast, stayed on the air after one minute's silence to mark the end of the days when pirates ruled the waves. From the Caroline ships at midnight came the civil rights battle hymn 'We Shall Overcome' and the new identification 'Radio Caroline International'. British disc jockeys Johnnie Walker and 'Admiral' Robbie Dale continued to broadcast despite the Marine Offences Act which now made them liable to two years in jail and a £400 fine. As the station played announcements for Broadside Free Radio Movement slogans including 'Make Wilson Walk the Plank' and 'Keelhaul Harold' went out over the air. (The Broadside Free Radio Movement had been founded in April 1967 among Oxford and Cambridge undergraduates by 21-year-old Cambridge history student Peter Philipson. Organisation on a national basis began in June when headquarters were set up in London and the

Movement secured airtime on Caroline. By the time the Marine
Offences Act went through Broadside claimed a membership of
80,000. The next month, however, it encountered serious financial
difficulties and collapsed in October with debts in the region of
£500. The Free Radio Association then took over the membership
of Broadside creating a single, unified free radio organisation with
more than 100,000 members.)

Ronan O'Rahilly breathed defiance: 'We fight on. The British
Government can do their damndest, but they won't sink us.'

Earlier in the day crowds in Ramsey had cheered five rebel disc
jockeys who left for the M.V. *Caroline* on board their tender *Offshore
III*. One, 21-year-old Dee Harrison from New Brighton, declared:
'We believe in free radio and are prepared to risk prosecution.' The
other disc jockeys were Mark Sloan, who had been with Caroline
South, British Martin Kayne, Canadian Don Allen and Australian
Jimmy Gordon.

But when the tender returned it did so with three disc jockeys
who were not prepared to risk prosecution – Tony Prince, Dave
Lee-Travis and David Williams, who all held British passports.
Also, Canadian Jerry King left the ship.

Radio Caroline South also lost some of its English disc jockeys.
Newsreader Gerry Burke left the ship before the Act came into
operation. Gerry decided to quit because of the threat of prosecution
if he attempted to land in Britain to see his wife and two young
children. Robbie Dale and Johnnie Walker who remained on board
the *Mi Amigo* faced a tough time. No longer would the tender be
allowed out from England, and the journey from Amsterdam to
the ship would take nearly twenty hours. If the two ever returned
to Britain they would risk prosecution and accordingly resigned
themselves to exile. Explained 22-year-old Johnnie Walker: 'It has
meant moving to Holland and not being able to visit my parents
in Hampton-in-Arden, Warwickshire . . . but this has become a
matter of principle.'

From the station's newly opened headquarters in Amsterdam,
Ronan O'Rahilly announced his plans to 'internationalise' Caroline.
Offices had been set up in Toronto, Paris and New York's Panam
Building. He also disclosed that the Foreign Minister of 'a certain
country' had offered Caroline's staff and disc jockeys citizenship,
and announced to the surprise of pressmen that an appeal would be
made to the United Nations: 'I think there is a good chance of the

*Two who carried on and became criminals under the anti-pirate law:
Johnnie Walker of Caroline (left) and Spangles Muldoon (alias Chris
Carey) also of Caroline, but who later went on to Radio North Sea
and Radio Luxembourg.*

United Nations condemning the British Government's action.' With a view to this he was visiting several foreign countries 'very soon'.

At the same time as Ronan O'Rahilly announced his plans, the European Commission for Human Rights fired a broadside at his intention of appealing to it. In a statement the Commission said: 'Mr O'Rahilly may be thinking of basing a case on Article 10 of the Commission's convention. This states that everyone shall have the right of freedom of expression, including the right to hold opinions and to receive and impart information and ideas without interference by public authority, and regardless of frontiers. But the article goes on: "This shall not prevent states from requiring the licensing of broadcasting, television or cinema enterprises".' The likelihood of any success in appealing to the Commission now became even more remote as that body seemed to have prejudged the issue.

The Caroline organisation claimed the day after the Act came into operation that international advertisers had booked £300,000 worth of advertising; enough to keep the station going for six months. The station continued to pump out advertisements, many for British companies and products and which were plainly 'dummy' advertisements meant to confuse the GPO monitoring the station's transmissions.

As the Marine Offences Act lays down heavy penalties for any British firm placing advertising with a pirate station, many firms were clearly embarrassed by fake advertisements. Horlicks, Nestles and Beechams all promptly denied that they were providing advertisements either from Britain or their offices outside the country.

A Beecham spokesman said: 'All our contracts with the station ended last November. All they are doing is using old commercials and putting them out without our permission.'

But a Caroline official denied that they were giving any free advertising at all and claimed that all advertisements were paid for. 'The contracts for the international products we are advertising were entered into before the Marine Offences Act. Some of the contracts are for more than a year and have been prepaid. We can say that some British firms have bought advertising space in defiance of what they feel is an iniquitous Act.'

Meanwhile confused GPO officials were reported to be listening to the broadcasts in an attempt to sort out the real advertisements from the fake ones.

Among Caroline's new, genuine advertisers were American religious broadcasters who had bought two hours of time per day and were widely regarded as having saved the station from extinction.

Radio ships go to rest: after the introduction of legislation against the offshore broadcasters the M.V. Galaxy (Radio London ship) was towed to her anchorage on the German North Sea Canal.

Radio ships go to rest: the Radio Scotland Ship was berthed at Vlissingen in Holland.

Radio ships go to rest: after being towed off the seas by the Wijsmuller Salvage Company, the Caroline ship ended of rotting in Amsterdam Harbour.

While it was obviously illegal for British advertisers to use Radio Caroline South on August 14th, confusion existed with regard to Caroline North off the Isle of Man as the Order in Council extending the Marine Offences Act to the island had not been delivered. So it was business as usual for the pirates, and its Dutch tender took out mail, papers, water, fresh milk and supplies. The Dutch skipper of the tender stated that he intended to go on supplying *Caroline* from the island until the Order arrived. A Manx Government spokesman also gave the assurance that no one aboard *Caroline* had committed an offence and neither had anyone who supplied her.

The mate on board the *Caroline* tender *Offshore III*, 29-year-old Manxman Harry Maddrell, told pressmen that he was ready to go into 'exile' to keep supplies running to the pirate ship when the Order was signed. 'I am ready to go and live in Ireland where the new supply base will be set up. I realize that when I set foot on British soil again I may be liable to prosecution, I am prepared to take the risk. There are principles involved.'

The fact that the Act had not been extended to the island did not prevent the GPO from placing an advertisement in the island's newspaper headed: "The Marine, etc. Broadcasting (Offences) Act, 1967 – how it may affect you'. It listed the new offences under the Act and set out the penalties which could be imposed upon the Isle of Man residents. The ill-timed advertisement served only to further exacerbate relations between the British and Manx Governments. The Speaker of the House of Keys, Mr Charles Kerruish, described it as 'an insult to the Manx people'.

The advertisement was in fact only one of many placed in no less than 70 newspapers, magazines and journals. The GPO spent £1,200 on a full-page in the American magazine *Time*; presumably in a bid to discourage potential American advertisers on Caroline. Other expensive advertisements were placed with *The Times*, *The Financial Times* and *Life*. The costs of these three alone ran into many thousands. Not only did the advertisements list the dangers of contravening the Act, but announced that the forthcoming BBC music programme would, 'the Government believes, meet the needs of these audiences'. Lavish expenditure, it may be thought, in order to tell people what they want.

As the Act came into force around the rest of Britain, Mr Kerruish and Sir Peter Stallard, Lieutenant-Governor of the island, were invited to the Home Office for talks with Miss Alice Bacon, the Minister of State at the Home Office.

On August 17th the talks took place, but Miss Bacon gave no concessions to the island on the issue of Radio Caroline, and told the delegation that the Order in Council would take effect on September 1st. Not surprisingly, the meeting left the island even more bitter than before. At Ronaldsway Airport, on his return to the island, Mr Kerruish said that relations between the two governments were now 'at their lowest-ever ebb'. He continued: 'I think that the island now has to demand an increase in its measure of independence without going fully independent. This could be achieved by associate-status in the Commonwealth. This would put the Isle of Man in a situation similar to the Caribbean Islands. This would give the islanders the right of independence if they so desired.'

On the decision of the House of Keys to refer the problem of the Marine Offences Act to the Commonwealth Secretariat he stated: 'I am saddened to think that the British Government should see fit, in the light of the representations we have made to the Commonwealth Secretariat, to go ahead and impose the Order in Council, while our appeal is still being considered. I wonder now whether the appeal will be allowed to reach the Commonwealth Secretariat by the Home Office.'

Asked if Radio Caroline would have to come off the air on September 1st he replied: 'As far as I am concerned there is no question of Radio Caroline coming off the air then.' In reply to questions on whether the station would be invited on land, he said that it would not, as that would be contrary to the wishes of the British Government. He added, however, that such an action 'would be welcomed by many Manx people'.

He did divulge, though, that the Manx Government was considering buying the island's legal, land-based Manx Radio. Preliminary discussions had already taken place between Government representatives and the station's owners – Mr R. L. Meyer's Isle of Man Broadcasting Co. and Pye Radio. Agreement on this was reached at the beginning of 1968.

As September 1st approached the GPO said that it would provide the evidence required for any prosecution in connection with Caroline North, and then ask the island's Attorney General or Chief Constable to take the necessary action. There seemed little doubt that the Marine Offences Act would be successfully imposed on the island, and plans for Caroline North to evade it were swung into action by the Caroline organisation who prepared to service and supply the ship from Greenore, the port owned by Ronan O'Rahilly's father in Eire. Ronan O'Rahilly stated: 'It will make no difference, apart from a little inconvenience.'

As Radio Caroline moved its offices to Amsterdam, it was known that the Dutch Minister of Culture, Mrs Marga Klompe, had before her plans for a national commercial radio service starting in 1968. This almost certainly appeared to indicate that in 1968 Holland would come into line with the Strasbourg Convention on broadcasting and introduce a Bill similar to the Marine Offences Act.

Caroline's own position in January and February of 1968 became increasingly insecure with legislation being proposed by the Dutch Government, loss of advertising and difficulties over insurance of the two pirate ships. The swashbuckling days when pirates ruled the waves indeed appeared to be drawing to a dose.

On Sunday, March 3rd, Radio Caroline South began transmissions as normal at 5 a.m. Shortly after 5 a.m. the Dutch tug Titan, owned by the Wijsmuller salvage company, hove to off the *Mi Amigo* and her Captain went aboard the pirate ship. Together with four crew members he burst into the studio and ordered chief engineer 'Ray' to 'close down, we're going to Amsterdam'. As the disc jockey prepared to tell listeners about the close down, the burly tugboat captain emphasised the order by grabbing the microphone cable and ripping it out of the panel. At 5.20 a.m., in the middle of the record, Radio Caroline International went dead.

In this way the last pirate ship was closed down – by an act of real piracy – as the Dutch Wijsmuller company hijacked simultaneously the North and South Caroline ships. While startled disc jockeys and engineers on the *Mi Amigo* were herded into the lounge and locked in by the tough Dutch pirates, off the Isle of Man the Wijsmuller tug *Utrecht* put a line aboard the M.V. *Caroline*. On both ships the crystals were ripped out of the ship-to-shore transmitters, the bridges locked and a long tow began. Not before, however, quick thinking disc jockeys and engineers on the South ship managed to destroy technical information and throw vital files overboard.

In an obviously carefully planned operation, which came as a complete surprise to the Caroline organisation on shore, the South ship was towed north up the East Anglian coast where a rendezvous was made with two other tugs. An erratic zig-zag course across the North Sea, to confuse mystified observers, was then followed. Twenty-four hours later the *Mi Amigo* was towed into Amsterdam where the M.V. *Caroline* later joined her.

The disc jockeys and engineers were puzzled and angry; millions of listeners were even more bewildered; Caroline's owners put a brave face on the situation and promised that the station would be back after repairs and reinsurance. As his staff were paid off, a broken O'Rahilly looked for a possible replacement for the home of the British 'pop' music explosion.

Poetic justice indeed; 'pirates' silenced by ... piracy. For her many faithful listeners, the disappearance of Radio Caroline from the airwaves became more mysterious with the passing of the months. Soon after entering Amsterdam harbour, the Caroline ships were moved to the Verschure shipyards, where they were berthed side by side. It gradually emerged that they were to become the centre of a legal battle over alleged non-payment of dues and, with writs nailed to the masts of the *Caroline* and the *Mi Amigo*, it was obvious that the 259 spot was to remain silent.

Soon after the enforced closure of the station, the Caroline organisation began to disintegrate. Ronan O'Rahilly's position had already become somewhat tenuous and, in the last few months of Caroline's life, his role had been relegated to that of a mere spokesman. Mr Philip Solomon, managing director of Major Minor records which had received so much exposure in the last few months of the station's life, had taken over control of the Caroline network.

Splinter groups of the organisation made a number of abortive attempts to refloat the station from other ships. In April, Caroline personnel, including O'Rahilly who was checked in at a local hotel in the name of O'Connor, made a number of trips to Whitby, where the Radio 270 ship *Oceaan 7*, was berthed and up for sale. The plan was to refloat *Caroline* from the small Dutch lugger on Easter Sunday but, at the last minute, plans fell through. Advance publicity in the press was blamed officially for the failure but, in fact, negotiations over the sale of the ship broke down, and rumours widely circulating suggested a daring attempt at blackmail and trickery. A number of wild schemes were embarked upon; would-be pirates in London offered strong-arm men money to go to Whitby and steal the *Oceaan 7* and, in May, generators and radio equipment were landed on the Knock John Fort in the Thames, from which Radio Essex had broadcast. Although this station had been prosecuted for broadcasting from the fort, which lies within territorial waters, it was reckoned that the authorities could be held off. Those involved, however, thought better of it – and just in time. Within an hour of removing their equipment from the fort Thames river police had surrounded and boarded it.

The last of the British pirates silent, Radio Veronica became looked upon by more and more British listeners as a very real alternative to Radio One. In fact. Radio Veronica's Hilversum office began to receive so many letters from English listeners that it decided, in June, to introduce some English programming into the station's format. 'Admiral' Robbie Dale was put under contract to broadcast an evening show four times a week and the innovation proved a great success with British listeners.

The gap left on the pop scene by Caroline's demise soon became apparent. At the end of March *Disc* predicted: 'Expect many of the small independent record companies to fold now there is no pirate radio.' Undoubtedly, the British pop music explosion, the pop culture of the sixties and the phenomenon of 'Swinging London' were attributable to the offshore stations, which injected exciting new sounds, zest and vitality into the pop scene, gave so many opportunities to unknown artists and fostered the growth of the small record companies. When Caroline came on the air in 1964, the market was monopolised by a few large record companies; the small ones, in fact, occupied only two per cent of it. With the help of the pirates, small record companies destroyed this monopoly and, in three years, managed to corner more like twenty per cent of the market.

The supposed replacement for the pirates. Radio One, was continually alleged, in pop circles, to be doing its utmost to kill the whole scene. In July, *Top Tops*, referring to 'that great current affairs programme, Radio One', forecast: 'By the time 1969 gets round we'll be lucky if there's such a thing as teenybopper music left. The forces of the establishment will have drowned us for ever. Radio One and Jimmy Young will be the masters.' In the same issue, one of the country's leading record producers, Steve Rowland, producer of the Dave Dee and Herd records, lashed out at 'the fuddy-duddy attitude of the BBC which refuses to play anything that does not comply with their idea of a record that makes a "nice programme" ... nobody wants to know non-chart names ... I feel very much like getting out'.

July 1968: almost one year after the British Government introduced the Marine Broadcasting (Offences) Act, When Pirates Ruled The Waves, the first book on the British pop 'pirates', was published amidst controversy. The legal situation surrounding a book in support of offshore broadcasters was a confused one, under the terms of the Act, and prosecution appeared possible after the Office of the Director of Public Prosecutions read it and declined to give any guarantee against it. Nevertheless, the book sold out within two weeks and there was no prosecution.

The offshore radio stations not only demonstrated a need for commercial radio, but also the central part played by radio broadcasting in the lives of young people today. Pop music, and the vast industry which surrounds it, has, in recent years, assumed an ever increasing importance in the lives of teenagers; for many, indeed, it has become the focal point of their lives. The stimulus for this trend, without a doubt, came from the offshore broadcasters who, during their short reign, reached the hearts of millions of young people, influenced them and brought a great deal of pleasure into their lives. As such the so-called pirates might be regarded as an important sociological phenomenon whose role in the lives of millions has, at best, been under-estimated and, at worst, totally ignored.

It is fashionable in certain circles to deride and belittle pop music. Both its sound and the appearance of those who perform it frequently come under violent attack and fears about its corrupting effect on young people are voiced. Sweeping condemnations of pop music all too often smack of a combination of intellectual arrogance, doubtful value judgements and an unwillingness, even a refusal, to try and understand an Allen culture.

But, nevertheless, the importance attributed to pop music in the lives of the majority of younger citizens cannot be denied. For many of them life is dull at the factory bench or on the assembly line, others have emotional and other problems which, at this time of life, can be at their most intense. Pop is for them something very positive and valuable. The pirate stations as disseminators of this sub-culture brought some joy where there may have been sadness, brought zest where there previously existed dullness and injected a little more excitement into their lives. Pirate radio, in fact, began to assume an importance almost as great as the very pop it propagated; the highly individual disc jockeys could be identified as symbols of the fight against authority.

Not surprisingly, the closure of the offshore stations by the government was seen by many of its young listeners as yet one more assault upon their much criticised interests and attitudes.

There now remained just one offshore radio ship for European listeners. Remarkably, this survivor, Radio Veronica, had outlasted all those stations which had broadcast from off the British coasts and she was to be the first of a number of Dutch-based radio ships. The story of Radio Veronica is no less fascinating than that of other offshore broadcasters.

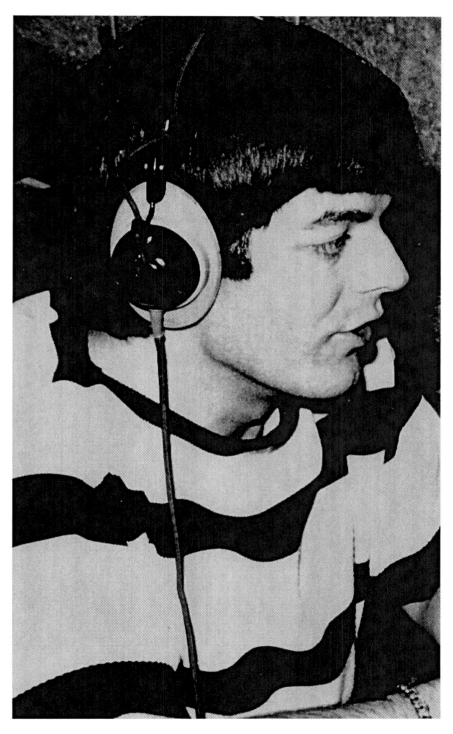

The DJs who fled to the legal BBC: Tony Blackburn rapidly became the 'darling' of Radio One.

The DJs who fled to the legal BBC: Ed 'Stew Pot' Stewart found a niche in Radio One's children's spots.

The DJs who fled to the legal BBC: Simon Dee (here in the Radio Caroline studio) enjoyed a meteoric rise (and fall) with his own TV talk show.

12

The *Veronica* saga

The story of Radio Veronica, that most durable pirate of them all, begins back in 1959 at a meeting of radio dealers in Amsterdam's Krasnapolsky Hotel. One of the wealthier Dutch dealers, Lambertus Marie Slootmans, called the meeting, principally to group all the dealers together for the purpose of fighting a German manufacturer, who was prosecuting retailers for selling his products below recommended prices. But a more daring venture grew out of that meeting on October 15, 1959.

Earlier in the year, Slootmans had been in contact with a man named Max Lewin, who was on the right-wing fringe of Dutch politics and who was interested in putting a radio transmitter on board a ship outside territorial waters. He saw both commercial and political possibilities in such a plan.

At the meeting that evening the two came into contact with a plastics dealer, Henricus Oswald. He, like a few others, had watched with interest the activities of Europe's first offshore radio ship, Radio Mercur, which lay off the Danish coast. He had nurtured in his mind the idea of such a station off the coast of the Netherlands. When the plan was put forward at the meeting, however, it did not meet with particular enthusiasm. Most of those there thought the plan fantastic, but they agreed, in principle, to go ahead with an investigation into the possibilities. The initials VRON (Vrije Radio Omroep Nederland) were adopted for the project, and the enthusiastic three had a busy few days before the next meeting, held on October 19. At the next meeting, 19 people agreed to invest about five hundred pounds each in the idea and plans went ahead.

Oswald took responsibility for the technical side and Slootmans was appointed financial manager. In the meeting, though as yet taking no part in the proceedings, was a textile manufacturer from Hilversum named Dirk Verweij. He saw the immense possibilities in the project but, for the moment, was content to wait in the wings for his chance.

Other men who were later to be dramatically involved in offshore radio became associated with the VRON. Amsterdam night-club owner Kees Manders was appointed 'artistic director' after applying for the position by telephone. He resigned only two weeks later, alleging Oswald, Slootmans and Lewin to be hopelessly incompetent; events were to prove his allegations only too true.

Shortly afterwards, Lewin left the team after Slootmans called a press conference and announced that he was 'unsuitable' and, therefore, to be dismissed. Lewin claimed it was because he knew rather more about the activities of Slootmans and Oswald than they cared to admit. Whichever was the truth the would-be 'pirates' had begun to fall out.

Shareholders gathered once again in the Krasnapolsky Hotel on November 16 and the first of a series of elaborate deceptions on the part of Slootmans and Oswald was perpetrated. The two announced to those present that they were to listen to the first test broadcast of the VRON. There was an amazed silence as Oswald turned a dial on a radio and the speaker crackled into life.

Good evening, this is the Vrije Radio Omroep Nederland with a test transmission from a ship on the North Sea . . . we wish you good reception and will be back shortly. The shareholders were both amazed and delighted. They would not have been quite so pleased, however, had they known that the transmission actually came from Oswald's offices but 200 yards from the hotel!

Two advertising men from The Hague now entered the picture, Will J. Hoordijk and J. Beeuwkes. They also had planned to set up their own radio station but lacked the capital. They had, though, discovered what they regarded as the perfect ship for such an enterprise, an old German light-ship which lay in harbour in Emden. They approached the men from the VRON. Slootmans and Oswald were keen on the idea of a lightship, and Hoordijk and Beeuwkes were promptly appointed advertising managers. A few days later Slootmans and shareholder Phil Krant from Bussum drove to Emden.

There they looked over the former German liphtship *Borkum Riff* which was built in 1911. A sturdily built ship, designed for lying at anchor over long periods, it was indeed ideal for the purpose and, a few days later, Slootmans purchased it on behalf of the shareholders for 63,000 guilders (about seven thousand pounds).

Meanwhile, Oswald had started to build the transmitter. Work went ahead in a German shipyard to prepare the old ship for her new role, a crew was laid on and, inevitably, the money began to run out. At this stage a newcomer entered the project, a man destined to become a central fieure in the Veronica saga; Norbert Jurgens. Jurgens and Dirk Verweij's brother, Hendrik A. 'Bul' Verweij, occupied themselves with the search for a 'flag of convenience' under which to float their radio ship. Initially, they met with a lack of success.

Representatives of the Panamanian Government in The Hague and Germany were approached fruitlessly. Eventually, however, the Panamanian Embassy in London agreed to provide a flag – at a price.

Simultaneously, shareholders set up a company, the Anstalt Veronica, in the tiny European country and tax-haven of Liechtenstein. Then the first of a number of setbacks was experienced. In December, as the transmitter was about to be removed to the ship in Emden, Oswald's offices in the centre of Amsterdam were raided by police and a Dutch PTT (Post Office) official named D. H. Neuteboom. Under Article 20 of the Dutch Telegraph and Telephone Law, pieces of transmitting equipment were seized. Oswald appeared indignant and, naturally, had to ask the exasperated shareholders for more money for a new transmitter. The facts of the incident, as they came out later, are a little different than they appeared at the time. Oswald himself tipped off the authorities that there was a transmitter on the premises and, when they arrived, they merely removed a lot of completely useless and worthless radio spares. Oswald duly presented himself to the shareholders with the sorry tale of how their transmitter had been seized and was given further funds.

Work on board the ship from late November until May, 1960, was supervised by Jurgens. By February, everything was ready for the installation of the transmitter and, on the 9th of the month, one of Oswald's relatives and an employee set off in a Mercedes delivery van from Amsterdam – destination Emden. In the back was the transmitter. Oswald spread the rumour that they would cross over the border near Groningen when, in fact, at the last minute, the drivers were instructed to go by another route.

Five hundred yards inside the German border, the van was overtaken by a police motorcyclist and requested to return to Dutch territory. As soon as it drove back over the border, the occupants were detained and the ubiquitous Mr Neuteboom arrived and announced he intended to confiscate the van and its cargo.

The transmitter was taken to PTT headquarters in The Hague and nothing further was seen or heard of it. The authorities revealed they acted on a tip-off, but where it came from was a matter of mystery.

The bulk of the organisational work was being carried out by Jurgens, Bul Verweij and Slootmans, while Oswald set about the construction of a new transmitter. Understandably, the shareholders were becoming concerned about progress on the technical side of the project, and Jurgens and Oswald decided on another deception to keep flagging spirits high. One night Jurgens took a transmitter to a deserted island on Lake Loosdrecht near his home. Shareholders were informed that another test transmission from their radio ship on the North Sea was to be made and, sure enough, they once again heard a beautiful and clear signal.

By April, however, Oswald was at last making progress. He drove to Denmark a number of times for consultations with the engineers of Radio Mercur, Europe's first offshore radio station. Unexpected opposition came from the German Funkamt in Hamburg (Post Office) who advised, in a shock letter, that the installation of a radio transmitter on board the *Borkum Riff* was an offence under German law. The would-be 'pirates' pressed on regardless and ignored the warning.

By the middle of the month arrangements were sufficiently far advanced for the converted lightship to leave harbour. The English tug *Guardsman* was ordered from Copenhagen, but, as it arrived in Emden, the owners of the radio ship were informed that it could not leave harbour; the papers were not in order. After a chase over half of Germany, in search of a senior Customs Officer the papers were stamped and everything seemed in order . . . until the harbourmaster chained up the ship 'on the orders of the Dutch consul in Emden'. Oswald telephoned the consul, who informed him he was acting on orders received from The Hague. But the Dutch authorities had made the mistake of assuming that the ship was to fly the flag of *The Netherlands*. Oswald informed the German officials that the ship was flying a South American flag, was owned by a South American company, and that he was acting as an agent for the Anstalt Veronica of Liechtenstein. The whole matter was nothing to do with the Netherlands. As a follow-up, an official of the Panamanian Embassy in London took up contact with the German authorities and protested vehemently at the detention of one of his country's ships. Bonn gave instructions to the Emden harbourmaster to withdraw the injunction against the *Borkum Riff*.

The English tug took up the tow and prepared to take the ship out onto the open sea. Once out of the harbour a Dutch police

1562 Kcs. - Output 5 Kw.

QSL

Zeedijk 27 a, Hilversum (Holland)

The two Radio Veronica ships: the first ship converted lightship
Borkum Riff *(above), and converted fishing trawler* Nordeney
(right) which took over later.

patrol boat took up position behind and followed closely. On board everyone was tense. From above, Oswald watched anxiously from a small plane.

Approximately seven miles west of the Dutch seaside resort of Noordwijk the Guardsman released her tow. On shore, jubilant shareholders broke out the champagne as the first real test broadcast came from Veronica. The power was only one kilowatt and the first programming very amateurish. Nevertheless, the reception was, in more ways than one, surprisingly good.

Many difficulties were experienced in the initial stages. There was no regular tender for the ship; at times crew members had to stay on board for weeks and supplies ran low. Once, Phil Krant had to go out in a private plane and drop supplies packed in a drum over the ship.

Another time, Jurgens took his speedboat from Lake Loosdrecht and went out to sea from the beach at Scheveningen. All went well until the small boat reached the shore again; some of its occupants had time to make off, but Jurgens was detained by two policemen. Customs officials arrived and Jurgens was charged with smuggling four persons into the country! After prolonged questioning he was allowed to go and, months later, was fined just ten guilders for the offence.

Soon after broadcasts commenced there came the predictable complaints from the PTT that the station was causing serious interference. It was alleged that the station was interfering with fishing vessels, pilot boats, coastal radio stations and rescue services, but the authorities refused an offer by Oswald to discuss the matter.

Official action against Veronica was taken on a number of fronts. Recognition as an 'n.v.' (limited company) was refused; Oswald's passport was withdrawn and the telephones of the directors were tapped.

The last straw came when a jamming station apeared on Veronica's wavelength, 185 metres. Oswald and a team of engineers tracked the jammer down to a Dutch naval radio station. The PTT prevented publication of the location in the press, but the newspaper columns contained a flood of indignation from Veronica listeners. Ten thousand young people in the Hague signed a petition in protest.

On May 7, in retaliation for alleged interference, radio communication between the *Borkum Riff* and the land was denied by the coastal radio station at Scheveningen.

On May 13, Radio Veronica ceased transmissions on 185 metres and returned two days later on 192 metres. The station was no longer disturbed.

244

The tender draws alongside the Radio Veronica ship amid a shower of spray.

The sophisticated anchoring system aboard the Veronica ship.

But the station's difficulties had only just begun. The Panamanian consul in Rotterdam found out that London had granted his country's flag to the Veronica ship and, on May 19, a telegram arrived from Panama demanding that the ship cease broadcasting. Jurgens, however, was unabashed: 'We are not bothered,' he claimed, 'we have a drawer full of flags.' In June the flag was changed, but the new one was not flown. The gentlemen of Veronica wisely kept their mouths shut.

By the summer of 1960, the general position was improving. There were more listeners and the advertisers were becoming interested. Hoordijk and Beeuwkes, busy on that aspect, brought in their first clients; Van Nelle tobacco and Lexington cigarettes. By the winter of 1961-62, after a few spectacular campaigns, the station was established as a recognised advertising medium. By this time a dramatic and lasting organisational change had been made. The management was now firmly in the hands of the three brothers Verweij; Dirk, Bul and Jaap, textile wholesalers and manufacturers from Hilversum. The previous November the station had run heavily into debt, even though things were just getting off the ground. The astute brothers saw their opportunity. They pumped money into the almost bankrupt station and set about running it in a more efficient and businesslike manner.

Slootmans was no longer involved in the day-to-day operations and Dirk Verweij dispensed with the services of Hoordijk and Beeuwkes as advertising representatives. Oswald also was dismissed. The Verweijs immediately set about building a respectable public image for the station, something which they were to carefully nurture for all of ten years before on" single foolish act was to discredit it completely. However, that was in the future. Taxes and copyrights were paid, heed was paid to customs and immigration formalities, and an efficient staff of over 40 people was employed. In the Spring of 1961 Radio Veronica acquired her own tender, the converted fishing vessel *Ger Anna*.

Advertising began to build up and was accepted by the station, with the exception of religion or politics. In Holland the two are interlinked at every level in society and the cautious Verweijs wished to avoid treading on any toes. Request records, contests, special programmes and non-stop popular music were all a novelty to the Dutch audience, accustomed to the output from the State transmitters.

In 1962 the Swedish and Danish offshore radio stations. Radio Nord, Radio Syd and Radio Mercur, were outlawed by the

The studio on board the Veronica ship. Note the reel-to-reel tape machines used in the 1960s and 1970s

Scandinavian governments. In July, 1962, an interdepartmental commission was set up by the Dutch Government to work on a bill to outlaw Radio Veronica, by making it an offence for Dutch citizens to work for the station. Things looked black for a while.

Then one of Holland's most popular journalists, Henk van der Meyden, initiated a campaign to save the station. The result was an overwhelming vote of confidence in the little ship Veronica, and a condemnation of the official attitude. No action was taken. In July, 1962, a foundation 'Vrienden van Veronica' was also set up. Many thousands of listeners paid a guilder to join and three months later 50,000 guilders (over £5,000) was presented to charity from this money. There were still criticisms. Some journalists alleged members of the committee personally made money from the organisation and one charity, the Queen Wilhelmina Fund, refused over £1,000 – yet it had just accepted the legacy of a Hague prostitute. Blonde Dolly!

Despite opposition things improved. In 1962 the station had an advertising turnover of 12 million guilders (over a million pounds), and an estimated audience of five million.

A threat to the station's future emerged in 1964 when a radio and television station was set up on an artificial island erected on stilts and anchored in the seabed four miles off the Dutch coast. The government acted almost immediately against the REM island, as it was known, but left Veronica alone. In 1967, the British offshore stations were outlawed and it was generally thought that Holland, the last remaining West European country not to have ratified the Strasbourg Convention against broadcasting stations on the high seas, would introduce legislation. But the pundits were wrong and the popular little station continued unimpeded.

In 1966 the *Borkum Riff* was towed into harbour and broken up. The old lightship was replaced by a large, specially converted motor trawler named the *Nordeney* which was much more luxurious and better fitted out. On board was a 10 kilowatt transmitter and the aerial system had been perfected. A special device was installed which enabled the ship to turn on its anchor in the worst of weather without twisting the chain. The strain of the long, heavy chain was taken up by a complex system of strong nylon 'springs' mounted on the deck of the ship.

Accommodation on board the *Nordeney* was designed with comfort a foremost consideration; fitted carpets and modern furniture being the order of the day. Next to the broadcasting studios, which housed a bank of tape recorders for playing back the programmes recorded on land, a newsroom and the transmitter room were constructed. For'ard was the generator room supplying the power for the whole installation. Veronica has always tried to avoid interfering with other stations and, therefore, power was not increased beyond 10 kilowatts.

In any case, power in itself was not the recipe for success in the offshore radio business. Radio Dolfijn broadcast in Dutch from the MV *Laissez Faire* anchored off the English coast for several months in 1967 with a power of 55 kilowatts. But in its short time on the air it never achieved anything like the impact of the well established Radio Veronica.

After March 1968, when Radio Caroline International was forcibly closed down by the pirating of the two radio ships by the Dutch Wijsmuller tug and salvage company, Radio Veronica became increasingly popular in England and former Caroline South disc jockey Robbie Dale was taken into service for a series of evening programmes. That same year the station moved into lavish new headquarters in a specially converted villa on the outskirts of Hilversum, Holland's broadcasting 'capital'.

All seemed blue on the horizon, but startling developments were in store which were ultimately to bring the carefully constructed Veronica organisation to its knees.

13

A floating circus

Congratulations were in order for Radio Veronica as it entered 1970, its tenth successful year of broadcasting. Almost part of the establishment in Holland, its position seemed assured and the future rosy. There was more advertising than the station could cope with, there was a huge body of loyal listeners and the station's carefully cultured public image had paid off. The politicians in The Hague no longer made loud threats. Everything seemed fine ... there were disconcerting rumours about a new Swiss-run operation but it was scarcely thought of as endangering Veronica's established position.

When the *Mebo 2*, a converted 570-ton Norwegian coaster, put out from Rotterdam's Slikkerveer wharf at the end of January, 1970, it was the most lavishly equipped shipborne radio station ever. It had everything from luxury cabins, fitted carpets and fountains in the urinals, through to a gleaming new RCA medium-wave radio transmitter with a power of no less than 105 kW. The only one of its kind in the world (serial number 001), it was one of the most powerful in the whole continent of Europe. This, in turn, was backed up by an FM transmitter and two 10kW. short-wave transmitters, which would give the station worldwide reception.

But the whole operation was cloaked in mystery. In a blaze of remarkably uncritical continental publicity the psychedeli-cally-painted radio ship, with its huge 140-foot aerial mast, nosed out of the Maas Estuary and into the January swell of the cold North Sea.

Its two 'captains' were as flamboyant as their radio ship. Two Swiss named Erwin Meister (32) and Edwin Bollier (34), they were the sort of characters who are a journalist's dream; flashy dressers with extravagant clothes who drove expensive Mercedes and divided their time between a fair share of the capitals of Europe. Owners of night clubs in Zurich and self-styled 'millionaires', their story of from where the motivation and finance for the station had emanated was eagerly devoured by the press.

'We paid for it all ourselves – nobody else's money was involved. It has cost us more than 4½ million guilders,' stated Bollier to journalists. Both Meister and Bollier continued to assert that they paid for the ship and its fitting-out with their own money.

Whoever actually footed the bill, it was a mighty large one. It probably, however, was not nearly as large as the claimed 4½ million guilders (approximately half a million pounds). Investigation shows that the invoices of the Slikkerveer wharf for the gutting of the former coaster, ballasting it for use as a radio ship, rebuilding the interior, installing and renovating the bridge and engine room and installing all the technical equipment, were for a total of 612,397 Dutch guilders and 93 cents (about £65,000). Purchase of the *Mebo 2* cost Meister and Bollier 220,000 Swiss francs (about £25,000).

A well-nigh incomprehensible initial blunder was made by the duo when they bought the *Mebo 1*, a vessel formerly used for inshore work in the Norwegian fjords. The ship was reregistered in Panama and gutted for conversion into a radio ship. After nearly 500,000 guilders had been spent on conversion work (studios were actually installed) the owners decided it was too small for a radio ship!

'It was too small and the round bottom made everybody seasick when we went out in it,' Meister later explained to me. And so the *Mebo 1* was relegated to the role of supply ship, for which it was too large, too expensive to run and altogether unsuitable. The larger, fast and relatively modern coaster the *Silvretta* (1954) was purchased for broadcasting.

This was not the first mistake, however, in what was to become one long catalogue of error, incompetence and misjudgement. There are about as many stories as to how RNI came to birth as there are explaining where flies go in the winter. The approved Meister/ Bollier version runs like this.

A Swiss advertising agency decided to set up an offshore radio station aiming at the European public and Meister and Bollier, self-styled experts in telecommunication, were put in charge of the technical aspects. The ship to be used was the former Radio London ship, MV *Galaxy*, which was lying near Hamburg in the River Elbe. Work was begun on the ship, but problems of finance and opposition from the German authorities meant that work on refloating the one-time American minesweeper had to be abandoned.

Meister and Bollier then decided to launch their own radio ship. Claims Bollier: the money came from Caritas (the Roman Catholic charity) which bought Japanese radio equipment from us in 1968 to set up a radio network in Biafra.' He also mentions a Jugoslavian contract as being lucrative and having provided a great deal of money.

*The coaster Silvretta, converted into the psychedelic radio ship
Mebo 2, leaves Rotterdam harbour for the North Sea.*

The RNI ship on an untypically calm day off the Dutch coast.

Other stories are far more romantic – and not entirely mythical. One recounts how the Biafran Government paid the two to set up a floating radio station for the tiny breakaway state. By the time it was completed, however, Biafra had fallen and the duo found a valuable property on their hands. A variation of this story alleges the ship was to be used not in African but in European waters, on behalf of the Biafran regime, to try and mobilise European public support. More sinister rumours hint at a political plot to use the station to unseat Labour Prime Minister Harold Wilson, who was lending British support to the official Nigerian Government. This story should not be entirely discredited in view of evidence which was later to come to light of Meister and Bollier's interference in British politics. There is probably a little truth in all the stories. But what is not admitted is that about five million Deutschmarks were advanced for the project by the Swiss bank ORBIS upon the order of a mysterious German group . . . a German organisation is to figure later in the story.

The radio ship *Mebo 2* immediately ran into stormy waters. The first transmissions went out on Friday, January 23, but were barely audible on land. A bad frequency technically and politically was chosen, 186 metres medium wave, at the end of the band near ship-to-shore wavelengths. There was steady interference from morse stations. In a Force 8 gale on the Saturday night the large and unmanoeuvreable tender, *Mebo 1*, collided with the radio ship and serious damage was done to both ships in transferring a 25-ton length of anchor chain. A porthole was broken on the *Mebo 2* and water poured into the transmitter room. All the English and German disc jockeys were reported as being seasick and trouble flared as some German journalists tried to board the pop ship. A crewman threw a press camera into the sea and blows were exchanged on the deck of the rolling radio ship.

The following Monday the Panamanian consul in Rotterdam struck the *Mebo 2* off the ship's register of his country. 'We want nothing to do with the radio ship,' he stated.

Test transmissions in English and German went on, but they were of widely varying quality. According to Meister, vital parts for the transmitter had still to be delivered. The trials and tribulations of the station were so many and various in the next few months that it would be tedious to go through them all. An abbreviated timetable of the disastrous series of events might read like this:

February 28th, 1970   Location of the *Mebo 2* four miles off the Dutch coast at Noordwijk. After a month of technical problems regular transmissions begin on 186m., 6210 kHz, (short-wave) and FM 102 mHz.

March 4   RNI interferes with Dutch pilot-service which has to move frequency from 187 m. to 182 m.

March 23   *Mebo 2* ups anchor and sails for the British coast.

March 24   Anchored off Clacton, Essex; ceases transmission after protests from Ministry of Posts and Telecommunications, Coastguards and Trinity House lightships authority. Broadcasts become irregular and, due to severe interference, medium-wave transmitter closes down for frequency adjustments.

March 31   Edwin Bollier visits Royal National Lifeboat Institution headquarters in London where his offer of a 'substantial four-figure donation' is turned down due to the Marine Offences Act.

April 10   RNI back on the air-on 190 m. Interference caused to Norway and Radio Veronica.

April 15   The Post Office, under Government orders, takes unprecedented course of action and begins to jam (interfere with the signal) RNI on 190 m. Minister Stonehouse states this done on request of Italy and Norway. Bollier threatens to retaliate by jamming BBC.

April 16   Medium-wave transmitter off the air.

May 1   RNI back on the air - on 217 m. Swiss government announces intention to act against nationals involved in ship-borne broadcasting. Station jammed again on 217 m.

May 13   Tests on 244 m., next to Radio One and causing interference.

May 16   Regular transmissions begin on 244 m.

May 21   Jamming of RNI recommences on 244 m.

May 30   Hundreds of pop fans demonstrate outside Beacon Hill naval radio station, Kent, where jamming transmitter is located.

June 1   Bollier announces imminent closure of German service and states RNI will close on June 19 if a Labour Government is re-elected.

June 13   Dramatic change of name for RNI. Intensive anti-Labour Party campaign launched as station renamed Radio Caroline International after talks with former Caroline boss Ronan O'Rahilly.

June 14   Thousands of demonstrators mass in Hyde Park and led by Ronan O'Rahilly and disc-jockey Simon Dee march on 10 Downing Street.

June 16/17   In the last two days before the General Election constant anti-Labour propaganda flows from the transmitters; O'Rahilly and an RNI double-decker bus tour London; jamming intensifies as Prime Minister personally authorises use of the most powerful radio transmitter in Western Europe – the one-megawatt transmitter kept at Droitwich for use in national emergency.

June 18   The Labour Party loses the General Election. We shall never be able to gauge accurately the effect of RNI, but many marginals in London and the South-east (where fluctuation of one or two votes in every hundred is vital) fall to the Conservatives. Young people under 21 voting for the first time. Evidence to hand suggests, in my opinion, RNI played a decisive role in the election and, perhaps, changed the course of British political history.

June 19   Station continues – under old RNI name. But jamming continues.

July 3   New Postmaster General, Christopher Chataway, meets RNI programme director Larry Tremaine but there is no indication of when jamming will stop. Norway begins to jam RNI's short-wave frequency.

July 23   *Mebo 2* ups anchor again and sails back to the Dutch coast in a bid to beat the jammers. Bollier states: 'Our mission in Britain is complete. The new Conservative Government is in favour of commercial radio!'

July 24   RNI recommences transmissions from off Scheveningen. The jamming has stopped.

July 27   RNI is now causing interference to Dutch Government 'pop* station Hilversum 3 on 240 m. PTT sends a telegram to station's head office in Zurich.

July 30   Now FM transmissions are interfering with Netherland's bus company's VHF communications. RNI leaves the air and returns on 245 m. but there is still interference to Hilversum 3.

July 31   Transmissions cease.

August 3   Station back on 217 m. this time. VHF channel also changed and now broadcasting on 31 m. as well as 40 m. short-wave band. Station soon leaves the air again for adjustments to the aerial.

August 17   Station goes off the air yet again.

August 23   Back on the air on 220 m., 100 mHz (FM), 49 m. and 31 m. short-wave.

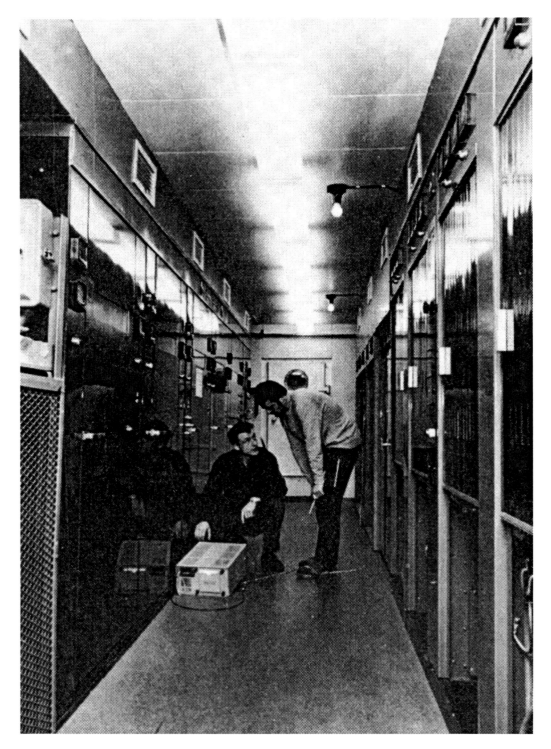

In the transmitter hall on board the Mebo 2

By this time the itinerant radio ship with the constantly wandering transmitter was already becoming something of a living legend. No other 'pirate' ship had met with so much determined opposition and continued difficulty. Around the end of July, I met Erwin Meister for the first time and we sat in the sun on the terrace of Scheveningen's plush Grand Hotel, where he and Bollier were in virtual permanent residence together. Three miles away on the blue summer sea the distinct, brightly painted outline of the *Mebo 2* was visible. We talked about the station and its future; Meister was confident that the tide would turn in his favour and things were improving. But the worst was yet to come. . . .

On August 12, Amsterdam night-club owner Kees Manders announced he had been appointed commercial director of RNI and that he was to seek advertising for the station. His tenure of the post was just about as long-lived as his period of office as 'artistic director' of Radio Veronica. Manders set about drumming up commercial support for the station, and all seemed to be going well until, on August 26, the RNI tender, *Mebo 1*, was arrested in Scheveningen harbour and chained up by a court officer. The night-club owner claimed he was owed over £3,000 by Meister and Bollier in the form of advertising commission; the much persecuted Swiss claimed they had never hired him and were not interested in his services.

The following day, acting on a tip-off (with no prizes for guessing who was responsible), officers of the PTT raided the Grand Hotel and removed radio transmitting equipment from the bedroom of Meister and Bollier. The equipment, it was revealed, was being used for communication between the hotel, the *Mebo 2* and Zurich.

It was in the early afternoon of Saturday, August 29 that the climax came in the conflict between Manders and the owners of RNI. At about twenty minutes past one that afternoon two ships were sighted from the bridge of the *Mebo 2* heading straight for the radio ship. One was a tug, the other a small launch. As they approached, they were identified as the tug *Huski*, registered in Curacao and flying the Dutch flag, and as the Panamanian launch *Viking*, owned by a well-known Dutch businessman named I. P. Heerema. Despite his close involvement with the disastrous REM television island fiasco he had again become active in offshore broadcasting.

The *Viking* drew alongside the pop ship and Manders climbed on board and asked to see Captain Hardeveld. For five minutes the two went into conference in the Captain's saloon; Manders

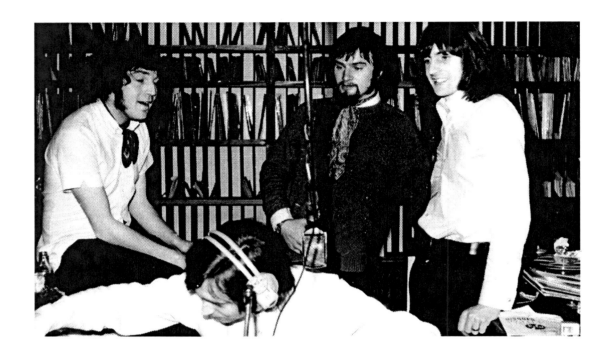

Disc jockeys on board RNI; (above, left to right) Andy Archer, Carl
Mitchell and Roger Day.
(Right) Carl Mitchell at the RNI turntables.

demanded that the ship be taken into Scheveningen Harbour and offered the Captain a substantial sum of money. When the Captain refused, the indignant Manders declared he would cut the anchor chain and forcibly tow the ship in. He was told, in no uncertain terms, that such an action would be regarded as piracy.

Manders left the ship and the launch drew away as those on board decided on their next step. On the *Mebo 2* crew and disc jockeys became concerned about the intentions of the visitors and an appeal was made over the air to listeners to alert the station's Zurich office and staff at Scheveningen's Grand Hotel.

'Amsterdam night-club owner Kees Manders wants to take over this ship and tow us into harbour ., . we are very worried ... please telephone the following numbers and ask for Mr Meister or Mr Bollier.'

The appeal over the air was so successful that the telephone exchange in Zurich broke down completely under the strain of international calls from all over Europe, and the one at Scheveningen was blocked for over an hour!

As the tug and launch approached the radio ship again, crew members and disc jockeys gathered together as much improvised armament as they could lay their hands on. Attempts to board the *Mebo* from the tug, which had more than twenty men aboard, foundered under a hail of missiles and, instead, attention was shifted to the anchor chain.

The appeals for aid over the station's transmitters became more insistent and the djs announced they had petrol bombs ready to throw at the attackers if they persisted in their efforts to cut the ship loose from its anchor. Those on shore were provided with a running commentary and the names of the two vessels were constantly announced, 'for the information of the authorities, this is an act of piracy on the high seas'. Kees Manders and Heerema heard themselves described to the European listening public as 'gangsters' and 'hoodlums' in some of the most entertaining and amazing Saturday afternoon radio ever.

Those on board the *Huski*, beaten off by the defenders, now made ready to use the powerful water cannon mounted on the forepart of the tug; it was set to pour a stream of high pressure water on the high antenna-mast of the *Mebo 2*, which would certainly have put the station off the air, probably toppled the mast and, most likely, would have killed all those on board the tug as the high voltage arced back through the water path.

Disc jockey Carl Mitchell warned: 'You will all die if you use the water cannon." Some water was used and the 31 and 49 metre band shortwave transmitters had to be closed down.

Fortunately, the attackers thought better of this plan and decided to attempt to board again. On the fifth run up to the *Mebo 2* the radio ship's tender. *Eurotrip*, was sighted approaching from the direction of Scheveningen Harbour. On board were Erwin Meister and programme director Larry Tremaine. At this point, Manders and his entourage made off at full speed, shouting that they would be back later. At twenty past three Larry Tremaine made a public statement over RNI's transmitters on behalf of the station's owners. He stated that Kees Manders had nothing to do with the station, that there was no contract between him and Mebo Ltd., operators of the radio ship, and what had occurred was an act of attempted piracy. The djs thanked all those who had assisted, including the crew of Radio Veronica who sent a boat to the help of the *Mebo 2* together with three crew members.

Meanwhile, Heerema and Manders hot-footed it back to Rotterdam where the latter dismissed the whole incident as a joke. 'We just went out to have a look,' he claimed. With an ocean going tug and twenty 'heavies'! The Dutch Royal Navy began an inquiry into the incident and, later in the afternoon, the frigate *Van Nes* anchored near RNI. It spent a watchful night in the vicinity before continuing on patrol.

Heerema, however, claimed that Manders was, in fact, a director of RNI. At this stage it was not clear as to the extent of Heerema's own interest and involvement in RNI. Things were far more complicated than they appeared.

As the summer of 1970 approached our two Swiss 'millionaires' had found the kitty running empty and the expenses mounting up. Moving the ship here and there, altering the transmitters and the absence of any paid advertising all contributed to a grievous financial situation. And so they approached I. P. Heerema.

Heerema and his company, Global Offshore Structures, had been two of the principals in the disastrous REM television and radio island fiasco. In 1964 he and millionaire Dutch shipbuilder and industrialist Cornelius Verolme got together, with a horde of dubious characters, and hatched a plan to set up a 'pirate' tv station on the North Sea. At that time there were no commercials on the Dutch state-supervised television and the market was reckoned to be wide open for such an innovation. As broadcasts were to be directed to a virtually flat country near perfect signal propagation from an offshore tower could be ensured. The plan seemed sound enough and the two went ahead with construction of an artificial island, to be located on stilts sunk into the sea-bed, at Verolme's shipyard near Cork in Ireland.

A company was set up under the name Reclame Exploitatie Maatschapij to operate the station and coordinate programming, advertising sales and so on. Capital to finance the operation was sought from the general public in Holland through an organisation which was named the Volksaandelen Trust (People's Share Trust). The share issue was handled by the Dutch bank Teixeira de Mattos and people quite literally queued in the streets to pay in their few guilders to become a part of this exciting new project.

Transmissions from the island started on September 1, but it came as a shock when the Dutch government announced it was to legislate against the station. On December 17, 1964, Dutch police and marines, led by Mr. J. G. Hartsuijker, the Public Prosecutor of Amsterdam, in a combined air-sea operation captured the island and forcibly silenced its transmitters; they were unmoved by pleas that the platform had become Panamanian property and that broadcasts had been taken over by a mysterious company named High Seas TV Ltd. of London, run by an appropriately named Mr. Bent.

There had been no inkling of the far reaching repercussions the whole shady episode was to have. The gamble that breaks the bank is fine in the music-hall song, but this one literally broke the bank. Teixeira de Mattos went spectacularly bankrupt. An estimated £7 million disappeared somewhere – nobody is quite sure where it all went to this day – one of the directors of the bank was jailed (a scapegoat, in the opinion of most informed observers) and a lot of fraud charges and rumour flew around financial circles in Holland; the organisers appeared to come out no worse than they went in, an awful lot of ordinary, trusting people lost a lot of money and, lo and behold, there later grew out of the whole rotten, shady shambles what is now one of Holland's largest and most respectable broadcasting organisations, the TROS. One story hinted very strongly at some sort of high-level pact with the REM island's operators.

Evidently, offshore adventuring still appealed to Heerema and he pumped money into the ill-fated RNI project; a sum believed to be in the region of £50,000. (Meister and Bollier admitted later he had

The REM Island off the Dutch coast.

a 12½% interest.) In August, however, he asked the Swiss to take on his colleague, night club owner Manders, as commercial director. A verbal agreement to do so was made, according to Heerema and Manders. The two Swiss, however, resisted any abrogation of their authority and the clash came.

After the attack on the radio ship Meister countered with a letter to Manders claiming damages of over £100,000. Damages were also claimed for the time the tender was chained up in harbour on Mander's writ. In November, Heerema served yet another writ on the *Mebo 1* on behalf of a Panamanian shipping company, of which he was the Dutch representative. Despite all the to-ing and fro-ing of paper and writs, the *Mebo 2* still floated safely on the North Sea keeping up its barrage of non-stop pop.

The first phase in the station's troubled life came to an end on September 24. It was sudden. At around nine the previous evening the small boat *De Redder* from Scheveningen drew alongside the *Mebo 2* with a message from the radio ship's Swiss owners who were in residence at the Grand Hotel. Its contents were short and to the point. The station was to close the next morning.

Disc-jockey Spangles Muldoon broke the news to listeners and a communique was read out at frequent intervals during the evening's broadcasting. A nice little myth in attractive packaging had been concocted in the Grand Hotel for the benefit of the listeners. In view of the political crisis over the 'pirates', RNI would close down in the hope that Radio Veronica 'so much loved by the Dutch people for the last ten years might be able to continue'. Everyone was very touched by the grand, unselfish gesture. Except those in the know.

RNI closed down at 11 on the morning of the 24th after a final hour loaded with all the emotion and nostalgia that could be worked into it by the imminently jobless djs. The imaginary advertisers who had never paid for a single spot, were thanked; Iberia, Toshiba, Sony, Camel and Bulova. The station's two themes, 'Peace' and 'Man of Action', played out. And then there was just the vacant crackling of the ether as the channel went dead.

That afternoon I saw Meister and later went out to the *Mebo 2*. Those on board had no idea why the station was really closing. Meister claimed the ship was sold to an African company and would shortly sail for a new anchorage in the Mediterranean. It would no longer broadcast to a European audience.

The future role of the ship was later enlarged upon in varying fanciful versions: it was to be sold to the Palestine Guerilla Organisation, El Fatah; it was to be taken to an East German port; it was to be used as a counterforce against the West's Radio Free Europe.

On the Friday night, however, we got at least half of the true story in discussions with Meister and Bollier at the Secretariat of the International Broadcasters Society, operators of shipborne Capital Radio, in Bussum. We talked over the possibility of taking over the *Mebo 2* in discussions which went on until four in the morning. Meister revealed that the African story was a sham and that they had been asked to close down by Radio Veronica! At this stage, however, he did not reveal that money had changed hands.

Bollier, who speaks only Schweizerdeutsch, that peculiarly indecipherable Swiss dialect, explained through Meister that everything had gone wrong with their radio dream since the very beginning. The plain result was that the money had run out. 'We do not know what to do.' It all sounded very plausible at the time. They are both extremely plausible characters, friendly in a quiet, typically Swiss way and with an attractive image of youthful naivety. But they are both sharp and perceptive to the point of cunning. Some of their mistakes, true, occurred as a result of inexperience and ignorance, but they fall into such a regular and recurring pattern that one cannot help but wonder if many of them were not made as part of some grand design. A grand design which has enabled them to use their radio ship to remarkable profit, though not from actual broadcasting.

For they had become such an embarrassment to the gentlemen of Radio Veronica, who saw their ten year monopoly of the seas threatened by the incomer, that the previous week they had gladly paid over to the Swiss 'with the big Dutch mouth' a 'loan' of no less than £100,000 for them to close down their radio ship.

And so, on September 26, Meister and Bollier left Schipol Airport for Zurich, their pockets £100,000 fuller (paid in Deutschmarks) and, apparently, with no further interest in their floating juke-box, which the obliging people at Veronica had agreed to staff with their own 'pirate' crew. But both sides had less of a deal than they bargained for.

The RNI story was remarkably uneventful for a few months, which gives us an opportunity to take a look at the trials and tribulations of another 'pirate' crew a few miles up the coast.

14

The pride of the Liechtenstein navy

High above, the red navigation lights of the London plane winked in the clear night sky as the Viscount circled for landing. I left the outskirts of the city behind and took the road to Aberdeen's Dyce Airport. The Mercedes glided almost noiselessly over the darkened road and within five minutes was turning into the airfield car park. Barely a hundred yards away the Viscount taxied to a halt and began to disgorge its load of passengers. I could make out the bespectacled features of the man I was to meet; Tim Thomason, Executive Director of the Dutch-based International Broadcasters Society.

My mind went back to our first meeting in the summer of 1969. In Hilversum, on a visit to the headquarters of Radio Veronica, I realised the headquarters of the IBS was in nearby Bussum. Its Executive Director, I remembered, had ordered some copies of my first book, *When Pirates Ruled the Waves*, and we had exchanged letters. A visit seemed worthwhile. Little did I guess what was to come of it.

We had a useful meeting at which I also met Thomason's wife, Berthe Beydals, who was then Editor of the radio and television section of Holland's largest daily paper, *De Telegraaf,* as well as being IBS Secretary-General. Also there, by a remarkable coincidence, was an American, Professor Frank Iezzi of New York's Hofstra University who had written a number of articles in academic journals on the legal and political aspects of offshore radio, and which I had read and studied with great interest.

The meeting turned out to be something of a communion of souls. Not only were we of a similar outlook on the main topic of conversation, offshore radio, but our views on the essential nature of freedom in broadcasting were in remarkable accord.

At that time, I knew little of the IBS and its work. Largely the brainchild of Thomason and his wife, it had been set up eight years previously in Holland as a private foundation, the International Broadcasting Service, to study broadcasting, generally, and, more specifically, the needs of the professionals involved in the industry. Activity, at first, was mainly in the fields of research and the organisation of programme exchanges. This initial activity was so successful, and the need for an association for professional workers in broadcasting, which was not in existence, became so obvious, that, in May, 1964, the International Broadcasters Society was formed.

Within three years, it had more than 2,000 members in most countries of the world. Services to members were concentrated in the fields of broadcast research assistance, book sales, travel and introductions, newsletters and special study projects. An annual Honours Ceremony was instituted, at which those who had made outstanding contributions in the field of broadcasting were awarded the shield of the Society. Thomason, personally, had been active in more unusual spheres; during the August/September, 1968, Czech crisis he had assisted dozens of Czech broadcasters in their flight to the West. New positions had been obtained for them, direct physical aid in the form of shelter and funds was extended, and an intricate liaison system set up.

After our August, 1969, meeting, Thomason and I kept in close contact. The letter marked 'Strictly Confidential' which arrived in the second week of October came as something of a bombshell; the IBS had made the decision to set up its own offshore radio station! Naturally, I found the idea of such a project, which was to have an ideological rather than a commercial basis, exciting, to say the least.

On October 31 Thomason flew into Aberdeen, where I was completing a four year Political Studies course at the university, and from where my Scottish-based publishing company was operated. In a series of intensive discussions, we hammered out the broad principles of the project. The practicalities were left for later. Firstly, we set ourselves guidelines for the operation. Certain members of the IBS were concerned about the trend towards increasing government interference in broadcasting throughout Europe. It was hoped, somewhat ambitiously, that through the powerful voice of an offshore radio station this trend could be slowed and good, professional radio, free of the constraints of the State could be demonstrated. On a more general level, we were worried about government interference in all aspects of the life of the individual, of left-wing trends in Western Europe, and the growing opposition to genuine free thinking, the concepts of commercialism (in the real sense of the word) and competition. It was decided to call the radio station Capital Radio.

The Confidential Memorandum compiled after that first meeting succinctly outlined the station's objects which were unashamedly

*political: . . . the purpose being to establish and maintain a responsible,
ethical and professional alternative radio service for European audiences
in keeping with the standards proclaimed by the Society. The radio station
will be commercial, but will seek only a limited annual revenue in order
to avoid over-commercialisation to the detriment of the programmes
themselves. The radio station will be legal . . . the basic format will be
MOR (Middle of the Road), an all music service, 24 hours a day . . .
all copyrights will be paid. The radio service will include two hours of
religious programmes daily. Time will also be made available for paid
political broadcasts . . . policy will be to promote law and order; respect
for the rights of the individual; the concept of free enterprise in general,
as opposed to state controls and monopolies; the concept of free radio as
opposed to state monopolies in broadcasting; freedom of expression and
freedom of the press . . . the editorial policy will be opposed to dogmatic
socialist and / or communist concepts. . . .*

The conceptual basis of the station was ambitious and idealistic;
but all the more exciting for that. Perhaps the whole operation
was a little too idealistic, but, then, my own fears were more on
the practical side – especially the problem of raising the estimated
capital of £50,000 which we reckoned would be necessary to float
the project and run it for a year.

This, however, was not nearly as difficult as anticipated. On
December 6 Thomason met with a wealthy Dutchman resident
in Switzerland; his name, Dirk de Groot, the representative of
a Liechtenstein-based international financial empire called The
Mississippi Trade and Investment Corporation, which is active
on a worldwide basis in many different spheres of business from
metals to property. After a preliminary discussion, he agreed to
invest some D.fl. 300,000 (nearly £40,000) in the idea. A few days
later, Thomason and the IBS lawyer flew to Switzerland and then
went on to the tiny tax-haven of Liechtenstein to finalise financial
details and arange the corporate structure of the enterprise.

It is, perhaps, worthwhile digressing for a few moments to
outline, briefly, why this minute 65 sq. ml. country (population
19,500) is so attractive to the international businessman and why
it is abhorred by so many of the governments of Europe (and their
tax authorities especially). Like Switzerland, Liechtenstein rigidly
upholds the bank secret and also has a unique system of company
registration. Common practice is for a businessman to set up a
company with the aid of Liechtenstein legal advisers, whose names

appear on the company's notepaper and on the official records as proprietors and directors of the business. Locked away in a bank vault, however, is a document, enforcable by law, in which the 'directors' agree to act only upon the instructions of the company's real founder. Thus, both anonymity and complete control of the company is guaranteed to the founding businessman. No tax authority can check out interests or holdings.

Liechtenstein tax is levied on the company - at incredibly low rates. Some types of company (such as the Establishment or Anstalt) are not even liable to tax on profits, and pay a mere 0.1% on capital and reserves. An initial fee is payable and at least Sw. Fr. 20,000 must be paid up, but all-in with the service is an office in Vaduz, the capital, and use of telex and telephone facilities. Currency is in the form of hard Swiss francs and the central position of Liechtenstein in Europe all contribute to make a company there extremely attractive for the businessman operating in the international sphere.

For an offshore radio operation, this little country with its anonymous, low tax company arrangement was the obvious choice. And so, the Kangaroo Pioneering Co. Est. of Kirchenstrasse, Vaduz came into being that December with two local lawyers as its directors. The real owners and operators were the Mississippi Trade and Investment Corp. and another Liechtenstein operation, the Saltwater Foundation, which was made up of people ideologically committed to the project, as opposed to commercially, and who wished to kep their names secret for a combination of financial and political reasons.

Back in Aberdeen, a bid was registered for a number of local trawlers impounded and rusting in harbour following a fishing strike. One was to be used as a radio ship, another as a tender and two others were to be outfitted and sent to Colombia, South America, where they were to be used in a development project using radio as the method of communicating with the underdeveloped population. But the bid was turned down as being too small. Shortly after Christmas Thomason flew into Aberdeen again and stayed over the New Year. In between the merrymaking which traditionally accompanies the Scottish New Year we developed our plans and Thomason flew on to New York for meetings with potential advertisers in the States. Five days later he was back in Aberdeen – with a contract for religious advertising worth nearly £50,000 a year!

Back in Holland, ships of all shapes and sizes were perused, surveyed and considered. Trawlers, coasters, minesweepers and even a destroyer were inspected. Towards the end of January, a 128-ton Dutch trawler *De Twee Gesusters*, built in 1916, was purchased for £4,000 and promptly renamed the *Kangaroo*. Fitted out with radar, radio, decca and depth meter, she was ideally suited for use as a tender.

Our future radio ship turned up at the beginning of February in Groningen Harbour. A coaster built in 1938, the *Zeevaart* (359 tons) was nearly 150 feet long and appeared to be in sound condition, both structurally and enginewise. Formerly used in coastal traffic between Britain and the Dutch and Belgian ports, she had made her last passage, from Norwich to Rotterdam, the previous December and was then tied up for sale. After some bargaining, she was bought from her financially embarrassed owner for some £5,000 and put into dry dock for plate riveting and the fitting of a new screw and rudder. This little ship, it was the plan, was to challenge the might of the governments of Europe and the name *King David* was decided upon. But things started to go wrong with the *King David* right from the very start.

In the cold February weather the water and pumps froze up and the launching was delayed. As she approached the lock gates in the harbour of Groningen, under the control of the pilot, in the strong wind and with no ballast, she was thrown against a German ship; the pilot misjudged her speed at the lock gates and she ran right into them, causing over £2,000 worth of damage. The *King David* was then detained by the harbour authorities until the insurance company lodged a guarantee sum.

That night the Captain took appendicitis. The heating broke down and everyone on board shivered in the cold winter night. Next morning a storm built up and it was too dangerous to leave harbour. Then came the tragic news that the chief engineer's brother was on board a trawler missing off the Dutch coast and the engineer left the ship to take part in the search.

Thomason laid on a new Captain and a new engineer, but the latter couldn't even start the compressor and promptly quit! There was another day's delay and a new engineer was found.

The ship still hadn't been officially renamed and was unregistered. The harbour authorities were both mystified and a trifle concerned by the no-name ghost ship, and tactfully suggested that she should

The M.V. Zeevaart, *later to become the Capital Radio ship, photographed in Groningen Harbour.*

fly a flag of some description. Thomason poked around some local shops, but all he could find which seemed remotely suitable for a Liechtenstein-owned ship was the Swiss flag, which was duly hoisted to the satisfaction of local officialdom! And so, with her old name painted out and flying the Swiss flag, the *King David* at last set sail for Zaandam, near Amsterdam, and shipyard conversion to a radio ship.

On Tuesday March 3 the *Kangaroo* left Ijmuiden Harbour, the Panamanian flag at her stern whipping to and fro in the stiff breeze; her destination, England. The same day a colleague and I travelled to Scarborough, on England's north coast, to make arrangements for the delivery and stowing of the vital cargo she was to collect.

We had known for some time that there was an RCA 10 kW. transmitter in store near Scarborough which had been used on board Radio 270. This radio station had broadcast for 13 months from Scarborough Bay until the Marine Offences Act had forced its closure in August, 1967. Although the radio ship, the *Oceaan 7*, had since been scrapped. I knew that the valuable transmitter had been removed. Its owners, Ellambar Investments Ltd., represented by northeast supermarket tycoon Wilf Proudfoot (later a Conservative MP), were only too glad to part with it, a sum was negotiated and we set arrangements in motion for it to be collected by the *Kangaroo*. At the same time we arranged for two 27 kW. output diesel generators to power the radio ship's electronic installation to be manufactured at the Dale Electric plant in nearby Filey (the plant's managing director, Mr. Leonard Dale, was Chairman of Radio 270 and had supplied generators for that station).

We hoped the equipment could be loaded at Scarborough but plans were changed at the last minute. The tide was not convenient for a deep-keeled vessel like a trawler, and altogether too much official interest began to manifest itself after we informed the local harbourmaster of the nature of the cargo. The local authorities rather surprisingly, and more or less correctly, assumed that a Panamanian ship collecting the old 270 transmitter and two new generators to power it must be a new pop radio ship.

On the Thursday morning, I went down to the harbourmaster's office to be greeted with a threatening, 'We know exactly what you're up to. This transmitter's not to be let out of the country!' Visions of policemen descending on the harbour waving copies of the Marine Offences Act came to mind and we drove back to the hotel to radio the *Kangaroo* not to try to enter Scarborough

The hold of the Zeevaart *is prepared for the addition of 200 tons of concrete as ballast.*

The former cargo ship is converted into a pirate radio ship: in the background are two Dale generators and in the foreground is the RCA BTA 10J 1 10Kw. transmitter.

Harbour. Fortunately, the Captain had already decided to make for Middlesbrough and the next evening we travelled there by taxi – loaded with all manner of electronic spares and sundry junk looted from the former Radio 270 store. Never before had such an amzaing sight been seen at the plush Marton Country Club as when our taxi arrived at the front door, bursting at the seams with amplifiers, lengths of wire, boxes of valves, loudspeakers, tuning coils, and a monster control panel bearing the legend 'RADIO 270' inscribed across the top in large letters. A procession of mystified and amused doormen and flunkeys helped carry the load to our rapidly filling bedroom. There came the inevitable comment, 'What the —— are this lot doing, starting a pirate radio station?'

On the Monday the *Kangaroo* loaded the transmitter and generators at Middlesbrough Harbour. A late addition to the cargo was four Landrovers lashed to the deck. These had been bought over the weekend for 'camouflage' purposes to confuse anyone who might become unduly interested in the electronic cargo. All to be used for a development project in South America, dockers were told. It might have fooled the authorities, but the dockers' foreman wasn't convinced, 'Looks like you're starting an effing pop radio ship to me!' The *Kangaroo* put out of the Tees and set course for Aberdeen, where she arrived the next afternoon to take on more electronics equipment. There was considerable interest expressed in the converted trawler flying the Panamanian flag but the jeeps served their purpose in that interest was focused more on them than the cargo below decks.

At the end of the week we sailed out of Aberdeen Harbour and onto the North Sea. Forty hours sailing away was the Dutch coast and our port of destination, Ijmuiden.

During March and April conversion work on the *King David* forged ahead at Scheepswerf Vooruit in Zaandam. First of all she was dry-docked, the bottom scraped and cleaned and zinc-plating attached to safeguard against the corrosive, electrolytic action which can damage the plating of a radio ship broadcasting from the sea. The next step was to pour 200 tons of concrete ballast into the hold which would ensure the stability of the *King David* at sea.

There were a hundred and one jobs to do; the plumbing had to be fixed, there was carpentry and electrical work, the old lifeboat was removed and replaced by a modern liferaft, the water tanks were cleaned and resurfaced, a stairway was built from the saloon down into the hold. The empty hold, which was to house the generator and transmitter rooms, the studio, a bar and three cabins, swarmed with welders, electricians and joiners.

As the work went on, and the bills came in it was realised, at this early stage, that costs were exceeding expectations and further discussions were held in Switzerland and Liechtenstein. A contract was drawn up between Kangaroo Pioneering Co, and the IBS under the terms of which Kangaroo were the owners of the two ships which were hired to the IBS for a monthly rental of D.fl. 100,000 (just over £10,000). Around this time we learned that the authorities in Liechtenstein, with the concurrence of Prince Franz Josef II, the country's ruler, had officially approved Kangaroo's intention of operating a radio ship and, for the first time ever in the country's history, granted the use of the landlocked principality's flag on a ship. The 'pirate' *King David* became the first ship in the Liechtenstein navy! A policy decision had been made earlier that uniforms should be worn on board by both officers and crew, in a bid to escape the 'pirate' image, and ranks were allocated. With a marine experience limited to knowledge of boating ponds, radio ships and one voyage on the *Kangaroo*, I found myself in the uniform of a Lieutenant-Commander, the sleeves heavy with gold rings and the third most high ranking officer in the Liechtenstein navy (the first and second being Franz Josef II and Tim Thomason respectively)!

Work on the *King David* intensified during the second and third weeks of April. The generators and transmitter were lowered into the hold and welded into position, air intakes and exhaust outlets were installed and work went ahead on construction of two 72 foot high steel masts to support the aerial system. We were still lacking, however, an electronics engineer with knowledge of the building and operation of antennae and so I called an old university friend named Ewan MacPherson who worked with the BBC in London. I put a few hypothetical and general questions to him about aerials, but his answers to my queries were hopelessly detailed and technical for my unpractical mind. It suddenly clicked with him: 'You're building a "pirate" radio station!' Within three days, he had a week's holiday arranged and arrived the following weekend in Amsterdam. After a critical look at the ship and much measuring and calculating, Ewan pronounced that the two mast system of aerial was unsuitable and inefficient, but he remembered reading in the BBC library an American military intelligence report on a totally new type of aerial design; an aerial termed 'the directional discontinuity ring radiator' and which was of a revolutionary circular design. After more calculations it was reckoned that for use on 270 metres, the ring aerial should have a circumference of 67 metres and should be mounted about 12 feet above the deck; its radiation potential would, in theory (if the reports were correct) be equal to that of a vertical mast 67 metres in height. Tests which had been carried out in America also indicated that the new aerial system had many advantages. The conventional, vertical mast radiates two signals-a ground wave and a sky wave. The former is designed for coverage of the primary reception area and the latter tends to be both wasteful and the cause of the interference which plagues the medium wave band. The ring, however, appeared to radiate a signal, over 90% of which was ground wave and, therefore, much more efficient. There would be a much stronger signal in our primary reception area, Holland and south-east England, and we would not cause interference with stations outside that area using the same frequency. Costwise the aerial would work out at about 20% of that of any other system. It seemed the perfect choice. But we reckoned without the practical construction problems posed by such a structure. As soon as we presented the new idea to the shipyard it was pointed out that passage through the North Sea canal to the coast was certain to be denied to a ship with a huge, unidentifiable ring structure projecting over 20 feet from each side. The ring would have to be hinged on each side and a system of pulleys was designed whereby the two sides of the ring could be hauled up manually; the whole structure to be held up by nylon ropes slung from the central mast and attached to the ring on the 'maypole system'. It sounded ingenious; but it was to take us a long time to perfect the design.

On April 25 the *King David* put out from Ijmuiden Harbour for a test broadcast; inquisitive officials were told the South American 'cover' story and that the ship was going on short sea trials. Within an hour of leaving harbour, the weather worsened and soon a Force 8 gale was blowing. In lowering the antenna the first lesson was learned; that the ring structure, in its raised position, possessed little rigidity. One side was lowered a fraction too fast, the whole ring twisted beyond repair and the *King David* had to return to Zaandam with pieces of metal hanging over the side. The Harbourmaster, who had his fill of enquiries about the mystery Liechtenstein ship berthed in his harbour, refused the battered vessel entrance to the port on the grounds of it being a danger to the safety of other vessels. The Captain cursed him roundly and steamed past to berth at Scheepswerf Vooruit.

On May 1 a more successful test run was made and an actual broadcast was put out; a test tape, bearing the identification of the BBC World Service, and onetime property of the Corporation! A strong signal was monitored on the Dutch coast and, no doubt, there was some headscratching at the BBC monitoring station in Kent.

Throughout May work continued on the ship and a crew was laid on – which included the innovation of girl sailors. Old salts reckon women on board ships to be bad luck; however, it would be too simplistic an explanation to blame our later troubles on the presence of girls. They certainly enlivened shipboard life which could so easily be boring on board a radio ship lying at anchor, and proved competent in both studio work and keeping the vessel shipshape. In the fishing villages on the Dutch coast the *King David* was later to earn the reputation of the sex ship of the North Sea. This was largely undeserved, although life was altogether more interesting, and the atmosphere healthier, than on board a ship full of males.

Simultaneously, in Amsterdam programmes and station identification tapes were being recorded, lavish new offices were being fitted out in Bussum and staff were being employed. No one beyond a small circle, however, knew of the plans for Capital Radio and the whole operation remained secret until the first official test transmission on Sunday, June 14.

In the evening of June 13 the *King David* anchored three miles north of the REM television island in 40 fathoms of water. Within hours the strains of Handel's Water Music, which had been chosen as the station's theme, were heard on 270 metres. The next day news of the new 'pirate' broke in the newspapers. Transmissions during the following week were intermittent. On the evening of the 29th one of the nylon aerial insulators blew up during transmissions. Three days later the *Kangaroo* went out with a welder and technical experts.

Around 10.30 on the morning of the 26th it was noticed that radiation from the aerial was slowly burning away one of the nylon support ropes. Third officer Ari van der Bent volunteered to go out on the ring and fix the stay. But as he edged out on the metal rim the whole structure lost its rigidity under his weight, collapsed into an s-shape and catapulted him onto the deck, knocking him

The Capital Radio ship under construction in Scheepswerf Vooruit, Zaandam. The picture above shows the final aerial system while the other (right) shows the original unsatisfactory system which was alarmingly prone to total collapse without a great deal of warning.

unconscious. Thomason decided that return to Zaandam for repairs was necessary, the anchor was raised and the engines started. Over the radio a doctor was requested to be on hand at Ijmuiden.

In talks with the shipyard it was decided to reinforce the ring and work was begun on a new design. On July 13 the *King David* again left Ijmuiden and took up her position on the North Sea. The next day Capital Radio was back on the air with a beautiful and clear signal. Any elation we felt was short-lived. That day a storm blew up and the *King David* began to drag her anchor. The Captain dropped the reserve anchor but she still drifted before the storm, rolling heavily and helpless. The salty spray and solid walls of water which passed over the radio ship began to affect the aerial and arcing started, which meant there was imminent danger of the insulators exploding. The storm subsided a little the next day and inspection revealed serious damage to the insulators. Later in the day, to make matters worse, a nylon cable on the starboard side of the antenna broke. Transmissions had to stop. The following day, repair work was carried out but our troubles had only just begun. In the following weeks problems were experienced with the transmitter; and vital parts had to be flown in specially from America. Then the aerial feeder cable burned through within minutes of going onto full power with the new parts. It turned out we needed a special cable as thick as a man's arm to carry the load; after a week of telexing and telephoning cable companies in the States, a length of suitable cable was located and airfreighted over.

We did not appear to derive enough generator power from the Dales; our stock of spares was too low due to budgetary limitations; the ship's ballast was too heavy and she was rolling too fast in the seas; the anchoring system was not heavy duty enough; the heating broke down; the pumps refused to work; crew and captains alike proved unsatisfactory. Every time the tender went out to the *King David* some new problem was produced.

By the end of August the teething troubles seemed to be ironed out and regular transmissions were officially started on September 1. On September 9 at 6.20 in the evening the radio in the office tuned to Capital Radio went dead. Twenty minutes later the telephone rang. 'This is Scheveningen Radio. We have an emergency call from the *King David*.' An insulator had exploded and the whole ring was in danger of collapse. The following day we tried to arrange for welders to go out to the ship but the shipyard insisted that the

The Capital Radio ship wallowing in heavy seas at her anchorage off the Dutch coast.

radio ship return to port for work to be carried out. We tried to call the ship to let those on board know, but Scheveningen Radio refused to put through the call to the 'pirate' ship.

The *Kangaroo* left Ijmuiden to take the news out to the *King David*. That night several unsuccessful efforts were made to pull up the two anchors which were hopelessly entangled. Meanwhile, a Force 8 gale had built up and the situation was becoming critical on board. First one anchor was cut loose completely and then work was begun on cutting the other one free.

The crew worked on the fo'c'sle of the rolling ship, the cold numbing their hands and the spray tearing at the exposed flesh of their faces. Suddenly, a metal hawser snapped without warning and the chain began to run out. The ship's 3rd officer, Ari van der Bent was unable to get out of the way and his leg was caught under the fast moving chain; it was horribly mangled.

A distress call was put out and a naval air-sea rescue helicopter set out from its base at Valkenveld. Captain van Dalfsen applied a tourniquet and the other crew members did their best to comfort the injured man. The difficulties of the situation were compounded when the rudder shaft sheered. The ship was now helpless before the seas and wind. But the arrival of the *Kangaroo* alongside helped the situation. The *Kangaroo* put a line aboard the drifting ship and pulled her round into the wind, so that the naval helicopter could perform the delicate rescue operation. Under the most hazardous conditions the helicopter *Pedro 1* hovered over the wallowing ship despite severe buffeting from the wind. A doctor was lowered onto the rolling deck and the injured seaman lashed to a stretcher and hoisted into the helicopter. By late afternoon An van der Bent was in the operating theatre, where his crushed leg was removed.

Meanwhile, the *Kangaroo* battled to save the powerless radio ship. Three times a rope was put aboard and three times it broke. The two little ships pitched and rolled in seas which towered above their bridges. Sometimes they were obscured from each other completely by towering green walls of water. On the third attempt to put a line aboard, a huge wave hit the *Kangaroo* broadside-on as she was closing with the *King David*. The old trawler was thrown violently against the radio ship. Amid a tearing and rending of metal the ring antenna collapsed and the hulls of the two ships ground together.

The dangers increased with every minute; the weather was worsening and was now so bad that even rescue tugs were unable to

The Capital Radio ship in calmer, summer weather.

September 1970: a disaster strikes when the anchor chain severs the leg of 3rd Officer Ari van der Bent. The Dutch naval helicopter 'Pedro 1' airlifted him from the rolling deck of the radio ship. In the left photograph the radio ship's tender Kangaroo *can be seen to have a tow-line aboard.*

leave Ijmuiden Harbour. Only after a long, difficult and dangerous tow did the battered radio ship reach Ijmuiden. For the next three weeks the *King David* underwent repairs in Zaandam; repairs which put a further strain on an already tight budget. A new anchoring system had to be purchased, a new half-ring constructed and dry-dock inspection was necessary.

The radio ship's stay in dry dock was punctuated by a visit from the water police and PPT officials led by no less than Mr D. H. Neuteboom, who had plagued Veronica. They stated that they were acting upon the instruction of the Public Prosecutor of Amsterdam under Article 20 of the Telegraph and Telephone Law, which prohibits the installation of transmitting equipment without government permission. A report would be made and submitted to the Prosecutor.

We decided it would be expedient to be on the high seas by the time the report was considered and, that night, left Amsterdam Harbour for Ijmuiden. Later in the day, a 5-ton anchor and chain was installed on board the *King David* in Ijmuiden Harbour. We were satisfied, at the time, that the chain was strong enough to hold her 600 tons in position. Oil, water and provisions were taken on board, but sailing was delayed by the weather.

The *King David* left Ijmuiden Harbour at four in the morning under cover of a thick mist. Before she left some additional and unusual equipment was brought on board; two of the latest model of West German machine rifles, two sten guns, a Browning high power machine gun and nerve gas bombs.

We had been aware for some time that a 'pirate' war off the Dutch coast was brewing after Kees Manders' attempted hijack of the Radio North Sea ship, and there were rumours of bad blood between RNI and Veronica. Only two weeks previously in Zaandam Harbour, an attempt had been made to blow up the *King David*; the cock on a tank of diesel fuel in the generator room had been opened in the middle of the night and the officer of the watch had discovered the room more than a foot deep in highly explosive fuel. We intended to take all possible precautions in protecting the *King David* from sabotage attempts or hijacking. And so some of the latest machine guns were smuggled in from West Germany.

The radio ship drew out of the harbour mouth in the thick mist and we began to lower the ring antenna before the two attendant tugs left. The port side went down smoothly but the starboard side of the ring stuck. When it did fall, it was with an all too familiar rending and tearing of metal as a weld near the bridge gave way; the steel shook and strained and then collapsed on the deck in a twisted mass of metal. Disappointed and exasperated, we turned about and returned to Ijmuiden yet again.

Two days later, the damage repaired, the *King David* again left Ijmuiden and Capital Radio came back on the air on Saturday, October 10. We hoped and prayed our trials and tribulations had come to an end. During October the signal improved and the listeners club which was started, the Vrienden van Vrije Radio, met with remarkable success, gaining 5,000 members by the end of the month. The listeners' mail began to build up, the first advertising contracts came in and the general reception to the Capital Radio continuous, unannounced 'sweet music' was better than we had dared hope. The Dutch Cabinet crisis over the 'pirates' which had been in the news during September had subsided after RNI left the air on September 24 and the threat of government action was receding with Radio North Sea's powerful and troublesome transmitters off the air. Following midnight crisis discussions with Meister and Bollier on September 25, they agreed to give consideration to handing over its management of the *Mebo 2* to the IBS if their agreement with Veronica should go by the board.

The time was approaching midnight and we decided to head back to Bussum; we had had quite a night in the clubs and discotheques off Amsterdam's Leidseplein and we got to bed well after two. At 4 a.m. the doorbell rang. It was Berthe Beydals, IBS Secretary-General.

'The *King David*'s lost her anchor. The ship's adrift!'

My sleep-dulled consciousness refused to take the information in for at least five full seconds. But within five minutes I was dressed and in the office below the flat.

It was the morning of November 10. The weather off the Dutch coast was bad, although not severe enough to justify any fears for the safety of the *King David*; at least so long as she lay at her anchorage seven miles off Noordwijk.

At 0200 that morning Captain Lain Plug took over the watch from seaman Bob Brown of Manchester. The ship had been rolling in the heavy seas all evening and the wind was now gusting to Force 9. Immediately after taking over the watch the Captain became concerned that the ship was taking the seas broadside on, instead of riding into the waves as she normally did at anchor. A horrible fear

A 'new' anchor is installed in Ijmuiden Harbour. It was to last until the first gale ...

flashed across his mind and he made his way for'ard up onto the fo'c'sle. Gripping the handrail, he peered down into the blackness. His worst fears were confirmed; the anchor chain trailed slackly into the foaming sea. The anchor chain, which had been installed only one month previously, had broken and the ship was adrift!

Plug immediately roused the crew. On board were four girl sailors, Bob Brown and electronics engineer Ewan MacPherson.

Efforts were immediately made to drop the emergency anchor but it was found that the pin holding it had inexplicably been hammered into position and it was a full half hour's work before it was successfully dropped. Even then it was far too light and did not hold on the sandy bottom.

It was now obvious to all those on board that the ship was drifting shorewards in the north-westerly gale. It was difficult to estimate her position, but lights on the coast were plainly visible. Captain Plug decided to send a Mayday and went to the bridge to call Scheveningen Radio.

'MAYDAY! MAYDAY! MAYDAY/ Dit is de *King David*.'

The transmitter appeared to function normally but those waiting anxiously on the bridge for a reply from Scheveningen just heard the vacant crackling of the ether. Ewan MacPherson examined the transmitter and only after about a quarter of an hour discovered that the transmit/receive switch had jammed; the distress calls had been heard, but those on board had been unable to hear the replies.

Shortly after 3 a.m. Captain Plug was in communication with Scheveningen Radio and then with the Wijsmuller tug and salvage company. The first distress calls had been received at Wijsmuller's communication centre in Ijmuiden by the night operator. The well-oiled Wijsmuller machine swung into action. The duty operator telephoned down to one of the tugs which lie like vultures at their wharf a hundred yards away. Within five minutes the Captain of the tug *Hector* was casting off on his way to the crippled radio ship – and a potential fat salvage fee. Meanwhile, Scheveningen Radio had alerted the Ijmuiden lifeboat, *Johanna Louisa*, and the Noordwijk beach rescue boat, *Kurt Carlsen*, and both launched to the assistance of the distressed ship. It was a race against time.

In the office half a dozen of us sat in a dejected circle. A communications receiver crackled away in the corner and the telephone rang with progress reports on the rescue attempts. Most of us realised only too well the full implications of the situation; if

The Capital Radio ship back in Ijmuiden harbour with a hopelessly twisted antenna damaged during the lowering operation at sea.

the ship ran aground it might be so badly damaged it would never float again. If Wijsmuller got a line aboard, the salvage claim would be so large the *King David* might never go to sea again.

On board, the crew were equally powerless as the *King David* continued her shoreward drift, the seas battering her broadside on. The girls made tea and the crew gathered in the saloon below the bridge. There was no diesel engineer on board to start the engines; he had walked off the ship and left on the tender the previous weekend. An apparent coincidence. There was nothing to be done.

At ten minutes past five the *Kurt Carlsen* came alongside and, one by one, the crew jumped from the rolling deck into the lifeboat. Captain Plug and the electronics engineer remained on board; the radio ship was now only 500 yards from the beach.

At five-thirty a shudder ran through the ship as she passed over the first sandbank; then another, before she finally came to rest hard and fast on the beach at the Dutch seaside resort of Noordwijk, only two hundred yards from the luxury Palace Hotel.

At 5.55 a.m. Scheveningen Radio telexed IBS Secretary-General Berthe Beydals in Bussum: '*King David* now high and dry on the beach.'

The rescued crew members were landed safely and taken to the local police station; by 7 a.m. we had arrived in Noordwijk. We drove along the beach promenade in the half-light of dawn. The stranded radio ship was hardly difficult to find. She lay only two hundred yards from the promenade, silhouetted in the dawn with the waves breaking over her. It was a macabre sight to see her lying there, her ring antenna still down and her lights blazing. She might still have been in the open sea but for the fact her precarious position was given away every time a fresh wave hit her and she lurched sickeningly on the sand. It was strange and curiously poignant to see her there; normally she lay so alone on the open sea but was now thrust ruthlessly ashore by the waves.

On the beach there was a huddle of men gathered in the chill early morning wind. One had a radio and I spoke to Captain Plug and Ewan MacPherson. There was no serious damage as yet and the two were in no danger. Low water was at 9 a.m. and it would be possible to go on board then.

Shortly before nine Thomason and crew members waded out to the ship; an initial inspection showed there to be little apparent damage. The tug *Hector* could be seen lying about a mile off-shore and hopes were high that the ship would be refloated at mid-day with the high tide.

We all repaired to the Palace Hotel for coffee and a discussion with Wijsmuller's salvage director, Mr van Brugghen. It was made obvious that an early salvage attempt was not possible; cable was not available and it had to be brought by lorry from Ijmuiden, fifteen miles away.

That morning, the lifeboat *Kurt Carlsen* took up position on the beach ready to take the cable out to the *Hector*, which, due to the depth of water it drew, was unable itself to approach the *King David*. We waited impatiently for the cable to arrive. High tide came and went. No cable appeared. The *King David* embedded herself deeper into the beach.

At five in the afternoon Mr Arthur Wijsmuller arrived in Noordwijk to make a personal assessment of the situation, and he had a telephone conversation with Berthe Beydals in Bussum. Wijsmuller agreed to pull the ship off without a further contract; Captain Plug had signed a contract granting salvage rights under Lloyds Open Form, but which was subject to the approval of the ship's owners.

Meanwhile, the grounded radio ship had become a major tourist attraction and throughout the day thousands of people had thronged the beach to stare at the curious sight of a crippled radio ship lying on the sand. The schoolchildren of Noordwijk were given the morning off and escorted to the beach by their teachers to stare at the scene. Police were called in to deal with the traffic on the promenade and two hotels, closed for the winter, threw open their doors! One hotel owner declared that the longer the radio ship lay aground the better it suited him! We, quite naturally, felt more than a little differently. The cable still had not arrived and early in the evening the *Kurt Carlsen* stood down. At nine in the evening the lorry arrived from Ijmuiden and Wijsmullers put a crew of no less than 14 men on the radio ship, who set about securing the cable and preparing for the salvage attempt.

The next morning, Wednesday, a special flat-bottomed vessel left Amsterdam Harbour and arrived off Noordwijk at 6 a.m. The skipper decided, however, that in the Force 7 wind and heavy swell it was too dangerous to take his ship alongside the *King David* to attempt the cable transfer to the *Hector*.

At 7 a.m. the ship left for Ijmuiden and Wijsmullers informed us that no attempts could be made that day in view of the weather. The whole day the *King David* was battered by the seas and on the Thursday there was still no improvement in the weather. It was a

On board Capital Radio in happier days. Three of the attractive girl sailors on the bridge of the ship and (opposite) Executive Director of the International Broadcasters Society, and operator of the station, T.D.R. Thomason, complete with Scottish Highland dress.

November 1970, and Capital Radio runs aground on the Dutch coast at Noordwijk. The lifeboat stands by (above) and crew members trek ashore (right)

Aground

The warships of many countries kept a watchful eye on the radio ships off the Dutch coast in the early '70s. Here the Dutch gunboat Bellatrix draws alongside the MV Kangaroo.

The link that broke ... in the 'new' anchor chain.

The radio ship is chained up in Amsterdam harbour on the orders of the court pending payment of the Wijsmuller salvage claim.

strange experience to walk about the grounded ship; each wave which hit the steel hull sent a sledgehammer crash and alarming vibrations through the whole vessel. The ship was tilted over at a crazy angle, the waves washed over the deck and the huge ring antenna shook under the strain.

The situation was now becoming more serious. The concrete ballast was beginning to fracture and water was welling up through the cracks. We had no idea how the plating under the ship was suffering and our fears were increased with every hour the vessel lay on the sand. Those on board, however, did manage to turn the ship that day by throwing out the emergency anchor and starting the engines. Although the ship could not refloat herself in the shallow water, she was at least facing into the waves.

We were becoming increasingly exasperated with Wijsmullers; at each high tide there was a fresh excuse as to why the ship could not be pulled off. The weather was too bad, the cable was not strong enough, there was no boat to take the cable out to the *Hector*, and so on.

On the Thursday morning our tender Captain, Huig Ouwehand, talked with the crew of the Nordwijk beach rescue boat who informed him that they were and always had been, willing to take the line out to the *Hector*. Wijsmullers were not availing themselves of the opportunity for reasons of which we were not quite sure. But the longer and more hazardous a rescue operation, the greater the salvage fee which can be claimed.

No thanks to Wijsmullers, at 7 p.m. that evening the *Kurt Carlsen* was launched and, in a difficult two hour operation, succeeded in transfering a polypropylene line to the *Hector*. It was hauled aboard and the cable between the tug and the radio ship was secured.

As 2 a.m. on the Friday morning an attempt was made to pull the *King David* off on the high tide. We watched from a bedroom on the top floor of the Palace Hotel; below us the crippled radio ship lay straddling on a sandbank-her stern sunk deep in the sand, and her bows pointing in the air. We watched, heart in mouth, as the ship strained and rocked in the sand; her deck was lit by floodlights and all else was black dark save for the lights of the *Hector* which could be seen in the near distance bobbing up and down in the swell.

The tug made attempt after attempt to free the *King David* but she would not budge. We were afraid that the strain would break her back, but the more imminent danger was of breaking the cable which had taken so much time and effort to transfer. After an hour of fruitless pulling and straining the salvage master decided to abandon attempts for the night. The huddled groups of onlookers on the beach, like so many mourners at a winter day's funeral, began to disperse. It occurred to me that it was Friday the 13th . . . we certainly seemed to be running short of luck.

We began to wonder if the *King David* was now too deeply entrenched in the sand to shift and later on the Friday morning we held crisis talks in Bussum. We decided to give Wijsmullers one more try; if it did not succeed at the next high tide, we would cut the ship open with oxy-acetylene burners, remove all the vital radio equipment and abandon her to the elements. All morning Wijsmullers prepared for the next high tide, which was at 2.30 in the afternoon. The salvage director reckoned the starboard side of the radio ship was too deeply embedded in a sandbank and he ordered a considerable quantity of sand to be shifted by bulldozer.

At 2.40 that afternoon the Captain of the *Hector* put his engines full ahead; the *King David* shuddered from end to end and was free! There was a cheer from the hundreds gathered on the beach and in the office there was a carnival atmosphere. If we had known what trials and tribulations the following months were to hold, we would have felt very differently.

At 7 p.m. the *King David* arrived in Ijmuiden Harbour leaking slightly, but otherwise undamaged. The formalities were carried out; a meeting was arranged with Arthur Wijsmuller to discuss salvage payment and we were told the ship could be moved anywhere except onto the open sea. The local police arrived and the ship's armoury of machine guns and light weapons was seized.

In Ijmuiden a disturbing piece of evidence with a direct relevance to the stranding came to light. Examination of the engine room showed that all the moving parts of the ship's engines had been 'lubricated' not with lubricating oil but with highly explosive diesel fuel. When exactly it had been done we could not be sure, but it raised our suspicions. Such an explosion would have wrecked the engine room and maybe blown a hole in the side of the ship; there was no rational explanation for the presence of the diesel fuel in the engine room. Attempted sabotage was the only explanation and our minds went back to the Zaandam incident in September. It was indeed fortunate that the engines had not been started in a bid to halt the drift of the ship. The convenient departure of the diesel engineer from the *King David* three days previous to the accident also left question marks in our minds.

The following week the *King David* was towed down the North Sea Canal to dry dock at Amsterdam's Westerdoek. Examination in dry dock revealed the damage to be very slight indeed and within two days it was repaired. Arrangements were then made for the vessel's transfer to another shipyard, Ceuvel Volharding in North Amsterdam, for the installation of a new anchoring system. Wijsmullers were informed of the intention to move the *King David*. Arthur Wijsmuller was abroad on business but an underling panicked when he heard that the radio ship was to be moved.

As the *King David* left Amsterdam's Westerdoek on November 26 the crew noticed a police boat and harbour launch move into pursuit. At her destination, in the North of Amsterdam Harbour, sheriff's officers came aboard, served a notice of the ship's arrest upon the Captain and chained up the wheel.

This symbolic act set the seal upon the *King David*'s fate. It severely prejudiced efforts that were being made to recapitalise the Capital Radio project. From the day that the ship went aground, it was obvious that further capital was necessary. The insurance company refused to pay out and claimed the *King David* was uninsured. A court case over this would probably have lasted up to three years. Wijsmullers made it clear they expected the equivalent of £15,000 sterling for the saving of the ship. The installation of a new anchoring system was to cost an estimated £5,000, and sundry other repairs another £2,000. All the time the ship lay in harbour the bills mounted up. Wages for the crew and office personnel; bills for fuel and food. And there was no income at all. Advertising contracts which were due to start lay in the files, unactivated. One contract alone, from an American religious organisation, worth nearly £50,000, would have paid the debts more than twice over, but Wijsmullers were inflexible. They required payment before the radio ship left for the open sea.

By the beginning of December money had run out completely and Executive Director Tim Thomason and his wife put their personal assets at the disposal of the IBS to pay crew members in a bid to keep the project going. Incredibly, the organisation managed to continue in a cohesive form right up to the month of March, 1971.

There was a tremendous spirit among those who had become involved in this exciting project. Everybody on the crew and in the office refused to believe that the daring adventure was doomed to failure. With only one or two exceptions everyone carried on without pay; some taking part-time jobs and sharing the money they earned.

Thomason raised personal loans to pay the staff, but the situation became more and more serious as creditors pressed for their money. Somehow enough money was raised to keep the telephone and light working in the office but there were no reserves for anything else.

We all hoped against hope that something would come of at least one of our attempts to gain fresh capital. The idea of operating a radio ship on the high seas appeals to many people, but few have either the finance or the enterprise necessary for such an operation. In the months following the stranding of the *King David* we approached, and were approached by, all sorts of people and groups.

Gus Jansen of Basart, the Dutch record company, who later made a deal with RNI, declined to take the risk. In January, Meister, in the midst of scheming to get the *Mebo 2* back on the air, offered £15,000 to get the *King David* out of dock if, upon returning to the air, we would consent to jam Radio Veronica. We had discussions with disc jockey Willem van Coten (alias Joost de Drayer) and Jan van Ween, son-in-law of former Veronica director Dirk Verweij, but they also later went into alliance with RNI. At the end of December, Executive Director Thomason flew to the United States in a bid to raise further capital, but this also proved unsuccessful.

Protracted negotiations went on during the latter half of January and into February with a representative of Will Hoordijk, who had been involved with Veronica on the advertising side, but they were unsuccessful. His representative, De Man of Oscar Film Studios in Amsterdam, had an interesting background. He had been involved in the abortive REM island project and had lost a great deal of money in the adventure. Shortly after the collapse, he was put under pressure by one of his creditors, a film producer by the name of Claude Berkely. An evening meeting was arranged at De Man's studio on the banks of Amsterdam's River Amstel. What exactly happened that evening no-one knows to this day. But Claude Berkely's body was found the next morning trussed up in a sack floating in the Amstel. He had been strangled. De Man was taken into custody by police and interrogated at length. The evidence against him was purely circumstantial and he was released.

The last bout of negotiations were carried on with a Belgian group operating under the name of Radio Marina. Meister and Bollier

An Aberdeen Corporation double-decker bus goes to work raising funds in an effort to get Capitol Radio back on the air. Here the bus is pictured in the very heart of Amsterdam outside the Royal Palace in Dam Square.

Chic female pirate crew members aboard the MV King David. *Chief radio engineer Ewan Macpherson is emerging through the hatch cover.*

also tried unsuccessfully to deal with this group but found them as slippery as we did. The two principals were a pair of remarkably skilled and experienced confidence tricksters, who had managed to fool a large number of supporters that they were seriously intent upon the operation of an offshore radio station.

They made their first approach in December but no concrete proposal was forthcoming and the next contact was in February. When I was in Belgium on business that month I paid a visit to a young man named Pierre Deseyn in Ghent. He was the organiser of the Belgian Free Radio Organisation and asked if I would meet the Radio Marina people – Valere and Cecile Broucke – again for further discussions. An initial discussion followed that afternoon in Ghent and the next day the Brouckes travelled to Holland for further talks in Bussum.

The following week a verbal agreement between Radio Marina, the IBS and the Kangaroo Pioneering Company of Liechtenstein was hammered out and Thomason, myself and Dirk de Groot of Kangaroo drove down to Ghent for the signing of the contracts. Under the contract drawn up, Broucke was to hire the *King David* for a period of three months at a price of five million Belgian francs (approximately £50,000).

We met on a pleasure boat named the *Benelux* in Ghent Harbour, which Broucke claimed to be his own. At the point of signing the contract, however, he stated that he wished to consult his bank director before committing himself in writing. Feeling rather frustrated, we left Ghent without the money but with Broucke in possession of the two copies of the contract, signed by Kangaroo. Payment was to be made the next morning.

The next day we waited for word of payment. The day after that, a Friday, we were still waiting and were unable to contact the elusive Broucke despite frequent and lengthy telex contacts with his bank director in Ghent, van der Hof of the Europa Bank. We were never able to ascertain fully the role of the bank in the episode but we later discovered that it was not exactly one of Europe's larger or more prosperous institutions. In fact it is not even listed in the official directories of European banking.

We only discovered what was going on when we received a telephone call on the Sunday morning from Radio Veronica's lawyer, Dr Borderwijk. The previous day, Valere and Cecile Broucke had arrived on the doorstep at Veronica in Hilversum and asked to speak to the station's commercial director. Bold as brass they produced the signed contracts and declared that the agreement would not go through if Veronica paid ten million Belgian francs! Surely, the intrepid pair asked, the gentlemen of Veronica did not want to see another Dutch pop ship lying next to them off the coast?

Jurgens reserved his decision until the Monday and contacted the station's lawyer. On the Sunday, Thomason informed both Jurgens and Bul Verweij that the IBS refused to be a party to any form of blackmail and that the contract was off. When the Radio Marina people visited Veronica the next day, they found that their attempted imitation of the RNI blackmail tactic was not going to work and the Brouckes disappeared.

15

Blackmail, bullets and bombs

On the morning of November 10, 1970, Radio Veronica once again became the sole radio ship broadcasting off the Dutch coast. Capital Radio squatted awkwardly across a sandbank in all of nine inches of water on the very doorstep of Noordwijk's Palace Hotel, and the RNI ship lay silent at her anchorage off Scheveningen after the abrupt September 24 closure. The rumours were still flying thick and fast. Most people in the business suspected RNI had closed as a result of Veronica pressure, but the full story was not yet known. In Zurich a number of conflicting statements were made. Bollier told journalists that the future of the *Mebo 2* was under active consideration and it was rumoured that the station would return on December 15. December 15 came and went. New Year's day was postulated. New Year's day came ... and at IBS headquarters there came a telephone call from Meister asking if Capital Radio would return to sea to jam Radio Veronica. A further 'silence payment' was due from Veronica's Liechteinstein company, World Wide Trade, and £15,000 could be made available to free Capital Radio from harbour. We were convinced that a full-scale 'pirate' war was about to erupt and we didn't act on the generous offer of the two Swiss. Hostilities were declared five days later. On January 6 a small boat left Scheveningen Harbour and drew alongside the *Mebo 2*. The master, Captain Onnes (who had been placed on board by Radio Veronica), was told that there was an urgent telephone call for him at the shipping agent's office in Scheveningen. He left the ship and within half an hour was at the agent's where his surprise rapidly turned to dismay when he realised how he had been tricked; there was no telephone call.

In the meantime, another boat had left the harbour; on board was Edwin Bollier, one of his Swiss engineers and two pistols. The two went on board the radio ship and told the crew of 'new arrangements', distributed drink and a party began. Bollier and colleague established themselves on the bridge with their guns, like latter-day cowboys, and awaited the return of the unfortunate Captain, who duly drew alongside in a hired boat. Predictably, he demanded his ship back and accused Bollier of piracy. But the superior firepower of the duo convinced him of the folly of attempting any sort of counter coup (especially with his crew below decks half-drunk) and he made off back to the shore to alert the gentlemen of Veronica in Hilversum.

Both Bul and Jaap Verweij, accompanied by the station's general manager Norbert Jurgens, drove to Scheveningen and went out to the *Mebo 2*. At the rail of the ship stood Bollier and technician, pistols in hand, obviously unwilling to countenance a piping-aboard ceremony. Bul Verweij told Bollier that the ship belonged to Veronica and that he was coming aboard. The latter replied with the ultimate and irrefutable argument: 'If you attempt to board, everybody on your boat will be shot dead.'

On January 7 two tugs from Rotterdam drew alongside the *Mebo 2* and, on Bollier's instructions, the anchor was hauled up and a tow began to a new position off the Belgian coast. Simultaneously, Erwin Meister checked out of Scheveningen's Grand Hotel and drove to Belgium. The plan was to broadcast as RNI from off the Belgian coast; this was clear of Veronica's 'patch' and, also, the Belgian organisation Radio Marina had verbally agreed to take substantial blocks of time. Both Meister and Bollier spent some time in the next ten days in Ghent discussing plans with Valere Broucke and the others involved in the Marina project. They rapidly realised the futility of negotiations with the slippery, elusive Broucke. In the meantime, the 'pirate' war was brought into the public gaze in Holland by a detailed and lengthy article in influential *Elseviers* Magazine. The article told how Veronica paid what it termed as 'ether blackmail', in the form of an estimated £25,000, to the Swiss owners of RNI, in return for which the station would stay off the air for three months. In December, as RNI made plans to return to the air, Veronica invoked a clause making the contract renewable.

The article also revealed something of the internecine conflict which had split Veronica itself. It told how Bul and Jaap Verweij had ousted their brother, and fellow owner, Dirk from he board of directors of the station; how they had sacked Dirk's son-in-law, top disc jockey Jan van Ween; how Holland's most popular d.j. Joost de Draier had also been sacked by the directors. This was, perhaps, the most critical article on Veronica published since the station's early years and it marked the turn of the tide; a shift of opinion against Veronica and the beginning of doubts about the ethical nature of the station's dealings.

The psychedelically-painted RNI ship was the most modern and sophisticated pirate ship ever launched. Her antennas facilitated broadcasts on medium wave, short wave and VHF. She housed an array of sophisticated technical equipment, the purpose of which was never clarified right up until the time she was taken over by Libya's Colonel Gaddafi.

On January 28 unannounced test transmissions came from the *Mebo 2* anchored off Cadzand on the Belgian coast. The following weekend the position of the ship was again shifted – back to Scheveningen, and 2 km. away from the Veronica ship. Meister and Bollier now occupied themselves with finalising arrangements for a more secure Dutch base for their operation. Negotiations began with Gus Jansen of Amsterdam's Strengholt Publishing and Basart record company. At three o'clock on the afternoon of Monday, February 8, a contract was signed betwen the two groups. Under the contract a new company was set up, 'Radio Nordsee N.V.' which was to be responsible for programming and advertising sales. Control in these two spheres passed to the Dutch parties involved, although ownership of the *Mebo 2* still rested with the Swiss. Full details were later announced to the press. The two former Veronica d.js Jan van Ween and Joost de Draier were appointed by the new company to take over programming, which would be in Dutch between 0900 and 1600 hours. The rest of the day it would be in English. The Dutch programmes would be taped on land; the English would be broadcast live from the radio ship.

Familiar names joined the English service. Alan West and Dave Rogers (who had been with the station previously); Tony Allan (former Radio Scotland, Grampian and Granada TV man); Stevi Merike who came via Radio Scotland, Caroline and Radio One; new man Crispian St. John and Martin Kayne (former Caroline d.j.).

The position of owners Meister and Bollier seemed somewhat vague. They claimed they were still involved in the running of the radio ship. 'We are working together', Meister told me at Schipol Airport on February to when we met to discuss an advertising contract. Jansen of Basart was sure he had gained complete control of the operation and put in former singer John de Mol to run it. He was not fully in the picture, however, as to all the various agreements Meister and Bollier had made, and was to find that other groups were to file notice of prior claims on the controversial radio ship.

Station production director Victor Pelli, a pop man from Zurich appointed by Bollier (also to run the station), welcomed listeners on the afternoon of February 21 to 'a new era in the history of RNI as official transmissions were commenced. He did this against a background of spectacular new developments.

The previous week the owners of Radio Veronica had announced they were to charge Bollier with piracy on the high seas. Bul Verweij revealed how Bollier had taken over the *Mebo 2*, which, he claimed, was under contract to Veronica. Bollier had threatened to kill him, and the Captain had had his command taken from him forcibly. The act was regarded as piracy and evidence had been submitted to the Officer of Justice in Utrecht. That same week a member of the Dutch Second Chamber called the attention of the BVD (Dutch Secret Police) to certain information which had come into his hands concerning Bollier's, and his radio ship's, connection with the East German government and the top secret Instituut fur Technische Untersuchunc in East Berlin. Rumours of this reached the Dutch press but the full extent or nature of the investigation was not perceived. The BVD commenced investigations and certain information was made available to the US Central Intelligence Agency in Amsterdam.

At the beginning of March the directors of Veronica issued a writ against Meister and Bollier. The writ asked the court to order the radio ship *Mebo 2* to cease broadcasting and enter the port of Rotterdam or, as a subsidiary request, to empower Radio Veronica to itself bring the *Mebo 2* into port. The writ further alleged that RNI was in breach of a contract with Veronica; the radio ship was under hire to Radio Veronica for a sum of one million guilders (over £100,000); Meister and Bollier were in breach of contract by tricking the captain off the vessel and taking forcible control of it; the contract also forbade Dutch language transmissions from the *Mebo 2*

On March 10 a hearing took place in the district court of Rotterdam, at which both sides put their submissions. In court for the event were both Jaap and Bul Verweij, Jurgens, and the two Swiss.

Veronica's lawyer, Borderwijk, put Veronica's case; the money had been paid over for RNI to stay off the air as its activities were politically harmful to offshore radio. RNI's lawyer explained that in December 1970 his clients attempted to repay Veronica so that they could recommence broadcasts. Despite the fact they had presented themselves with a suitcase stuffed with £100,000 worth of Deutschmarks, Veronica refused to accept the money. Having offered return of the money they were entitled to recommence broadcasts, their lawyer maintained.

The judge was obviously unimpressed by both sides and commented: 'This is a fight between two parties as slippery as eels in jelly.' The contract was unclear, he thought, and he anounced he would give a decision in the case on March 25. When the court reconvened two weeks later he adjudged that having offered return of the money, RNI could continue with its broadcasts.

The gentlemen of Veronica were understandably angry. They had genuinely believed they would win the court action and the result had been little better than a slap in the face. There was a general air of embitterment towards RNI in Veronica's headquarters. The elections were approaching and the end of all offshore stations was in sight if RNI's 'big Dutch mouth', as the Verweijs termed it, wasn't closed for good.

One station executive murmured confidentially in my ear: 'One night there's going to be an accident out there!' We both laughed. I thought he was joking. He wasn't.

In June, 1966, the radio station Radio City, located on a Second World War fort complex in the Thames Estuary, was boarded and occupied by a group of hired thugs. The pirate war spilled into the columns of the press and a premature end for the offshore broadcasters was announced the following month, when the Marine Broadcasting (Offences) Bill was put before Parliament. The dramatic events around, and consequences of, the Radio City affair were later to be mirrored off the Dutch coast in the violence which exploded around the *Mebo 2*.

There was no reason for those on board RNI on the night of Saturday, May 15 to suppose that it was anything other than a normal evening. On board the radio ship, which wallowed in a gentle swell, all was quiet; crew and off-duty disc-jockeys relaxed before the television; in the transmitter room, Kurt, the Swiss electronics engineer, checked the brightly glowing tubes and, all over Europe, millions of listeners, at home and in their cars, were tuned in to 'the Summer Sound of RNI'.

Four miles away, however, on a stretch of lonely beach near Scheveningen, three frogmen were silently inflating a rubber boat and affixing an outboard motor. Silently they pushed it out into the oncoming surf and wriggled themselves aboard as the outboard motor spluttered into life. The leader of the three, 24-year old 'Captain Thorn', as he is known in Scheveningen, took the helm and set course for the radio ship. There was a little mist but within a quarter of an hour the hull of the *Mebo 2* loomed up. The motor cut out and they paddled their way across the silent sea and under the stern. On board there were lights and the sounds of laughing and joking. There was no-one on watch; Thorn gripped the handrail and pulled himself onto the deck. He knew the *Mebo 2* well. His small diving boat *De Redder* had served as the station's tender for several months. Since the September close-down of RNI, however, he had fallen on hard times and his diving business, 'Duikwacht Holland', had gone bankrupt.

It was the work of seconds to find their way down the metal stairs into the engine room. Two of them wrapped oil-soaked rags round the fuel lines, affixed over a pound of dynamite and lit the rags. At ten minutes to eleven, as they prepared to lower themselves back into their rubber boat, there was a huge explosion. A blast of searing hot air hit the diver still on the deck and he was blown from his feet, over the rail and into the sea. As crew and disc jockeys tumbled onto the deck they saw the small rubber boat drawing away from the ship. There was an acrid, burning smell and they immediately understood what had happened.

In a series of dramatic broadcasts amazed listeners all over Europe heard of the radio ship's plight. Disc jockey Alan West interrupted transmissions: *'Mayday! Mayday! This is the radio ship* Mebo 2, *four miles off the coast of Scheveningen, Holland . . . we require assistance urgently due to a fire on board this vessel caused by a bomb being thrown into our engine room . . . Mayday! Mayday! This is an SOS from Radio North Sea International!'*

For the next half hour listeners were given a minute by minute report on the critical situation aboard the now blazing 'pirate' ship. Captain Hardeveld, the master of the ship, repeated the distress calls in Dutch and disc jockeys made the situation clear for listeners, in what must go down as some of the most exciting radio of all time.

This is an act of piracy on the high seas . . . you have bombed a Panamanian ship on the high seas . . . we do not know how long the Mebo 2 *will stay afloat . . . we may have to abandon ship. . .!*

Urgent appeals were made for the Zurich office of RNI to be alerted and the telephone number was given out over the air. Meanwhile the fire was spreading throughout the whole stern section of the ship; at one stage, crew members believed they had it under control but it flared up again and reached the bridge. Vital telecommunications equipment was removed from the bridge as it filled with smoke.

The appeals for assistance became even more dramatic. *'The entire stern end of the ship is ablaze . . . we are having to abandon the* Mebo 2 *. . . this is the* Mebo 2 *on fire . . . Mayday! Mayday!'*

Danger High Voltage! Unforeseen dangers were ahead for RNI.

Clip from Dutch TV film of the RNI ship burning after frogmen attached explosives on the instructions of rival neighbour Radio Veronica.

Periods of silence were punctuated by the station's theme tune 'Man of Action'. Three quarters of an hour after the attack the Captain came on the air to give the crippled ship's position and announce that the crew and disc jockeys were in the lifeboats. The last announcement came from the station's Swiss engineer. Coughing in the smoke-filled studio he gave a report on the situation in Schweizer-deutsch for the ship's owners in Zurich. Seconds later, RNI's medium wave, VHF and short-wave channels went dead as the huge transmitters were closed down.

On land a massive rescue operation was swinging into action. The distress calls had been monitored at the Wijsmuller salvage company's telecommunications centre ten mile up the coast in Ijmuiden, and the tug *Titan* put to sea within minutes of the attack. The tug *Smitbank*, owned by the rival concern of Smit & Tak in Rotterdam, simultaneously left harbour for the distressed pop-ship. Lifeboats from Scheveningen and Noordwijk were launched. First vessel on the scene was the tug *Eurotrip* from Scheveningen, used for tendering by RNI. The *Eurotrip* took on board the disc jockeys and crew who had taken to the life-rafts and then set about tackling the blaze.

Shortly afterwards she was joined by a firefighting tug, the *Volant*. A later arrival on the scene was the Dutch Royal Navy frigate *Gelderland*, with 250 marines on board. As flames leapt high in the air over the after-end of the ship the tugs closed in on the ship and trained high-power hoses on the fire. The Captain, transmitter engineer and ship's engineer remained on board throughout the blaze. After two hours the situation was brought under control and the damage, it was discovered, was not as serious as was feared initially. The whole of the after-end of the ship, including the bridge, was gutted, but the studios, transmitter room and disc-jockeys' quarters were untouched.

When it was found that there was no further danger to the safety of the vessel, the disc jockeys and crew returned on board and transmissions were resumed ... as normal. On land, police immediately began an investigation into the mystery attack. The first news reports on the attack were confused and conflicting, and this factor led to the police receiving an invaluable lead. Captain Thorn's sister, who had heard her brother talk of making the attack, heard a news report that the Captain of the *Mebo 2* had died in the explosion on board. In a shocked state she telephoned the police and, early Sunday morning, Thorn was pulled from his bed in The Hague by officers of the Rijkspolitie. Events now moved rapidly. Later in the morning, two more divers suspected of taking part in the attack were arrested. On a stretch of lonely beach near Scheveningen police discovered divers' suits, and the remains of a rubber boat, which had been partially destroyed.

The police were of the opinion that the damaged radio ship should return to harbour and they visited the vessel. The management of the pop station, however, were not so keen on the idea (probably mindful of the queue of creditors with writs in hand who would doubtless gather). Director John de Mol told reporters in Scheveningen, 'We must continue our programmes.' Police announced that the divers would be charged with piracy on the high seas, a charge carrying a maximum penalty of 12 years imprisonment. Their competence in bringing such a charge was questioned, but it was pointed out that three Dutchmen, using a Dutch boat, had carried out the deed and, under The Geneva Convention of 1958, such interference with a ship and its crew on the high seas amounted to piracy – a charge which any national police force was able and dutybound to press.

Amsterdam police commander Theo Nelissen told reporters at a press conference later in the day that the operation was well-planned and that police believed the motives of the divers, two of whom had confessed, to be financial. There was one big question in everyone's mind. What was the reason for the attack? What was behind it? On the Sunday few people guessed at the sensational developments of the following 24 hours.

On the Monday morning police revealed that they believed a wealthy Dutch businessman to be behind the bomb attack, and that afternoon officers of the Amsterdam water police travelled to the village of Loosdrecht, Holland's 'purple patch,' and made a sensational arrest. The morning papers the following day carried the screaming headlines: TOPMAN VAN VERONICA IN ARREST', 'VERONICA BETAALDE AANSLAG NOORDSEE'.

No less than Norbert Jurgens, general manager of Veronica, had been arrested on suspicion of having ordered and paid for the bomb attack on rival station RNI. Amazement was expressed throughout Holland that ultra-respectable Veronica, almost part of the establishment, should be suspected of being involved in the weekend gangsterism on the North Sea.

A lengthy police statement was issued, which lifted the lid off the pirate war. Each of the divers was to receive from Jurgens, upon the successful completion of their task, approximately £3,000. An advance of over £1,000 had already been made for incidental costs. The plan was to set fire to the ship and damage it so badly that it would have to enter harbour, where it could be made subject to an arrestment order.

It was further revealed that Jurgens was the Dutch representative of a Liechtenstein company Worldwide Est. which was the owner of the Veronica ship *Nordeney* and which had, the previous September, signed the contract with the Swiss owners of the *Mebo 2* for the hire of the RNI vessel. The plot was thickening.

Commented Nelissen of the Amsterdam police; 'It is not easy to know whether we should speak of the Veronica organisation or World Wide. It is indeed a strange thing when two different companies can sit under one roof, and, in fact, be one and the same.' Most of the tax authorities throughout Western Europe would have agreed with him! (The nature of the structure of Liechtenstein companies, where the names of those involved remain a secret, is a constant source of irritation to them.) Jurgens told the police that he never gave instructions for explosives to be used and that evening the directors of Radio Veronica issued a statement saying that they had absolutely nothing to do with the attack. The police, however, thought differently.

On television on the Tuesday evening Bul Verweij admitted having paid Jurgens about £10,000 to have the *Mebo 2* brought within Dutch territorial waters, but denied any knowledge of, or responsibility for, the events which ensued.

But on Wednesday evening Bul Verweij, known affectionately to staff and listeners alike as 'Uncle Bul', was arrested by police and taken into custody. Each day headlines in the Dutch press announced sensational new developments. One paper printed a story that the Capital Radio ship, lying in harbour after its November stranding, would replace the *Mebo 2*. More notable was a story carried by the Amsterdam evening paper *Het Parool* on May 21 headed 'Dirk Verweij once again Veronica director'. The story broke the news that the displaced brother, with Bul Verweij and Jurgens now in jail, had been asked by shareholders to resume his duties as a director of the station. Jaap Verweij, whom the police saw no reason to suspect of complicity in the bombing, remained a director. For the personnel of Veronica the arrest of two of their bosses came like a bolt from the blue.

The same day as Dirk Verweij took over in Hilversum, the Officer of Justice in The Hague, Mr. Dr Van t'Veer, announced that he was ordering an official investigation into the circumstances of the stranding of Capital Radio ship the previous November. As a result of the RNI bombing, he stated, new evidence had come to light and the circumstances of the grounding appeared suspicious. 'I have received information that something irregular happened,' stated the Officer of Justice.

Elsewhere in The Hague there was unease over the outbreak of the pirate war, and moves in the Second Chamber for ratification of the Strasbourg Convention, outlawing offshore broadcasting, gathered momentum. On May 27 Dutch Premier Piet de Jong announced that a Bill for ratification of the Treaty would be placed before Parliament before the eud of the year. He denied it was a direct result of the sea attack and stated that further complaints of interference with shipping and other vital services had been received from Scheveningen Radio and from the governments of Britain and Norway. He also claimed that complaints had come from as far away as Australia! The weak transmitter of Radio Veronica was not responsible, but the powerful, worldwide equipment of RNI was causing chaos.

Meanwhile on May 24 the Dutch courts were, in their own way, sealing the pirates' fate. In the district court of Amsterdam the final nail was hammered into the coffin of Capital Radio as the International Broadcasters Society, operators of the station, were officially declared bankrupt. In court in The Hague, the Officer of Justice laid evidence of the complicity of Bul Verweij in organising the RNI attack. Verweij, personally, it was alleged, had given over £200 to one of the divers for the purchase of an outboard motor. Verweij told the judge that he knew of the plan to bring the *Mebo 2* within territorial waters, but thought that the dynamite was to be used to part the anchor chain. The charges were laid before the court by Dr H. van t'Veer: 'I accuse the three divers, as perpetrators of the attack, of piracy; Heer Verweij and Heer Jurgens of complicity in the crime.' The judge ordered that Verweij be kept in custody in prison in Utrecht.

Over the heads of all five detained men there hung the possibility of a twelve-year prison sentence.

The whole affair would have sounded fantastic in that small smoke-filled room in Amsterdam's Hotel Krasnapolsky ten years previously.

But on September 21, 1971, Hendrik 'Bul' Verweij, Norbert Jurgens and the three divers were all found guilty in organising and participating in the attack on the Radio North Sea ship. They were each sentenced to one year in prison.

16

Police, politics and sabotage

During the summer and autumn of 1970 a pirate war had broken out off the Dutch coast, evidenced by a whole series of dramatic events; Kees Manders' attack on the *Mebo 2*, the mysterious close-down of RNI, the seizing of the RNI tender, the writs which flew like confetti and the secret contracts designed to liquidate competitors.

Against this background, on November 10, the Capital Radio ship parted company with her newly installed anchor chain and was wrecked on the Dutch coast. The last in a long series of 'accidents' and 'coincidences' which befell the MV *King David*. I have in my possession documents and a detailed report made by IBS Executive Director T. D. R. Thomason. They detail a remarkable chain of coincidences; three attempts to blow up the *King David*, both at sea and in harbour, by the device of flooding her generator and engine room with highly explosive fuel oil; the 'new' anchor chain which was installed, to break only four weeks later; the mysterious activities of a certain crew member who walked off the ship the weekend before grounding, flew to London two hours after the accident and never returned to service. There can be no doubt that attempts were made to sabotage the radio ship and that there were too many coincidences for the grounding to be dismissed as an accident. Capital Radio fell – a victim of the vicious pirate war.

Dutch police spent some time during June, 1971, investigating the grounding. Thomason spent two days in The Hague with senior police officers and crew members were interviewed, as were other parties involved. After the inquiry was completed the police felt as we did; there were too many coincidences. There had been foul play. There were even suspects but insufficient evidence for a conviction. And so Capital Radio perished.

There has been high-level police interest in a number of European countries in the activities of RNI and its owners. In 1969, when Meister and Bollier launched an abortive attempt to refloat the MV *Galaxy* (the former Radio London ship), it was made plain that their presence was not welcomed in West Germany, and the ship was impounded by the authorities. It is not unlikely that they were worried about the duo's connections and activities east of the Iron Curtain.

In Holland, plainclothes men of the Dutch BVD (Secret Police) have questioned people they suspect may be able to cast any light on the mysterious activities of RNI. A close watch was maintained in Scheveningen on their tender, and on personnel departing for and leaving the *Mebo 2*. When the *Mebo 2* upped-anchor and sailed for the Essex coast in April, 1970, the British authorities began to take an interest. The station's remarkable participation in the British General Election campaign led to an intensification of this interest. Free Radio Association Chairman Geoffrey Pearl was among those questioned by Scotland Yard's Special Branch: 'They seemed particularly interested in where the money came from to finance the station. I told them I had no idea.'

In June, 1970, Swiss Urs Emmenegger, at that time styled 'managing director' of RNI, arrived at London's Heathrow Airport and was refused entry to the country. His successor to the post of managing director was American disc-jockey and programme director Larry Tremaine. After the September close-down of the station he came to Britain and was promptly deported, on Home Office instructions, back to the United States.

In the light of all this official interest in the station, it is, perhaps, interesting to re-examine this curious jamming episode when RNI's signal was interfered with by transmitters of the Ministry of Defence and Navy Department. This, obviously, was not a course of action lightly embarked upon.

In fact, more than one political correspondent at Westminster indicated that the decision to jam the station was taken at Cabinet level. Now the British Cabinet is a busy and hard-pressed body of men who discuss only the most important questions of the day. Even though Britain has passed legislation which seeks to suppress broadcasting from the high seas, I would seriously doubt whether they would really be worried by or feel impelled to take action against a harmless pop radio ship. Such a vessel three miles from the British coast might be regarded as a minor embarrassment but certainly no more. Yet the indications are that the British Cabinet sat down and seriously discussed what action could be taken against the Swiss-owned pop ship. The implication is, I think, very clear. The British authorities, at a very high level, had information to hand about the activities of RNI, Meister and Bollier which disturbed them – so much so that they have never made this information public. The jamming episode, the deportation of those involved with the station and the activities of Special Branch indicate that there was more going on than met the eye. When jamming was authorised the Prime Minister and Cabinet must have realised that the use of such an expedient, almost universally condemned in the world of broadcasting, would bring severe criticism to bear. It is highly unlikely they undertook such a serious measure merely to spoil the enjoyment of a few teenage listeners; there was, without a doubt, a more carefully considered motivation. They wanted this floating electronic wonder, with all its mysterious Communist connections and shady characters, well clear of the British coast, for while it was there it was regarded as no less than a threat to national security.

A number of British disc jockeys employed by the station have been questioned at length by Essex police about their activities. In September, disc-jockey Mark Wesley was interrogated at Southend police station, and, a month later, disc jockeys returning to Britain through Harwich were stopped and questioned. Although there was a clear case for prosecution, under the Marine Broadcasting Offences Act, in both these instances, no action was taken. Clearly the authorities were not interested in pressing a prosecution under the Act. They were interested in finding out all they could about RNI.

On board the *Mebo 2* there was a telecommunications room with complex electronic equipment. The radio ship was fitted with a teleprinter and, through this, instructions received direct from the station's Zurich office. An operation in contravention of regulations laid down by the Swiss Postal and Telegraph Administration. A radio or teleprinter link is, of course, the only link that a radio ship in international waters can have with the land, save by boat, in view of the fact that government operated coast radio stations refuse to handle traffic from a pop ship. A most elaborate communications set-up was implemented at the time of the British General Election of June, 1970. The radio ships intensive election campaign was backed up on land by the Free Radio Association, run by 33-year-old Geoffrey Pearl of Rayleigh, Essex, which coordinated action betwen the ship, public and owners of RNI.

The station asked those who were willing to organise support in their particular area to phone the F. R. A. Pearl noted the names, addresses and telephone numbers of those who responded and, in turn, phoned them on to a secret number. The information was then radioed to the *Mebo 2*, off Clacton, illegally by radio. Within minutes the names, addresses and telephone numbers were read out over the air. The whole operation was directed by an on-the-spot Swiss representative of RNI in London.

What is remarkable about the British Government's jamming campaign against RNI is the tenacity with which it was pursued; which, in itself, gives the lie to any belief that it was pursued against the activities of an unthreatening pop pirate ship.

The jamming was organised and coordinated like a military operation which, to a certain extent, it was; an enemy of the country was being fought and no effort or expense was spared – as the following evidence will suggest. I am unable to divulge my source for the information given here, but any examination of the official files relating to it, which under present regulations will have to wait half a century, would verify it.

The first jamming transmitter operated from the Post Office communications station at Ongar in Essex and interfered with RNI's broadcasts on 188 metres. This was found to be ineffective and operations were shifted to the naval radio station at Rochester. Two forms of jamming were employed. In technical terms, a continuous tone, keyed modulated carrier wave type of interference and, also, through the creation of a heterodyne (in layman's language a 'bleep, bleep' and a 'whistle'). So strong was this interference, that in Rochester and Clacton it was impossible to receive the broadcasts of BBC Radio One and serious interference to television programmes was caused.

As Election Day neared, the Cabinet realised, too late, that the jamming was proving largely ineffective against the superpower transmitters of the Swiss, and the Post Office and the armed services were instructed to set up a new and more powerful transmitter in a bid to stop the transmissions, which threatened to be instrumental in the Labour Government's losing the Election. By this time. Premier Wilson had before him the most disturbing reports from opinion pollsters which suggested that marginal constituencies in London and the South-east (still effectively covered by RNI's anti-government broadcasts), vital to the Labour Party if it was to remain in power, were undergoing swings in the region of 3% – enough to effect a change of government.

Political floating radio stations: The Radio North Sea ship bears the scars of its fire-bombing on the orders of neighbours, Radio Veronica.

*Political floating radio stations: in November 1969 the Peace
Ship was docked in New York at 63rd Street while her owner, Abe
Nathan, raised funds for his nascent radio ship project. John Lennon
signed this publicity photograph for the project and donated money to
Nathan. The Voice of Peace would broadcast to Israel and the Middle
East for more than a decade before its owner would tire of the project
and sink it in the Mediterranean.*

As a result of instructions thus received, less than a week before polling a plot of ground, owned by the Marconi company and located near Southend Airport, was taken over by the authorities. Army trucks began to pull into the empty field at Canewden in Essex; two marquees were erected and massive security precautions put into force. In one marquee there were installed powerful RCA transmitters and in the other generators. Two days before the Election the station came on the air with an estimated 200 kW. (twice the power of RNI). The site was closely guarded by police, army personnel and dogs. No photographs or observation was permitted. Any persons who loitered in the vicinity were stopped and questioned.

One hour after polling closed the 'last ditch' attempt to foil RNI left the air. By this time, it was clear the Conservatives would win the Election and they had secretly pledged to end the jamming.

The jamming, however, recommenced (from the naval radio station at Rochester); and it did not stop. Even with a new government in favour of commercial radio, and which had so vehemently opposed the introduction of the Marine Offences Act ending the reign of the pirates. There is only one rational explanation why; once in government, information and papers of a top secret nature, unavailable to the Conservatives while in opposition, had become available.

How RNI established its ship-to-shore link between its London-based Swiss Director, Urs Emmenegger, and the radio ship has never been revealed. It went something like this.

Less than a month before the election Erwin Meister contacted former Caroline man Ronan O'Rahilly and asked him to arrange the vital link. O'Rahilly phoned a contact man (a radio ham) in Clacton, only 4 miles from the *Mebo 2*, who agreed to furnish the service. Later, Meister arrived in Clacton with an ultra high frequency transmitter and receiver of Japanese design and manufacture. Designed for operating on frequencies above 600 mc/s., this piece of equipment was so complex and revolutionary, that it would be impossible for the British Post Office to detect. Thus absolute secrecy of communication could be assured. A 'substantial sum of money' (believed to be well into four figures) changed hands and the equipment was installed in a wardrobe. This transmitter was used constantly during the Election Campaign for communicating messages to the radio ship concerning the British political situation and the election campaign; messages received by telephone from Emmenegger, located in O'Rahilly's office in Hays Mews in London's plush Mayfair, were transmitted to the ship. On board the *Mebo 2* was O'Rahilly's personal link man made available to the Swiss, Irishman Jim Duggan. After the campaign was over, however, O'Rahilly heard nothing more from the elusive Swiss; he was left with a huge printing bill for thousands of posters and stickers and a top-level Scotland Yard enquiry; and the name of the station was changed back from Caroline to RNI. He had served his purpose.

It is odd to think of the course of British political history being tampered with from Central Europe by a group of foreigners.

The British police have long been trying (and to the best of my knowledge still are) to find out what actually was going on in those weeks preceding the General Election. In the case of Geoffrey Pearl, papers were referred to the Director of Public Prosecutions.

Amateur radio enthusiasts have also been incensed by the station's activities. For a while ship-to-shore communication was conducted between Scheveningen and the Mebo on the 20 metre band reserved for amateurs. An illicit amateur radio station broadcast from the radio ship on the 80 metre amateur band.

It is also rather curious to note that although Meister and Bollier have been operating under the company name of MEBO LTD. (compounded from the letters in their own names) since the beginning of their joint radio enterprise, the company MEBO AG was not registered until March 24, 1971. It was registered to 'trade in all kinds of goods' with a share capital of 50,000 Swiss Francs divided into 50 fully paid up bearer shares. The Board of Directors consists of Bollier (President) and Meister.

This was not, however, the duo's first business involvement in Zurich. Bollier took up residence in the Mebo offices in Zurich's Albisriederstrasse in 1964. A radio technician, he specialised, at first, in the supply and repair of motorcar radios, including two-way equipment. During the Biafra war he worked with Caritas and set up a private broadcasting station which was used to establish radio links between Switzerland and Biafra.

Later he became involved in the manufacture of miniaturised 'spy-bug' transmitters; this turned out to be a particularly fruitful field until, in 1969, the Swiss authorities passed a Federal Law forbidding their further manufacture, and production had to be abandoned.

Around this time, Bollier's radio ship operation was under way and he was working with a 32-year-old colleague, Erwin Meister.

Meister, unlike Bollier who was married with two children, was a bachelor and citizen of Benken in Zurich. For a number of years he had been living at Billeterstrasse 15 and operating a successful radio repair business (again specialising in motorcar radios) from Badenerstrasse 557. Along with Bollier he made the remarkable transition, in January, 1970, from smalltime radio repairman to big-time pirate radio ship operator. The strange saga of the radio repair men from Zurich becomes increasingly fascinating the longer it is studied.

At the end of September 1971 former RNI disc jockey Andy Archer revealed in a front page article in leading Dutch newspaper *De Telegraaf* that coded messages were being transmitted at night from the *Mebo 2*. These were being broadcast on the shortwave bands. The station's use of the 31 and 49 metre shortwave bands has always been something of a mystery for, commercially speaking, they are not interesting. The number of listeners to radio programmes broadcast on shortwave is extremely limited. One might, therefore, assume that the broadcasts from the radio ship which took place after closedown of regular programmes were, perhaps, more important than the daily diet of pop music.

Meister and Bollier dismissed charges of espionage made by Archer and *De Telegraaf*.

Complex electronic equipment was being sold internationally from Zurich's Albisriederstr. Much of it went to Eastern Europe – to countries such as East Germany and Jugoslavia – and Meister and Bollier's international radio operation begins to acquire more sinister undertones.

The position of an international electronics dealer is something like that of the more publicised arms dealer. Many West European countries and the United States have an embargo upon domiciled companies selling sophisticated electronics equipment to the East, where techniques and knowledge may be less advanced. There is nothing illegal, however, about selling equipment to a Swiss organisation. In Switzerland there are few trade or commercial restrictions and a Swiss company can then sell the goods to a Communist country. Meister and Bollier openly admitted selling to the East, which for them was not illegal, but a few governments could be very embarrassed if delivery slips detailing consignments were published.

Not only was equipment flown out of Zurich, but electronic devices have been shipped from Amsterdam's Schiphol Airport to East Berlin; which raises the curious business of the *Mebo 2*'s connection with a mysterious East German government department – the Instituut fur Technische Untersuchun-gen, PO Box 216, Ausstelle Bernau, East Berlin. Even curiouser when security services suspect that the Instituut's activities include work of an espionage and counter espionage nature.

When one examines the stormy history of RNI closely all sorts of oddities present themselves. Accounts and wages bills for the station settled in Deutschmarks; the PTT raid on the Grand Hotel in Scheveningen revealed not only sophisticated ship-to-shore radio equipment, but also miniature 'spy' bugs – no less than £25,000 worth; the intervention in the British General Election; the tender which was purchased and fitted out as a radio ship and which turned out to be 'too small'; the apparent lack of interest, in the first nine months of operation, in obtaining advertising; conflicting evidence about the initial source of capital to build up the station – ranging from Biafran Government money to finance from the Japanese electronics moguls; what were the precise roles in the financing of the operation of the Zurich bank Orbis (which deals in German 'flight' capital) and the Swiss advertising agency named Gloria International? What were the precise connections betwen the sales of equipment to Eastern Europe and the radio operation, both mounted from Zurich's Albisrieder-strasse? What was the significance of the plethora of frequencies RNI could transmit upon? The 49 metre short wave band was especially suited for espionage use.

All these factors are curious in themselves, but when woven together they make up a strange tapestry indeed. On Thursday, July 8, 1971 a remarkable story was published in the Dutch newspaper *De Telegraaf* which revealed, for the first time publicly, what I, and others, had heard rumours of for some months.

In the Polish seaport of Gdansk, according to CIA sources in Bonn, ten radio ships were under construction under the supervision of Russian and East German electronics engineers. The information came to light as a result of the strikes in the Polish seaports a few months previously. These were bloodily repressed and the information was leaked to American agents by workers in the yards. It was also believed that a number of such stations were under construction in East Germany.

The radio ships, it was surmised, were to be used off the coasts of Europe, North Africa and the Middle East as part of a massive Communist propaganda offensive. And, I understand, who should be involved in the technical organisation of the whole operation but the mysterious Instituut fur Technische Untersuchungen in East Berlin. The radio stations, with powerful transmitters like those on the *Mebo 2*, were being constructed on board former Russian trawlers.

The potential effect of such an operation on the delicate balance of East-West power might be literally termed world shattering.

It was certainly regarded as a matter of concern by the security forces and intelligence chiefs of a number of Western countries. CIA chief Helms is believed to have visited Israeli Premier Mrs. Golda Meir in the summer of 1971 to discuss this very problem, for it was feared that American-Israeli relations would be one of the prime targets for attack. The CIA leaked the information during June in the hope that such a leakage might make the intelligence services of the Warsaw Pact countries, preparing the operation, feel the plan was compromised. If the operation had been launched, the presence of ten Communist-backed radio ships around the coasts of Europe would have represented a grave embarrassment to the NATO alliance. Outside the jurisdiction of the Council of Europe's Strasbourg Convention, these vessels could have survived indefinitely, supplied by half a dozen East European navies. They would then have become a valuable political bargaining counter; perhaps to trade for the removal of Radio Free Europe and Radio Liberty which, CIA backed, have broadcast from studios in West Germany to the East since the early 1950s. These two very powerful radio stations have been a source of constant irritation to the Communists with their diet of uncensored news and current affairs programmes.

In August of 1970, Herr Willy Brandt, the German Chancellor, signed a Moscow-Bonn friendship treaty in the Russian capital and political experts observed at that time that pressure was being exerted from the Communist side with a view to the permanent removal of Radio Liberty and Radio Free Europe. It was strenuously argued that the presence of these radio stations was quite out of sympathy with the development of detente in Western Europe. Nevertheless, US pressure may be assumed to have succeeded in keeping the stations on the air. It is not unreasonable to venture that ten radio ships around European coasts would have been an instant and viable bargaining counter with which to trade silence for silence.

Everything was lavish about the RNI operation – even the toilet and shower facilities, which were in marked contrast to any other pirate ship.

Paul Harris, author and quondam publisher, alongside the radio ship Mebo 2

As for the connection between Radio North Sea International and this plan, it is for the reader to draw his own conclusions on the basis of the evidence; evidence of equipment sent to East Germany to an organisation involved in mounting this massive propaganda attack, the controlled leakage of information by the CIA and statements by those actually working on board the radio ship concerning its transmission of coded messages and array of unconventional radio equipment.

From the evidence available, it is far from unrealistic to suggest that the radio ship *Mebo 2* had become a pawn in European politics; a part of the power struggle between East and West, between communism and democracy. There can be very little doubt, I would maintain, that through its not insignificant effect upon the British General Election campaign of 1970, Radio North Sea International influenced the result of that election and, by implication, changed the course of British political life. At the time, the British Government regarded its activities in a most serious light – as can be gauged from its response. Behind the apparently harmless exterior, the euphoric pop and meaningless banalities of the disc jockeys there lay sinister and ulterior motives; the psychedelically-painted radio ship, lying at her storm-tossed anchorage in international waters beyond the reach of government and ordered society, was a political radio station which had interfered in the politics of one European country and which had mysterious and unexplained connections with East Europe.

My second book on offshore broadcasting, *To Be A Pirate King*, voiced these fears and was published in November, 1971. Prior to publication in book form in Britain, it was serialised in the leading Dutch daily newspaper *De Telegraaf*. Simultaneously, disc jockey Andy Archer made statements to that newspaper about activities on board the radio ship; he alleged its use as a spy ship and gave evidence of coded and secret transmissions. The whole question of the activities of the *Mebo 2* became headline news throughout Holland and the Dutch Prime Minister felt obliged to make a public statement on television. He confirmed the suspicions of intelligence chiefs in regard to the strange vessel.

I was in the south of England at the time but upon returning to my office in Scotland I was interviewed at length by a gentleman from the 'Ministry of Defence – Security Service'. In an interview, which I taped secretly, it became plain that my fears about the role of RNI were shared by the Security Service and that there had been in-depth liaison between the British secret service and the BVD.

Meister and Bollier materialised in Holland and gave a press conference in denial of the various allegations but, from now on, they were to maintain a much lower profile than hitherto and they largely disappear from the spotlight. It might be postulated that their cover was now 'blown'; probably their precise objectives and activities will never be known for sure.

But Bollier, at least, would dramatically re-emerge in the late 1980s, almost two decades later, as the man who supplied the timer for the bomb which blew up flight Pan Am 107 over Lockerbie, Scotland ... Again, more questions than answers.

17

A phoenix from the ashes

On the morning of Monday, October 18, 1971, the Capital Radio ship, the *King David*, was exposed for sale at public auction in Amsterdam. The bidding was far from fast and furious and after only a few minutes she was knocked down for 20,700 guilders (little more than £2,000 sterling) to a Rotterdam scrap-dealer, Mr. J. Boele, who promptly declared the vessel's broadcasting days to be at an end. A sad end indeed to a £100,000 investment and brief five month broadcasting history.

Events appeared set to repeat themselves on Monday, May 29, 1972, when the Radio Caroline ship *Mi Amigo*, which had lain rusting for five years in Amsterdam Harbour, under an arrestment order from the Wijsmuller tug company, was exposed at public auction. She was purchased for 20,000 guilders by the Dutch shipping agency, Hofman's, and it was generally assumed that the radio ship would be broken up. It was announced, however, that the Dutch Free Radio Organisation had taken her over as a pirate radio museum. At a berth in Zaandam a group of enthusiasts set to work with scrubbing brushes, paint and elbow grease. Gradually, the evidence of five years of neglect and looting was removed.

At this point former Caroline boss Ronan O'Rahilly arrived in Amsterdam and sought out the project organiser, Gerard van Dam. The result of the meeting was to become apparent in September, 1972, when the *Mi Amigo* left her berth and was towed down the North Sea Canal towards the North Sea. Harbour authorities in Ijmuiden were told that the 'pirate radio museum' was headed for England. But on September 3 anchor was dropped off Scheveningen, within sight of the Veronica and North Sea ships. At the end of the month test transmissions commenced and continued, without identification, through October and November as those on board prepared for regular broadcasting. At this stage the whole operation was still shrouded in mystery.

What had happened, in fact, was that O'Rahilly, through a company registered in Liechtenstein, had eifectively taken over the radio ship from van Damor, more precisely, had wrested control out of the hands of the band of eager but naive enthusiasts who had saved her from the scrapyard. Gerard van Dam is now, understandably, bitter. He borrowed the money to buy the ship from his aged mother and organised the refurbishing; his free radio organisation lent legitimacy to the operation and O'Rahilly came along and took over bowling over the free radio 'freaks' with his charisma and undoubted ability to get ship back on the air under the Caroline banner.

It was far from plain sailing now the ship was back on the sea and the events of the ensuing months were to be marked by chaos and lack of proper organisation. On November 13 the *Mi Amigo* broke free from her anchorage in a tremendous storm and the aerial mast collapsed. On December 22 the first announcement came from the ship, "This is Radio Caroline". Caroline was back! But at the end of the month serious trouble struck.

During his afternoon programme on December 28, disc jockey Andy Archer announced that there were 'visitors' and, later, that fighting had broken out on deck. In fact, the Dutch crew who had earlier deserted the ship in search of their wages on land had returned, empty-handed, and were now proceeding to fight it out with the disc jockeys! A Royal Netherlands Navy ship drew alongside and the incipient mutiny was quelled ... for a while. On December 30 the Dutch captain returned to the *Mi Amigo* by tug, promptly severed the anchor chain and towed her to Ijmuiden. The next day she was boarded by officials of the shipping inspectorate who declared her a 'wreck'. Simultaneously, the Haarlem District Court ordered the ship impounded and granted an injunction in favour of the unpaid crew members.

Meanwhile, O'Rahilly busied himself in raising the funds which were vital if the situation was to be retrieved and repair work commenced on the ship. A settlement with the crew was reached on New Year's Day 1973 and the ship was freed.

Over the course of the next few months transmissions became more regular with English at night and Dutch during the day. But there were many generator and transmitter breakdowns, a fire in the engine room and financial problems.

On April 2, 1973, conditions in the southern part of the North Sea were among the worst in living memory. Remarkably, the anchor on the *Mi Amigo* held but all was not well a few miles away. At 8.45 p.m. that night Scheveningen coastal radio station received

*The two Radio Caroline ships lie rusting in Amsterdam Harbour
before being refloated in September 1972.*

a Mayday call from the Radio Veronica ship; she had broken free from her moorings and was adrift. The station left the air and the crew were taken off by lifeboat. By 11.30 the *Nordeney* was aground only fifty yards from the entrance to Scheveningen Harbour. In fact, conditions were so bad that the lifeboat was unable to enter the harbour until ten the next morning.

The salvage company Smit-Tak was instructed to take charge of the salvage operation. It was clear it would be far from easy and a deep channel had to be dug through the beach and the ship turned. At this juncture Caroline came to the rescue and offered to broadcast the Radio Veronica programmes. At a particularly critical time, from April 11 to 18, the *Mi Amigo* kept the sound of Veronica alive. At 4 a.m. on the 18th the *Nordeney* was refloated and transmissions recommenced within the hour.

On board the Caroline ship transmissions did not settle into a steady routine. From July to October, 1973, transmission time was rented out to Belgian businessman Adriaan van Lanschoot who operated Radio Atlantis from the ship. Programming was directed at the Netherlands and Flemish-speaking northern Belgium. At the end of October van Lanschoot purchased his own ship, a former Icelandic trawler named the *Jeanine*, and also the transmitter which had been used for radio broadcasts from the REM island. An anchor was installed in the German port of Cuxhaven and the new radio ship dropped anchor off the Belgian coast at the end of December 1973.

In July, 1973, an English language 'progressive' music station started from the *Mi Amigo* under the name of Radio Seagull. This was silenced in October when the aerial collapsed again. A new mast was constructed at sea and on December 28, 1973, tests commenced under the identification Radio *Mi Amigo*.

As in the case of Atlantis, Radio *Mi Amigo* was the brainchild of a Belgian businessman; in this instance, Sylvain Tack. The Belgian government had outlawed offshore broadcasters as long ago as 1962 (after the Radio Uilenspiegel experience) and, therefore, programmes were prepared and taped in Holland. An interesting circumvention of the law was developed whereby Belgian goods and services were advertised by the reading of advertisements from Belgian magazines; this was deemed to be information given by the disc jockey to the listener and not advertising. The station rapidly became popular in its coverage area.

April 1973: the Radio Veronica ship hard aground on the beach at Scheveningen. (A.N.P. Foto.)

On February 23, 1974, the transmissions of Radio Seagull ceased and Radio Caroline returned, broadcasting an English language service during the night hours. April 14, 1974 was the tenth birthday of Radio Caroline and a special celebratory programme was broadcast.

Many factors though had now combined to produce a situation where offshore broadcasting was to be tolerated no longer – even in the free and liberal political and social atmosphere of Holland. The Radio North Sea bomb attack and the rumours of blackmail and gangsterism had turned many liberal politicians against the 'pirates'. Similarly, the proliferation in the number of stations, as in the UK during 1966, had rendered government reaction inevitable. Finally, the very diffuse nature of Dutch politics, marked by its many small parties and interest groups, which had worked in favour of the universally popular Radio Veronica, in the end of the day led to the passing of legislation to end the offshore broadcasters. During the early seventies Holland faced, along with other Western European democracies, economic and social problems requiring concerted action and the various political parties found 'log-rolling' an essential part of political life – and one of the issues on which more liberal elements found themselves allying with the left was on an offshore broadcasting ban – in return for support on other issues.

Perhaps most importantly it might be noted that in a general context the social atmosphere of the seventies bore little resemblance to that of the heady sixties. The zany extravagance of the pop culture of the sixties with all its spin-off activities disappeared as Western Europe sank into recession in the early seventies. Inevitably, this economic trend reflected in social attitudes and produced a situation in which it became politically possible for the Dutch Government to embark upon a course of action which, four or five years earlier, would have pro-produced so much popular antagonism as to be counter-productive.

The radio ships, especially Radio Veronica, mounted a spirited campaign to fight off legislation. Only hours after the refloatation of the *Nordeney* on April 18,1973, a parliamentary hearing took place in The Hague. Despite a massive public demonstration of support by 150,000 people, when the vote was taken on June 28 it represented a massive thumbs down for the pirates. The Dutch Marine Broadcasting Act did not take effect until September 1, 1974 but both Radio Veronica and Radio North Sea International announced they were to close. The former station launched a campaign to raise support for omroep status (broadcasting organisation) within the legal Netherlands structure (Veronica moet aan land). There was no intention to linger on and fight.

Radio Veronica closed at 6 p.m. on August 31 after an emotional final hour. Disc jockey Rob Out bade farewell: "With the end of Veronica dies a piece of democracy in the Netherlands – and that is a pity'. The National Anthem and a jingle followed. And then dead air ... the end of fifteen years of broadcasting for a radio station which had become part and parcel of the Dutch way of life.

Radio North Sea International closed two hours later . . . and then there was one. On the afternoon of August 29 the *Mi Amigo* had upped anchor and sailed for the English coast, broadcasting as she went. As the Dutch legislation came into force Radio *Mi Amigo*, the Dutch language service, was beamed to Holland and Belgium from a new anchorage off the Essex coast.

Broadcasts defiantly continued and European police activity around the radio ship intensified. Belgian police swooped on a farmhouse, confiscated recording equipment and tapes and made a number of arrests. In Britain, the Home Office and Scotland Yard took an increasing interest in Caroline's apparent survival against all odds and, in Holland, the offices of companies whose advertisements were still being broadcast were searched and employees questioned. The mailing address of both Radio Caroline and *Mi Amigo* was now in Playa d'Oro, Spain, and studios were established in the Spanish holiday resort. But provision of tapes, records, supplies and personnel was now a major headache. A tender run was attempted from Bilbao but this turned out to be a hazardous three day operation through the treacherous waters of the Bay of Biscay and it was abandoned in favour of the quite illegal but less harrowing shorter run from ports in south-east England, Holland and Belgium. In conditions of the utmost secrecy disc jockeys and engineers boarded fishing boats and other small craft to be transported illegally at the dead of night to the rusty wallowing radio ship.

On September 18, 1975, the first prosecutions were brought under the Marine Broadcasting (Offences) Act, 1967. Six men, including three disc jockeys, faced charges in connection with Radio Caroline broadcasts. Disc jockeys Andy Archer and John Mair were each fined £100 with £50 costs when they admitted the charges at

August 31st, 1974; the emotional final hour of Holland's beloved Radio Veronica is played out on air. With the glasses, 'Uncle' Bul Verweij, Veronica owner, and behind him, top DJ Rob Out. (A.N.P. Foto)

Southend Magistrates Court; another broadcaster, Michael Baker, was also fined £100 when he admitted supplying records to the station. The owner of a boat used to carry a disc jockey to the station was also fined. All had been arrested after police kept watch on a boat which went out to the radio ship and returned to the River Crouch, on the Essex coast.

There was another interesting series of events the following November when the radio ship went adrift. The *Mi Amigo* drifted right across the Thames Estuary from her moorings 12 miles off the Essex coast. An emergency anchor was dropped on November 9 and a couple of days later an American tug, sent out from Spain, delivered a new anchor. On November 13 transmissions resumed. Those on board were under the impression they were still in international waters but there was to be a rude awakening.

On November 14 a police launch left Sheerness and arrived alongside the *Mi Amigo* that afternoon. The vessel was boarded and searched under warrants issued under the Marine Broadcasting (Offences) Act 1967 and the Wireless Telegraphy Act, 1949. As a result four men were arrested and removed from the ship; the Dutch captain, two disc jockeys and an engineer. All four were bailed for £1,000 and were obliged to surrender their passports.

On December 11 the Captain and two disc jockeys were fined a total of £475 and a remarkable order was made by the magistrates 'to deprive the convicted persons of property used in the offence'. They added that this order could be taken to include the whole vessel (which had meantime been moved further out into international waters). The validity of this judgement, however, was extremely questionable referring as it did to a Panamanian ship in international waters although, presumably, the order could be held to apply in the event of a repetition of the offence within territorial waters.

But by far the most remarkable prosecution was yet to come. On April 30, 1976, at Liverpool Magistrates Court, three men were found guilty of promoting and publicising Radio Caroline. This was a prosecution which set an important precedent, pertaining as it did to an untested section of the Marine Offences Act. A hotel manager was charged with booking a discotheque calling itself the Radio Caroline Roadshow; another defendant was charged with running the mobile discotheque and the third, quite incredibly, was charged with the criminal offence of displaying a Radio Caroline sticker in the window of his motor car. The prosecution called no less than 25 witnesses to establish that Radio Caroline was broadcasting off the Essex coast while these offences were committed in Liverpool. The hearing lasted five days and cost an estimated £5,000; a remarkable committal of resources to deal with a series of quite trivial 'offences'.

The case has set a most unfortunate precedent which raises wider issues of censorship and freedom of information in a democracy. Apart from material which might be deemed grossly obscene, I know of no car sticker the display of which incurs criminal prosecution. Apart, that is, from the display of one publicising an offshore radio station. One must assume, as a logical development of this sequence of events, that any material giving publicity to a 'pirate' radio ship might lead the party publishing or displaying it to prosecution under the 1967 Act. The successful Liverpool prosecutions represent an open door for the police, Home Office and others engaged in enforcing the Act. Any witch-hunt on these lines is clearly iniquitous in a free society and represents a most dangerous precedent impinging on the freedom to communicate information.

Despite these various legal moves Radio Caroline has continued to broadcast, and in June 1976 began an all day English language service on 192 metres – in addition to the existing English service on 259 metres. The new service quickly atracted three major international advertisers – Coca Cola, Levi Jeans and Wrigleys Gum – all well placed to engineer advertising orders through offices in the United States well out of the reach of European legislation.

And so, as 1976 drew to a close, Radio Caroline remained – the grand old lady of 'pirate' radio. Her survival was quite remarkable in a Europe which, with the exception of Spain, has made her a complete outlaw with no base and no hiding place. The small rusting radio ship somehow managed to survive in a situation which was logistically increasingly impossible, strategically undefendable and in which her suppression would be politically acceptable.

The *Mi Amigo* was, perhaps, the last tangible relic of the sixties and became something of a social anachronism. She was a reminder of the free and uninhibited days of the Sixties; the era of swinging London, the mini skirt, Biba, Mary Quant, the Beatles, Union-Jack-on-everything and . . . pirate radio ships. Her isolated, lonely position in the seventies was symptomatic of a Europe increasingly characterised by a simple absence of joy and a reduction in the general level of tolerance of any activity not completely controlled by the State.

Maverick pirate radio operator Edwin Bollier leaves Rotterdam on January 16 1977 aboard his pirate ship the Mebo 2. RNI may be dead but he has sold the ship to Libyan leader Colonel Muammar Gaddafi and it is en route to the Mediterranean where it will broadcast extracts from the Koran before being sunk as target practice for the Libyan air force. Bollier himself will re-emerge ten years later in connection with supplyng the timer for the Lockerbie Pan Am bombing.

351

Original Appendix

The Offshore Stations: A Few Facts

Note: Audience figures, except where otherwise indicated, are those determined by a survey carried out in July 1966 by National Opinion Polls Ltd. Advertising rates also those current in July 1966.

RADIO CAROLINE (South) formerly Radio Atlanta

Ship: 470-ton M.V. *Mi Amigo;* used until 1962 by the Swedish pirate station Radio Nord.

Position: 3½ miles off Frinton-on-Sea, Essex.

On the air: May 9th, 1964 as Radio Atlanta, merged with and became Radio Caroline in July 1964.

Frequency: 200 metres as Atlanta, later 259 metres.

Technical details: Crystal controlled 50 kW. Continental Electronics transmitter plus 10 kW standby transmitter. Two generators. 163 ft. high, ¼ wavelength aerial.

Estimated cost to put on air: £150,000.

Audience: 8,818,000 together with North ship.

Advertising rates: £90 for 30 seconds peak time.

Owners/directors: Joint managing directors: Ronan O'Rahilly (programming and sales), Barry M. Ainley (administrative and financial). Sales director: Brian Scudder; also Directors: Jocelyn Stevens, Philip Solomon, Herman Good and R. L. Trapnell. Radio Atlanta run by Allan Crawford and Major Oliver Smedley.

Station identification: 'Caroline - the Sound of the Nation'. After August 14th, 1967 became Radio Caroline International with headquarters at Singel 160, Amsterdam, Holland.

Programme schedule after August 14th, 1967: 5-30 a.m. - 2 a.m. on 259 metres.

RADIO CAROLINE (North) formerly Caroline South

Ship: 763-ton M.V. *Caroline;* formerly the Danish passenger ferry *Frederika.* Position: Moved from off Frinton, Essex, July 1964 to 3½ miles off Ramsey, Isle of Man. On air: March 28th, 1964. First offshore station. Stayed on the air after August 14th, 1967.

Wavelength: 199 metres, later became 259 metres.

Technical details: Two crystal controlled 10 kW. Continental Electronics transmitters coupled together in a combining unit to the aerial. Two generator sets. 168 ft. high aerial of ¼ wavelength folded dipole construction, with a sausage aerial forming the other leg. Estimated cost to put on the air: £¼ million.

Audience: 8,818,000 together with South ship.
Advertising rates: £90 for 30 seconds peak time.
Owners/directors: As Caroline South.

RADIO CITY formerly Radio Sutch
Location: On Shivering Sands Fort in the Thames Estuary, 9 miles off Whitstable.
On the air: As Radio Sutch, May 1964. Five months later became Radio City. Closed down February 8th, 1967 at midnight.
Wavelength: 299 metres.
Technical details: 20 kW of power claimed to be used after September 1965, before then only low power. Transmitting equipment built by two Radio City engineers, Ian West and Phil Perkins. Aerial mast 240 ft. high on top of fort 117 ft. high.
Estimated cost to put on the air: As Radio Sutch, £4,000. Bought in September 1964 for £5,000. Estimated value in July 1966, £200,000.
Audience: Claimed 3 million listeners.
Advertising rates: £30 for 30 seconds.
Owners: Pop singer Screaming Lord Sutch until he sold out to his manager Reginald Calvert in September 1964. Calvert shot dead in June 1966 after a raid on the fort and his wife, Mrs Dorothy Calvert took over the management of the station. Station identification: 'Radio City - the Tower of Power.'

RADIO 390 formerly Radio Invicta and King Radio
Location: Red Sands Towers in the Thames Estuary, 8½ miles off Whitstable.
On the air: As Radio Invicta on June 3rd, 1964. Closed down December 18th, 1964. Renamed King Radio in January 1965 and became Radio 390 on September 25th, 1965. Closed down on July 28th, 1967.
Wavelength: 390 metres.
Technical details: 35 kW of power developed by two RCA transmitters. Often ran only 10 kW. Four Gardner diesel generators running the transmitters. Aerial mast 200 ft. high on top of fort 85 ft. a.s.l. As Radio Invicta used only low power, 1 kW transmitter.
Estimated cost to put on the air: Improvements carried out in September 1965, after King Radio was taken over and became Radio 390, cost £150,000.
Audience: 2,633,000 listeners.
Advertising rates: £50 for 30 seconds.
Owners/directors: Radio Invicta: Tom Pepper and partners Charlie Evans and John Thompson. Pepper met his death in December 1964 when he mysteriously drowned leaving the fort. His partners then started King Radio, but sold out in September 1965 to Estuary Radio Ltd. Managing

director: Edward Allbeury. Company secretary: David Lye, who took over from Mr Allbeury in February 1967. Directors: John Henry La Trobe, Michael Mitcham, John Goething, Christopher Blackwell.

Station identification: 'Eve, the Woman's Magazine of the Air.' 'Radio 390, Your Family Station.'

RADIO LONDON

Ship: 1,000-ton M.V. *Galaxy;* former U.S. minesweeper. Position: 3½ miles off Frinton-on-Sea.

On the air: December 19th, 1964. Regular transmissions began

December 23rd. Closed down 3 p.m. August 14th, 1967. Wavelength: 266 metres. Technical details: 50 kW RCA Ampliphase transmitter. Initial power used 17 kW, gradually increased to maximum 75 kW, shunt-fed to a 212 ft. high mast. Cost to put on the air: £½ million. Audience: 8,140,000 listeners although the station claimed 12 million in Britain and 4½ million on the continent. Advertising rates: £56 for 30 seconds peak time. Owners/directors: Owners, the Marine Investment Co. Inc. of Grand Bahama Island backed by American investors.

Station represented in Britain by Radlon (Sales) Ltd.

Managing director: Philip Birch. Station identification: 'This is Big L', 'Wonderful Radio London.'

RADIO SCOTLAND

Ship: 500-ton former Irish lightship *Comet* built on the Clyde in 1904.

Position: January to May 1966 4 miles off Dunbar in the Firth of Forth. May 1966 to March 1967 3½ miles off Troon in the Firth of Clyde. Moved to Irish waters for three weeks and then moved back to the Firth of Forth, anchoring off Fife Ness.

On the air: January 1st, 1966. Closed down at midnight on August 14th, 1967.

Wavelength: 242 metres.

Technical details: Two RCA Ampliphase transmitters type B10J, each one developing 10 kW and fed via a combining unit to a 145 ft. high omni-directional folded dipole aerial.

Estimated cost to put on the air: £150,000.

Audience: 2,195,000 listeners.

Advertising rates: £28 for 30 seconds peak time.

Owners/directors: City and County Commercial Radio (Scotland) Ltd. Managing director: T. V. Shields. Joint deputy-managing directors: Alan Carr and Stanley Jackson.

Station identification: 'Swinging to you on 242.'

RADIO ESSEX

later BBMS (Britain's Better Music Station)

Location: Knock John Tower in the Thames Estuary, 18 miles off Southend.

On the air: September 1965. After the prosecution of the station in December 1966 it was renamed BBMS. Closed down after its appeal failed in January 1967.

Wavelength: 222 metres.

Power: Very low power used, initially 25 watts later increased to 1.75 kW. Equipment built by the owner of the station.

Audience: Confined to the County of Essex.

Advertising rates: £8 10s for 30 seconds peak time.

Owner: Roy Bates.

Station identification: The Voice of Essex Broadcasting 24 Hours a Day.'

RADIO ENGLAND later Radio Dolfijn and Radio 227

Ship: 480-ton *Laissez Faire;* former U.S. liberty ship *Olga Patricia.*

Position: 3½ miles off Frinton-on-Sea.

On the air: May 1966 until November 14th when it commenced broadcasting in Dutch as Radio Dolfijn. Became Radio 227 in March 1967. Closed down on July 23rd, 1967.

Wavelength: 227 metres.

Technical details: 55 kW transmitter fed to an aerial mast 210 ft. high which was shared by both the stations on board the ship.

Cost to put on the air: Together with Britain Radio £1,450,000.

Estimated audience: 2,274,000 listeners.

Advertising rates: £56 for 30 seconds peak time.

Owners/directors: Peir Vick Ltd, backed by American investors. Managing director: William E. Vick. Station coordinator: Jack Nixon. In March 1967, a year after Peir Vick Ltd. was formed, a liquidator was appointed and the two stations on board the *Laissez Faire* were taken over by Carstead Advertising Ltd., with Edward Allbeury as managing director and John Withers as director in charge of sales.

Station identification: 'Swinging Radio England.'

BRITAIN RADIO later Radio 355

Ship: Same vessel as Radio England, 480-ton *Laissez Faire.*

Position: 3½ miles off Frinton-on-Sea.

On the air: May 1966 until March 1967 as Britain Radio. Became Radio 355 after the *Laissez Faire* was taken over by Edward Allbeury's Carstead Advertising. Closed down on August 6th, 1967.

Wavelength: 355 metres.

Technical details: As Radio England. Fully automatic standby studio on

board; for use in bad weather when station staff unable to man equipment properly, enabling them to switch over to pre-recorded tapes.
Audience: 718,000 listeners.
Advertising rates: £56 for 30 seconds peak time.
Owners/directors: As Radio England.
Station identification: 'Britain Radio - Hallmark of Quality.'

RADIO 270

Ship:160-ton *Oceaan 7*; converted Dutch lugger.
Position: 3 miles off Scarborough, later Bridlington, Yorkshire coast.
On the air: June 1966, closed down at midnight on August 14th, 1967.
Wavelength: 270 metres.
Technical details: 10 kW RCA transmitter type BTA-10JI. Two Dale generators. 154 ft. high aerial mast; aerial of vertical bird cage construction.
Estimated cost to put on the air: £70,000.
Audience: 4,750,000 listeners according to a National Opinion Poll survey carried out in June 1967.
Advertising rates: £30 for 30 seconds.
Owners/directors: Operated by British registered Ellambar Investments Ltd. 50 shareholders, mostly local Northeast businessmen. Chairman: Leonard Dale. Managing director: Wilfred Proudfoot. All capital loaned to a Panamanian company, Progresiva Compania Comercial SA, principal shareholder. Jack Lament. Agent in Britain, Australian disc jockey Noel Miller.
Station identification: This is the Super Hit Sound of Radio 270.'

RADIO VERONICA

Ship: M.V. *Veronica II*; this is the second ship from which Radio Veronica has broadcast. Transmitted for six years from a converted 485-ton German lightship, *Borkum Riff.*
Position: 3½ miles off the Dutch coast between Scheveningen and The Hague.
On the air: April 1960.
Wavelength: 192 metres.
Technical details: 10 kW transmitter. T-type antenna, double-thread, length 2 x 24 ft. and 66 ft. high.
Audience: In the Netherlands and Flemish speaking part of Belgium. Since close-down of Radio Caroline in March 1968 has attracted a large English audience.
Advertising rates: 12-15 guilders per second.
Owners: The Verweij Brothers of Hilversum.
Note on programming: The studios of Radio Veronica are located in Hilversum and all programmes are recorded on tape and sent out to the ship.

MANX RADIO

Britain's only landbased commercial radio station

Location: Studios in Douglas, Isle of Man. Medium wave transmitter at Foxdale, 800 ft. a.s.l. VHP transmitter on Snaefell, 2,034 ft. a.s.l.

On the air: November 24th, 1964.

Wavelengths: 232 metres in daylight hours; 188 metres in hours of darkness. VHP transmitter in use throughout.

Technical details: Power used 1 kW. Studios and transmitters by Pye.

Audience: Restricted to the Isle of Man; 40,000 listeners (R.M.A. Research Unit figures).

Advertising rates: Offpeak, £1 for 30 seconds. 30s. for 30 seconds peak time. 12s. 6d. for an offpeak 15 second spot.

Owners: Purchased in 1968 by the Manx Government from the Isle of Man Broadcasting Company and Pye Radio.

Future plans: Takeover by the Manx Government expected in many quarters to precede an increase in the station's transmitting power. Speculation over the possibility of a high powered Manx Radio broadcasting to the English mainland.

A Note on Currency in the United Kingdom.

Until decimalisation of the British currency in 1971,

One British Pound, written as £1, was equivalent to Twenty Shillings, written as 20s.

One Shilling was equivalent to 12 pence, written 12d.

A portion of a Pound was written, e.g., as 12s 6d.

Printed in the United Kingdom
by Lightning Source UK Ltd.
125360UK00001B/84/A